THE ROAD TO GLORY

BURNLEY'S FA CUP TRIUMPH IN 1914

MIKE SMITH

Grosvenor House
Publishing Limited

This book is published by
Grosvenor House Publishing Ltd
28-30 High Street, Guildford, Surrey, GU1 3EL.
www.grosvenorhousepublishing.co.uk

A CIP record for this book
is available from the British Library

ISBN 978-1-78148-690-0

The Prize and the cause of our Labours.

Contents

About the Author vii
Acknowledgements ix
List of Figures xv
Introduction xix
Turf Moor - Home of Burnley Football Club xxiii

Chapter 1: The Green and Whites 1
Chapter 2: The Birth of the Clarets 36
Chapter 3: Burnley Are Back 66
Chapter 4: January 1914 118
Chapter 5: The Third Round 143
Chapter 6: The Semi-Final 170
Chapter 7: Cup Fever 212
Chapter 8: Send them Victorious 241
Chapter 9: Player Profiles 311

APPENDICES **337**

Bibliography 338
Some Facts about the 1913-14 FA Cup 343
UK Currency in 1914 345
The Cost of Watching Football in 1914 346
Calculating Burnley's Attendances from Gate Receipts. 348
Burnley's progress in the FA Cup 1885 - 1914. 350
The First Division's Top Ten Goal Scorers. 355
1913-14 FA Cup, Round by Round. 356
Cup Winners Record Profits 357

About the Author

Mike Smith lives in Burnley and has supported Burnley Football Club since he was five years old. Mike's career began in the electrical engineering industry before he moved into teaching and management in further and higher education. *The Road To Glory* is his second published work and follows, *Tommy Boyle - Broken Hero* published by Grosvenor House in 2011.

Acknowledgements

At Burnley Football Club, I'd like to thank Adam Riding for his work on the Road To Glory extracts given in the club programme that ran through the 2013-14 season. My thanks also go to Darren Bentley for giving the Cup story its prominence in the Club programme all season and also to Burnley FC's Historian, Ray Simpson, for his advice. I'd like to thank Mike Benyon for providing the digital copies the 1913-14 Burnley programmes and to Programme Monthly for their article where I appealed for any information on the Cup Final and its memorabilia. Many thanks to George Chilvers for producing the colourised images for the cover and to Getty Images for giving permission to use the images of the Cup Final. Thanks to Valia Lamprou at the London Transport Museum and to Javis Gurr at English Heritage for use of their images under licence. Mostly I'd like to thank the sports journalists of the day who normally went by their pen names of; Sportsman, Brunbank, Lancastrian, Orion, Tityrus and many others. In the days before radio, television and the internet, their accounts of football matches gave a colourful insight into what football was like at the time. Finally I'd like to thank the staff at Burnley Central Library for their help and for access to their excellent resources, without which this work would not have been possible.

There must be a beginning of any great matter
but the continuing unto the end until it be thoroughly
finished yields the true glory.

– Francis Drake 1587

For Julia and Clare

List of Figures

Fig 1: The old Burnley Crest.   iii
Fig 2: Turf Moor in the 1920s. (English Heritage)   xxiii
Fig 3: The Burnley Football Team 1908-09.   5
Fig 4: Tottenham Hotspur Team 1908-09.   12
Fig 5: Alec Leake and Billy Meredith.   17
Fig 6: 1910 Manchester United Funeral Card.   31
Fig 7: In Memory Of Manchester United Postcard.   31
Fig 8: Yorkshire Street, Burnley.   36
Fig 9: Which Cup or Both? Cartoon.   38
Fig 10: The Roll-Call cartoon.   42
Fig 11: Burnley Are Cock Of The North.   48
Fig 12: Manchester United Team 1913-14.   83
Fig 13: Burnley vs. Newcastle United Programme.   90
Fig 14: Burnley Programme Adverts and League Tables.   90
Fig 15: Burnley vs. Newcastle Teams.   91
Fig 16: Robert Kelly.   93
Fig 17: The Baseball Ground, Derby.   104
Fig 18: Burnley Team at the start of 1914.   118
Fig 19: Crowd at Ewood Park on New Years Day 1914.   119
Fig 20: The Burnley Bulldog cartoon.   143
Fig 21: Burnley and Bolton Mascots.   145
Fig 22: The Quarter Final Captains. (Athletics News)   155
Fig 23: Burnley Fans Sat On the New Cricket Field End   162
Fig 24: Burnley Cup Team Postcard.   170
Fig 25: Burnley Ladies Play The Game.   174

Fig 26: English and Scottish League Teams. 176

Fig 27: Programme for the International Match. 177

Fig 28: Burnley Players Enjoy the Sea at Lytham. (Getty) 182

Fig 29: Football Training at Lytham. 182

Fig 30: FA Cup Semi-Final Programme at Old Trafford. 186

Fig 31: Burnley Attack in the Semi-Final. 188

Fig 32: Tommy Boyle Leads out The Clarets at Goodison Park. 193

Fig 33: The Semi-Final Replay Programme. 194

Fig 34: Herbert Sydney Bamlett, Cup Final Referee. 207

Fig 35: The FA Cup. 212

Fig 36: Burnley Players Train on the Green at Lytham Seafront 220

Fig 37: Burnley Players Outside Gaskell's Hotel in Lytham 221

Fig 38: The Liverpool Squad 224

Fig 39: Charterhouse Square and Hotel, Smithfield, London. 231

Fig 40: The London Palladium Programme 1914 231

Fig 41: The Royal Arms 241

Fig 42: London Underground Poster (London Transport Museum) 246

Fig 43: Piccadilly Circus 1914 (London Transport Museum) 246

Fig 44: Lady Ottoline Morrell outside the House of Commons 248

Fig 45: The Crystal Palace 251

Fig 46: Crystal Palace Entrance 252

Fig 47: The Crystal Palace Dinosaurs in the Lower Lake 253

Fig 48: Poster for the Cup Final (London Transport Museum) 255

Fig 49: The Official Cup Final Programme   255

Fig 50: Eddie Mosscrop's Shirt with the Royal Arms.   257

Fig 51: His Royal Highness, King George V.   258

Fig 52: The King in the Pavilion.   262

Fig 53: The Two Teams   266

Fig 54: The Final Gets Underway.   270

Fig 55: Action During The Match (Getty)   271

Fig 56: Freeman Scores!   273

Fig 57: Tommy Boyle Is Presented With The Cup   276

Fig 58: Crowds Outside The Newspaper Offices
            in Burnley   277

Fig 59: The Connaught Rooms. Inset Lord Kinnaird.   279

Fig 60: The Connaught Rooms Banqueting Hall.   280

Fig 61: Phillip Morrell MP and Lady Ottoline Morrell   280

Fig 62: Burnley Team Relaxing   288

Fig 63: Daily Mirror Front Page 27/4/1914   289

Fig 64: Tommy Boyle on Rosegrove Station Platform.
            (Getty)   295

Fig 65: The Procession Departs Rosegrove.   297

Fig 66: The Procession Reaches The Mitre.   298

Fig 67: The Scene Outside Burnley Town Hall at
            4:30 pm (Getty)   300

Fig 68: Burnley and Liverpool Teams at Anfield.   304

Fig 69: Burnley Team With The Cup.   306

Fig 70: Burnley on Tour in Earby.   307

Fig 71: Burnley Players Outside the Thorn Hotel
            in Burnley.   308

Fig 72: Flowerbed in Scott Park Burnley.   310

Fig 73: The Treaty of Commerce and Ronnie
            Sewell inset.   311

Fig 74: Tommy Bamford, Jerry Dawson and Dave
            Taylor (Getty)   313

Fig 75: George Halley   315
Fig 76: Tommy Boyle   316
Fig 77: Billy Watson   317
Fig 78: Billy Nesbitt   318
Fig 79: Richard Lindley   319
Fig 80: Bert Freeman   320
Fig 81: Teddy Hodgson   322
Fig 82: Eddie Mosscrop   323
Fig 83: Jimmy Bellamy   325
Fig 84: Bob Kelly   326
Fig 85: Harry Windle   328
Fig 86: John Haworth   329
Fig 87: Jackie Chew and Billy Morris with the 1914
        Cup Final Ball.   334
Fig 88: Artists Impression of the Proposed New Crystal
        Palace. (ARUP)   336
Fig 89: A Souvenir of the Cup Final.   337

Cover Image - The Burnley team arrive outside Burnley Town Hall on the 27th April 1914.

Inset: Burnley captain Tommy Boyle with The Cup. (Getty Images, colourised by George Chilvers)

---xxx---

Introduction

In England, the Football Association Challenge Cup as a national football tournament has no equal. Since the competition began in November 1871, the FA Cup has won a special place in the hearts of football players, clubs and their supporters. The competition has survived two world wars and become part of English sporting heritage. It remains the one major football trophy that lies within the grasp of thousands who take part in the competition every season. From village and works teams, through the amateur and semi professional leagues, all the way to The Premiership. Each team has a chance. It might be a slim one, but each team believes they have a chance to win and go through to the next round, or, like some have done, go all the way. That is what's so appealing about the Cup. There is a disregard for class and pampered overpaid superstars. The unpredictability of the Cup is what gives it its excitement. Who would have backed Wigan in 2013, Wimbledon in 1988', Coventry in 87', Southampton 76' or Sunderland in 73?' You can go back even further than that, to the early part of the 20th century and find Cup winning underdogs like Southern League Tottenham Hotspur in 1901, Second Division Wolverhampton Wanderers in 1908 and Barnsley in 1912 and these are only upsets caused in the Final.

Ask any supporter or player what their most memorable match was and it will most likely be a Cup tie. They'll describe in detail everything that happened on the day. The goals, the players, the stadium, the chanting, the lap of honour, the joy. An unforgettable day when grown men hug each other and cry like children. But winning the Cup is more than just the games played. The honour, prestige and glory not only go to the winning team, but is also bestowed on the town and community the team represents. Everyone stands a little bit taller and that bit prouder. For the winners, there's a heroes homecoming. A once in a lifetime experience with an open-topped bus tour, flag-waving crowds and a civic reception fit for a visiting head of state.

It all happened in my hometown, Burnley, on a special day in April 1914, when its football team won the Cup for the first time. In a hundred years, it remains Burnley's one success in the competition and as such it is unique. It was a very different world then. Burnley's victory took place only four months before the outbreak of the Great War. It was a world without radio, television, Sky Sports and the internet. The main source of football news then was the newspaper or old fashioned telephones that you wound up. Football supporters would wait anxiously outside newspaper offices on a Saturday afternoon for the football results to arrive, before they were hastily printed up as the 6 o'clock sports specials, the 'Pinks.'

Burnley have been in the Cup Final three times. In 1947, Cliff Britton's newly promoted Burnley played Charlton Athletic at Wembley but lost to a single Chris Duffy goal in extra-time. My father told me stories of what Cup Final day was like in 1962 when Burnley met Tottenham Hotspur at Wembley and lost 3-1. Just before he died, he passed on to me one of his most prized possessions; his 62' Cup Final programme, community song-sheet and match ticket that he'd kept in prime condition for almost fifty years. My own Cup experience with Burnley goes back to 1974, when as a teenager I watched the Clarets in the Semi-Final where we met Newcastle United. The atmosphere inside Hillsborough that afternoon was unforgettable, with 56,000 screaming fans packed inside. Two second half Malcolm MacDonald goals put Burnley out, and I can still remember the feeling of dejection on the way back from

THE ROAD TO GLORY

The Road To Glory celebrates the centenary of Burnley's 1914 FA Cup victory. We look at how Burnley got there, from the club's first Cup match in 1885 through to the 1908-09 season. The year when Burnley, according to reports were, 'robbed' of a first Semi-Final place following a quarter-final tie against Manchester United at Turf Moor. A match becoming infamously known among Burnley supporters as the, '*Stop the Game it's Snowing*' match. We progress from there to the 1912-13 season which saw Burnley reach the Semi-Final stage for the very first time. We then take a match-by-match view of the 1913-14 season to look at what happened, how the Cup team evolved from the League campaign and all the other events that took place in the build-up to arguably Burnley's greatest ever achievement. Evidence is gathered from match reports of the day from local and national sources, football programmes, photographs and other information from that eventful season.

The 1914 Burnley Cup-winning team of; Sewell, Bamford, Taylor, Halley, Boyle, Watson, Mosscrop, Lindley, Freeman, Hodgson and Nesbitt are legends. Heroes. They went all the way and won it and the reason why Burnley's name is inscribed on the Cup, and in the history books. Those eleven heroes did it first and every other Burnley team must follow. Hopefully one April day in your lifetime and in mine, their feat will be repeated and another great Burnley team will travel all the way down the road to glory and bring the Cup back to Turf Moor.

One day.

Mike Smith
April 2014

Turf Moor – Home of Burnley Football Club

Figure 2: Turf Moor in the 1920s

This photograph taken in the 1920s is the earliest aerial shot we have of Turf Moor as it would have appeared in 1914. The stand in the foreground is the Brunshaw Road Stand which opened in August 1913 at the start of the 1913-14 season. The stand was demolished and re-built again in 1973-4. It is currently The Bob Lord Stand, named after the former Burnley chairman. To the right of the picture is the Bee Hole End, a huge open terrace which was named after the colliery that overlooked the ground from Brunshaw Heights. This is now the Jimmy McIlroy Stand. To the left of the picture is the covered Cricket Field End that was completed during 1914. In match reports this was sometimes called the Town End and is currently the David Fishwick Stand. Burnley Cricket ground backs onto Turf Moor and you can see the old cricket pavilion in white in the distance.

The long, raised cinder banking opposite the Brunshaw Road stand was formerly home to the tiny Star Stand which covered only half the length of the pitch. The Star Stand was demolished in 1914 and the cinder-banking raised and extended to cater for larger crowds which increased the ground capacity at Turf Moor in 1914 to 40,000. It was not until the mid-1950s before this side of the ground was terraced and roofed which became the famously known among Burnley fans as 'The Longside' and is now the James Hargreaves Stand.

---xxx---

CHAPTER ONE

The Green and Whites

Loud without the wind was roaring
Through the waned autumnal sky;
Drenching wet, the cold rain pouring
Spoke of stormy winters nigh.

– Emily Bronte

Twenty miles north of Manchester, Burnley lies on the low western slopes of the Pennine hills. In the 19th and early 20th centuries the town was a key contributor to Britian's economy and one of the country's major providers of cotton and coal. Burnley's close proximity to Manchester and the damp climate attracted a number of cotton manufacturers and output grew rapidly from 1850 to the end of the century. As the demand for cotton grew, so did the population, reaching a peak of 106,765 by 1911. In 2009, a former Burnley manager commented that the town's population would now fit inside Old Trafford. Such had the town changed. In 1911, the working population lived in tightly-knit communities in mainly two-up, two-down terraced houses, in streets that fanned out from the mills and factories. Homes were gas lit, warmed by coal fires and were without electricity, hot running water or inside toilets.

The cotton mills, pits and factories ran repeating shifts, a six day working week that finished at 1:00pm on Saturdays. After a backbreaking 48 hour week, the workforce could then unwind. To quench the workers thirst, Burnley had six brewers supplying, 49 private clubs, 73 beerhouses, 87 hotels and taverns and 91 off-licences. In addition to a multitude of drinking establishments, Burnley had a variety of facilities for indoor and outdoor sport and recreation. From the mid to late 19th century, Burnley had held its own regular race meeting, The Burnley Stakes on Towneley Holmes. The 1912 Ordnance Survey shows a fine athletics stadium with a grandstand, a cycling and running track, in the Fulledge ward of the town. The town had 15 cycle shops, six billiard halls, three cycling clubs, two tennis clubs and two prominent cricket clubs (Burnley and Lowerhouse) that played in the Lancashire League. There were scores of amateur football leagues with teams from mill and works teams, churches and lads clubs that played on Saturday and Sunday afternoons. And representing the town, one professional football team, Burnley Football Club.

Burnley Football Club were one of the twelve founding members of the Football League which began in 1888. With the start of the League, football matches got a more competitive edge and the local population started taking more interest in Burnley's fortunes against other League clubs. The start of the Football League raised attendances at matches and with Saturday afternoons off and an excellent railway network, Burnley's supporters could travel up and down the country cheaply and follow their team with ease. But despite the League's arrival, and the fact that there was a League Championship trophy at stake, the League never set the pulse racing like the FA Cup did as a competition. The older Football Association Challenge Cup to give it its full title was *the* premier competition, football's holy grail and the one trophy all football clubs wanted to win.

Burnley's first entry into the Cup (commonly named the 'English' Cup in the newspapers) was in 1885, some fourteen years after the competition began in 1871 and three years before the birth of the Football League. Local village sides Padiham and Clitheroe had both entered the Cup competition several years before Burnley. Burnley's entry into the First Round on the 17th of October 1885 should have been a special day for the Turf Moor club who were drawn away against Darwen Old Wanderers. Because of the Football Association's rules of which prohibited professionals from playing, Burnley had to send a makeshift reserve team. Darwen Old Wanderers, (not to be confused with Darwen F.C. or Lower Darwen F.C. who were also drawn in the First Round), were an experienced Cup fighting outfit. From the result it looked like Wanderers must have done all the fighting. The match finished Darwen Old Wanderers 11, Burnley 0. As bad as that result was it wasn't the worst defeat of the day. Rotherham took that honour after a 15-0 thrashing by Notts County. It must have been a hard lesson for all those who played that day and for the football club. The following season the Football Association relaxed its rules and allowed professional footballers to enter.

Despite reaching the Third Round if the Cup in 1897-98, up to the 1908-9 season, Burnley struggled in the competition and were regularly knocked out at either the First or Second Round stage. Burnley had some notable First Round victories to their credit. A 6-1 win over Arsenal in 1895-96, followed by a 7-1 win over Newton Heath in 1900-01 (shortly thereafter changing their name to Manchester United) and an emphatic 8-0 win over Keswick in 1903-04, but it wasn't until the 1908-09 competition did people sit up and take notice of Burnley's progress. One reason for the poor form in the Cup co-incided with Burnley's decline in The League.

In April 1900 after a poor season in Division One, Burnley were relegated. Following relegation the club got into quite serious financial difficulties. In 1901, one young Burnley supporter, Harry Windle, who worked as a clerk for Abraham Altham, a Burnley tea merchant and travel company, began a fundraising campaign to fund a new player. Windle's efforts managed to raise £50 for the club. It helped, but with falling attendances and rising debts, the club directors had to dig into their own pockets to keep the football club afloat. On the pitch things got worse as Burnley dropped down the Second Division. At the end of the 1902 - 03 season, Burnley hit rock bottom, ending the season seeking re-election to the Football League. The Athletics News describes how bad things had got,

"There was a time when Burnley were without money, when they discharged their players, trainer and groundsman and the secretary alone remained because he was content to work without drawing a salary. That secretary was Ernest Magnall who was amazed if such a sum as £50 was taken for a League match. There was one occasion when to raise funds, Turf Moor was hired to a travelling wild beast show for £20. The club only received £10 because the elephants couldn't pull the caravans onto the pitch. That situation was only ten years ago." (Athletics News, 16/3/1914)

Magnall stayed on at Turf Moor through the bad times until October 1903 before he resigned after being appointed manager at Manchester United. The Burnley board appointed the 32 year old, Spencer Whittaker from Accrington, as their new manager. Around the same time as Whittaker arrived, the Burnley board formally invited Harry Windle to chair a fundraising committee. Four years later in July 1907, Windle was invited onto the board as a full director. The average age of the Board was 50. Windle was 33, a young man with modern ideas of how the Club should be managed. The ambitious, business-minded Windle became Vice Chairman in 1908 and on June 11th 1909 he was elected Chairman.

With Windle and Whittaker in the football club, things began to move forwards. The football team steadily climbed the Second Division table. An 11th place finish in 1905, 9th place in 1906, 7th in 1907 and again the following year. Attendances increased and the sixpences rolled in through the Turf Moor turnstiles. Windle turned the club finances around and by 1909 Burnley was back in the black. In 1907, Whittaker found a promising young goalkeeper, Jeremiah Dawson, the son of a Cliviger blacksmith. Dawson was so good he went straight into the Burnley first team. Whittaker signed more youngsters including Tommy Bamford a full-back from Darwen, Richard Lindley an inside-forward from Oswaldtwistle Rovers and Billy Watson a centre-back from Southport Central. The talented trio would begin in the reserves before breaking through into the first team.

Whittaker's biggest coup was the capture of two former England internationals, the 36-year old veteran Alec Leake from Aston Villa in 1907 and 32-year old Walter Abbott, a £200 transfer from Everton in 1908. Leake had won a Cup Winners medal with Villa in 1905 and five England caps in the same year. Abbot had also won a Cup winners medal with Everton the following year in 1906. Whittaker was building a Burnley team with a blend of youth and experience. Despite making progress up the Second Division table, in the Cup, Burnley's performances had not been so successful, but that was all about to change the following season.

BURNLEY.
Holden (Tr.)   Moffat.   Cretney.   Dawson.   Leake   Abbott.   Parker.
Morley.   Whittaker.   Barron   Smith, R.   A. A. Bell.   Smith, A.   Howarth.

Figure 3: Burnley Football Team 1908-09

The 1908-09 FA Cup

The First Round of the 1908-09 FA Cup kicked off on the 16th January 1909. Burnley travelled to Bristol to play Southern League side Bristol Rovers. The team travelled down to Bristol by train on the Friday afternoon, staying overnight in Cheltenham before continuing their journey on Saturday morning. While out for a Friday evening stroll, the Burnley centre-forward Dick Smith found a horse-shoe in the street. Footballers being a superstitious bunch, Smith collected the shoe and gave it to one of the Burnley directors and claimed the shoe was a good luck omen. In addition to the lucky shoe story, the Burnley Express's Sportsman in his football column told the tale of a Burnley Lane resident who had had a 'vision' three days before the Bristol game. The Burnley Lane man claimed Burnley would beat Rovers with a scoreline of 4-1 and Ogden would be among the scorers.

Bristol Rovers v Burnley FA Cup Round One, Eastville, 16th January 1909 Kick-Off 2:30 pm

The teams lined up
Bristol Rovers: Cartlidge, Appleby, Floyd, Smart, Strang, Higgins, Peplow, Gerrish, Corbett, Roberts, Dargue.
Burnley: Dawson, Barron, McLean, Cretney, Leake, Moffatt, Morley, Ogden, Smith, Abbott, Smethams.
Referee: Mr G. H. Muir (Southampton)

It was a sunny afternoon in the West Country but the ground was heavy after rain during the week. The conditions favoured the visitors, playing in their familiar green shirts. Burnley captain Alec Leake won the toss and played with the wind. Burnley took the lead through Dick Smith on 22 minutes whose run and shot hit the roof of Rovers net. Despite pressure from the home side, the score remained 1-0 to Burnley at the interval.

6

In the second half, Rovers attacked and Dargue had beaten Dawson and put the ball in the Burnley net only to be ruled offside. Fifteen minutes into the half a Smethams centre found Ogden to score the second goal. Two minutes after that Burnley made the game safe with a second goal for Ogden. Mid-way through the second half the Smethams – Ogden combination worked again. Smethams cross finding Ogden's head to give the inside-forward his hat-trick. Ten minutes from time, a long shot by the Rovers' Strang, caught the wind and flew into Dawson's net to give the home side a consolation goal.

At Full Time: Bristol Rovers 1(Strang), Burnley 4 (Ogden 3, Smith)
Attendance: 7,000

---XXX---

The lucky horse-shoe had worked its magic and the chap from Burnley Lane had his vision fulfilled. In Round Two, Burnley were drawn away again, this time against another Southern League side, Crystal Palace. It was Burnley's first ever visit to huge the arena of The Crystal Palace, home of the Cup Final. Burnley travel companies, Abraham Altham's and Whittaker's, were both running excursions to London for the Cup tie. The Burnley team and directors travelled down on the Friday morning. The lucky horse-shoe mascot travelled with them. Sportsman reported that the journey from Burnley to London was the fastest time he had ever experienced, arriving at Euston in 5 hours 14 minutes after setting off from Burnley Bank Top station. It was a frosty dawn on the Saturday morning in Sydenham but once the sun rose above the giant bowl-shaped stadium, the pitch thawed. By kick-off time the manicured surface looked more like a cricket pitch. There was a good home crowd and a number of travelling supporters cheering on Burnley when Alec Leake's men appeared shortly before the 3:00 pm kick-off. Burnley fielding an unchanged team from the First Round tie at Bristol.

Crystal Palace v Burnley, FA Cup Round Two, The Crystal Palace, Sydenham, 6 February 1909. Kick-Off 3:00 pm

The teams lined up
Crystal Palace: Johnson, Needham, Collyer, Innerd, Ryan, Brearley, Garratt, Lewis, Bauchop, Lawrence, Woodger.
Burnley: Dawson, Barron, McLean, Cretney, Leake, Moffatt, Morley, Ogden, Smith, Abbott, Smethams.
Referee: Mr J. W. Bailey (Leicester)

Alec Leake won the toss and Burnley playing in their regular strip, all green shirts and white shorts and played with the wind. The Southern League side began well and Woodger gave Jerry Dawson plenty to do in the first 15 minutes. Burnley came more into the game once they learned what their opponents were capable of. On 30 minutes, Burnley's Ogden had a goal-scoring opportunity. Johnson in the Palace goal managing to clear off the line. A Crystal Palace penalty claim when Fred Barron brought down Lawrence, was turned down by Mr Bailey.

In the second half, the Burnley travelling crowd started singing their songs, "Oh Antonio" and "Cock Robin" to try and lift their side. Morley and Smethams for Burnley had chances but their efforts were thwarted by Johnson. Jerry Dawson played well all afternoon according to Sportsman and the game drew to a goalless conclusion which was a fair result in the end. As soon as the final whistle went, part of the Burnley crowd invaded the pitch to try and 'chair' the players. The crowd caught hold of Dawson and shouldered him all the way to the dressing room.

At Full Time: Crystal Palace 0, Burnley 0
Attendance: 20,000.

---xxx---

THE ROAD TO GLORY

The Burnley team returned to their hotel for tea before visiting the Tivoli and afterwards caught the midnight train from Euston back to Burnley, arriving home in the early hours of Sunday morning. Sportsman gave the opposition a lot of credit, and thought that "for a Southern League side," they were, "a quite good side".

The two teams met again the following Wednesday afternoon at Turf Moor. Burnley fielded the same side while Palace had one change, Collins coming in at full-back and replacing Lewis. The referee was also changed from the previous encounter. Mr Herbert Bamlett from Gateshead turning out at Turf Moor to replace scheduled referee Mr Bailey.

The cold weather in Burnley had thawed over Monday and Tuesday making the Turf Moor pitch heavy, quite different to the cricket-pitch like conditions Palace had enjoyed at Sydenham. Sportsman gave the pitch and the strange surroundings as two reasons that troubled the visitors on their journey north. Rain early on Wednesday morning made the pitch even heavier. Before kick-off the skies around Burnley were a grey-black. It was cold, windy and teeming rain fell that continued throughout the first half.

Burnley v Crystal Palace FA Cup Round Two Replay Turf Moor, 10th February 1909 Kick-off 3:00 pm

The teams lined up
Burnley: Dawson, Barron, McLean, Cretney, Leake, Moffatt, Morley, Ogden, Smith, Abbott, Smethams.
Crystal Palace: Johnson, Collins, Collyer, Innerd, Ryan, Brearley, Garratt, Lawrence, Bauchop, Woodger, Needham
Referee: Mr H. S. Bamlett (Gateshead)

Mr Bamlett brought the two captains together and Alec Leake lost the toss. Palace played in their claret and blue shirts toward the Bee Hole End. In the first half, Sportsman counted that Palace had only three attacks in the first 45 minutes. The play having been mainly at the Cricket Field End as Burnley adapted far better to the wind, the rain and the mud. On five minutes, centre-forward Dick Smith opened the scoring for Burnley. Fifteen minutes later, Smith struck again and made it 2-0, nodding in a cross from Ogden. Three minutes later Moffatt made it three-nil. On 35 minutes, Burnley attacked again down the left flank, Morley centred and Abbott volleyed the ball past Johnson to make it 4-0. With a minute to go before the interval, a superb long-range strike by Cretney flew past a statuesque Johnson to make it Burnley 5, Palace 0 at half time.

Many teams, having scored heavily in the first half, rarely repeat their form in the second period. Changes of tactics by the opposition, fading strength and desire, tired legs all being factors. If that was some sort of text-book rule, then Burnley had not read it. The Palace defence managed to hold Burnley's forwards at bay for 21 minutes. Even though the rain had ceased, the goals came thick and fast. Abbot made it 6-0 on 66 minutes. On 71 minutes, Smethams got on the score-sheet scoring number seven followed shortly by another from Cretney by which time the crowd and Palace were simply stunned. Eight-nil. A dejected Palace were hoping Bamlett would blow the whistle. But Burnley were not finished. Burnley went on the attack as Dick Smith twisted the knife in deeper. Smith sensing his hat-trick, got it with minutes remaining to make it 9-0. And shortly after referee Bamlett blew his whistle and finally put Crystal Palace out of their misery.

At Full Time: Burnley 9 (Smith 3, Abbott 2, Cretney 2, Moffatt, Smethams), Crystal Palace 0
Attendance: 12,161 (Gate receipts of £393 15s 5d)

---xxx---

It had been an amazing afternoon for the twelve thousand who witnessed it. Sportsman had never seen a performance like it, "...even the most ardent admirer of Burnley never dreamt of anything approaching either the brilliancy of the exhibition or the heavy scoring. Dick Smith probably played the game of his life!"

Burnley had been drawn away again for Round Three. It was another long trip to the capital, this time to play fellow Second Division side Tottenham Hotspur. This would be a much stiffer test. Tottenham had gone all the way and won the Cup in 1901 when they were a Southern League side. Burnley had already played at White Hart Lane in December in the League and had come away on the wrong side of a 4-2 scoreline. With home advantage, the London newspapers were confident of a Tottenham victory at White Hart Lane.

The Burnley team arrived at London Euston early on Friday evening in high spirits. The team, directors and wives made the short journey to Smithfield and their normal base when they played in the capital, the Charterhouse Hotel. After dinner, the Burnley party went to the Adelphi Theatre for an evening of light entertainment and saw, 'Cinderella' starring Dan Rolyat, John Humphries and Phyllis Dare.

Around 700 travelling Burnley supporters on one special train, made the journey, arriving in London just before noon. According to Sportsman, "the Burnley spectators were not ashamed to make themselves known by voice and badge. During the morning I saw a few excursionists, wearing, 'Of the Green' in the Strand and they were evidently proud of the fact."
While one Burnley group were taking in the sights of London, a horse attached to a vehicle threw a shoe. A Burnley supporter spotted it and picked it up and gave it in to the club whose lucky horse-shoe collection now equalled four shoes. 'Lucky' Burnley were again unchanged from the side that had so easily disposed of Crystal Palace.

Figure 4: Tottenham Hotspur Team 1908-09

Tottenham Hotspur v Burnley FA Cup Third Round, White Hart Lane,
20 February 1909 Kick-off 3:30 pm

The teams lined up
Tottenham Hotspur: Hewitson, Coquet, Burton, Morris, D. Steel, Darnell, Walton, Minter, V. J. Woodward, B. Steel, Middlemiss.
Burnley: Dawson, Barron, McLean, Cretney, Leake, Moffatt, Morley, Ogden, Smith, Abbott, Smethams.
Referee: Mr A. Adams (Nottingham)

D. Steel the Tottenham captain led out the Spurs team wearing their cream jerseys and dark blue knickers followed by Alec Leake leading out 'The Greens.' At 3:31 Mr Adams got the match underway.

The pace of the game was fast and furious. The intention of the home side was clearly to put the visitors on the defensive.

Woodward, the Spurs centre-forward and celebrated amateur England international, tested Jerry Dawson early on but Leake was equal to the England man in defending. Burnley eventually settled and managed the occasional attack of their own. Following a foul by Darnell for elbowing, Morley had a goal opportunity that Hewitson only just managed to save.

Alec Leake managed his forces well, breaking up Tottenham's short-passing game plan, marking close and not allowing the opposition to put their combinations together. After ten minutes of stalemate, Sportsman picked up on the restless home crowd who thought their side should have been in front. Burnley continued to repel the Spurs attack. Middlemiss did manage to put the ball past Dawson, for the crowd to roar GOAL! Only to discover that a Spurs player was offside. For the next fifteen minutes Burnley took the game to their hosts. Dick Smith had a run on goal. He passed to Morley on the left, Smith running on and receiving Morley's return pass. It was a clever move but the Tottenham full backs cleared the danger and at the interval the scores were level at 0-0.

The second period began with another quick burst from Vivian Woodward and the Spurs forward line. Dawson saved splendidly from Minter, finger-tipping the ball over the crossbar. Burnley had chances of their own, mainly from Smith and Ogden. Some good combination work between the front Burnley pair drew applause from around 'The Lane.' One clever Burnley effort led to Smith stepping over the ball hoping Ogden who was behind him would have a crack at the Spurs goal, only for the defence to clear. It became an afternoon of chances missed for both sides and Burnley had had enough of their own to have won the contest. The match became a 0-0 stalemate, Burnley came away from White Hart Lane the happier team and the teams would meet again the following Wednesday at Turf Moor.

At Full Time: Tottenham Hotspur 0, Burnley 0
Attendance: 21,372 (Gate receipts of £1,390)

---xxx---

On the day of the replay, a number of Burnley firms had decided to close at lunch-time. Stuttard's gave their workers a vote to either work or watch the match. The mill engine was stopped shortly after. The same happened at Valley Mills and at Nelson's which closed on Wednesday dinner-time. Trainloads of spectators arrived in Burnley from as far as Bolton, Leeds and Bradford. One Southern group of Burnley supporters who had followed the team at Crystal Palace, had travelled all the way to Turf Moor from Southampton. At 2:30 pm, Turf Moor was bulging and a decision was made to close the turnstiles with thousands locked outside. Inside the ground there were banners, flags and one Burnley spectator managed to get a 20-foot green and white striped pole through the turnstiles and was waving it in the air.

A number of other Football League clubs were represented at the match. The Manchester United team who would meet the winners of the replay were present; Billy Meredith and his team mates sat on benches along one touchline. The weather was a perfect afternoon for football. It was cold and bright, but with no wind or rain. The pitch was on the soft side and had been sprinkled with sand in the goal areas and the centre-circle. Burnley were once again unchanged while Tottenham had one team change, Brough replacing Morris at half-back.

Burnley v Tottenham Hotspur FA Cup Third Round Replay, Turf Moor, Wednesday 24 February 1909 Kick-off 3.00 pm

The teams lined up
Burnley: Dawson, Barron, McLean, Cretney, Leake, Moffatt, Morley, Ogden, Smith, Abbott, Smethams.

Tottenham Hotspur: Hewitson, Coquet, Burton, Brough, D. Steel, Darnell, Walton, Minter, V. Woodward, B. Steel, Middlemiss.

Referee: Mr A. Adams (Nottingham)

Mr Adams once again got proceedings underway as the Spurs captain, Vivian Woodward, won the toss and elected to play toward the Bee Hole End.

Like the first game, Spurs began with their short quick-passing moves while Burnley were happy to spread the play out and go long, bypassing the midfield. The opening exchanges were fairly even. Hewitson in the Spurs goal was called on first, saving a Dick Smith effort. Eleven minutes into the game, Smith found Smethams on the right whose forward run won Burnley their first corner. Smethams centre into a packed penalty area found Walter Abbott who scored with a glancing header to give Burnley the lead to wild cheers around Turf Moor. Burnley held onto their advantage and Dawson had little to do, the half-backs keeping Spurs at bay. Then Smith won the ball in the Spurs half and rounded Coquet. Smith only had Hewitson to beat but the full-back (Coquet), "committed one of the most glaring offences of the game," said Sportsman. Mr Adams awarded Burnley a free-kick which should have put them further ahead but the ball was cleared. Burnley's Barron and McLean were called on close to half-time and safely cleared the danger. At the interval, 'the Greens' led the Spurs by Abbott's early goal.

The second half began with Spurs winning a quick corner at the Cricket Field End, the centre cleared by Fred Barron. Burnley came forward, attacking the Bee Hole End. Smethams fed Smith whose shot flew inches off the floor, just wide of Hewitson's post. But what happened next was something special according to Sportsman.

"Dick Smith received the ball from the right and though Hewitson did all he knew to cover his goal leaving Smith a task something approaching the threading of a needle, he was equal to the task and amid a scene which will not be forgotten for a long time by those who witnessed it, he found the net with a brilliant shot after four minutes."

Straight from the restart, Burnley's midfield challenged the Spurs attackers and won the ball back. The ball came out to Ogden who lost his half-back, ran in on goal and shot low past Hewitson and make it 3-0 to Burnley.

"Burnley were all over their opponents," said Sportsman. Shortly after the third goal Morley should have made it 4-0 but skewed his shot wide. Spurs eventually came more into the game but continued with their short-passing style which Burnley easily broke up and robbed them of the ball on the now churned up surface. With twelve minutes to go, Moffat the Burnley defender was judged to have pulled up Minter inside the penalty area. Coquet took the penalty kick for Spurs who shot straight at Dawson who got a hand to the ball but couldn't prevent it going in. Spurs attacked in the final ten minutes but had left it too late to pull any more goals back. The Greens deservedly won 3-1 and entered the Fourth Round of the Cup for the first time.

At Full Time: Burnley 3 (Abbott, Smith, Ogden), Tottenham Hotspur 1 (Coquet pen)
Attendance: 23,000 (Record gate receipts of £1,152 for a Turf Moor Cup Tie)

---xxx---

The Quarter-Final draw now read,

Burnley v Manchester United
Derby County v Nottingham Forest
Newcastle United v Sunderland
Glossop North End v Bristol City

It would be an interesting contest at Turf Moor for reasons other than football. Throughout the match, sat on the touchline, was United's Billy Meredith, the Wales international. Meredith had kept a keen eye on one player in particular, Burnley's captain, Alec Leake.

The two men had a mutual loathing and hatred of each other.

Figure 5: Alec Leake and Billy Meredith

Their mutual dislike of each other stemmed from an incident that had taken place between the two men four years previously in 1905. Leake was then captain of Aston Villa and Meredith captain of Manchester City. In the final game of the 1904-05 First Division season, Aston Villa played Manchester City at Villa Park. If City won the match, they could pip Newcastle United to the Championship.

The press reports stated that the game was quite a vicious affair. City's Sandy Turnbull and Villa's Alec Leake came to blows during the match (which City lost 3-2) which the Football Association later investigated. During the proceedings Leake claimed that Meredith had offered him a bribe of £10 for his team to throw the match. The Football Association began a further investigation, (Harding, 1998)

"The Football Association banned Meredith from August 4, 1905, to April 30, 1906, which constituted a season-long absence. The player told the *Daily Mirror* shortly after the ban was imposed that he was "perfectly innocent" and added: "Would any man risk his reputation for a paltry £10? Certainly not. I should not be such a mug to ruin my future and blight my character. If I had not been a Welshman it would have been all right." (Hackett, 2011)

"During his suspension, Meredith persistently and improperly requested that City pay him his £6 weekly wages - £2 above the salary cap - in addition to any win bonuses. Meredith threatened the club of the consequences should they fail to meet his demands but, in February 1906, City notified the FA of the player's blackmail attempt. It was an unwise strategy, and Meredith was to claim that he had made the £10 bribe on behalf of the club's secretary-manager, Tom Maley, and with the consent of several players. "I was only the spokesman of others equally guilty," he wrote in a letter to the *Athletic News*. He also credited City's success to "the fact that the club put aside the rule that no player should be paid more than £4 a week". (Hackett, 2011)

Meredith's whistle-blowing sent shockwaves through the Football Association. As a result, the Manchester City manager Tom Maley, and a former chairman were both banned from English football, sine die. Five City directors were dismissed, two directors were suspended for seven months and 17 City players were banned for six months (including Sandy Turnbull). For his trouble, Billy Meredith received the longest ban of all. He was banned from playing football for a total of eighteen months (extending his season-long ban by six months).

A year after the FA's inquiry, Meredith signed for neighbours Manchester United in May 1906, but he couldn't play again until his ban was lifted on New Years Day 1907. There he made his debut in a United shirt alongside Sandy Turnbull who had also signed for the Reds. A Meredith inspired United won the Football League Championship the following season. In the 1908-09 FA Cup, United had beaten Brighton in the First Round (1-0), Everton 1-0 in Round Two and Blackburn Rovers 6-1 in Round Three to reach the Quarter-Final. Turf Moor was all set for a showdown between Meredith, Turnbull and Leake.

Following the victory over Tottenham, to squeeze in more spectators for the Quarter-Final, the Burnley Board sanctioned some much needed ground improvements.

The wood and corrugated tin built Star Stand was dismantled and moved back from the pitch 15 yards to create an enclosure for 2,000 people. The stand was then re-built and extended to create additional covered seating for 1,700 more people. Hundreds of tons of mill ashes were brought into the ground to raise the banking all round the stadium while an extra twelve turnstiles were added at the Belvedere Road end. Work went on around the clock to get Turf Moor ready for the visit of United. The admission prices were raised, doubled in fact. Ground admission for adults up from sixpence to a shilling with sixpence for boys and ladies.

Despite two of the harshest winter months having passed, from mid-day on Friday to Saturday morning before the game, an arctic cold-front swept south across Britain. Temperatures fell below freezing and snow came to the high-ground in blizzards. With deep drifts in the Peak District, the first Quarter-Final called off was the Derby County v. Nottingham Forest tie. The pitches at Newcastle and Glossop were cleared and would go ahead. (With poor weather conditions right across the country, out of 23 League One and Two matches that kicked-off on that Saturday, only 13 managed to play to a finish.)

Burnley v Manchester United FA Cup Quarter Final, Turf Moor Saturday 6 March 1909 Kick-off 3:30 pm

The Turf Moor turnstiles opened quite early at 11:30 on Saturday and from then on a steady stream of spectators from Burnley, some wearing the green and white and a number from Manchester in their red and white favours, filled the ground. Before the start, match referee Herbert Bamlett came out to inspect the Turf Moor playing surface. He was accompanied by Charlie Roberts the United skipper and Burnley's Alec Leake. The pitch was already covered in snow and Bamlett asked the ground staff for the side lines to be swept clear. He was satisfied the match could begin at the scheduled time. The Daily Graphic of 13 March 1909 carried a photograph showing the Turf Moor crowd in jovial mood with little sign on the terraces of how poor conditions on the pitch actually were. Snow continued to fall, and as 3:30 pm approached the temperature dropped further as the teams lined up to kick-off. Burnley were once again unchanged from the side that had beaten Spurs and it was clear early on that the awful weather had kept a lot of people away.

The Teams lined up:
Burnley: Dawson, Barron, McLean, Cretney, Leake(c), Moffatt, Morley, Ogden, Smith, Abbott, Smethams.
Manchester United: Moger, Stacey, Hayes, Duckworth, Roberts(c), Bell, Meredith, Halse, Turnbull J., Turnbull A., Wall.
Referee: Mr H. S. Bamlett (Gateshead)

Alec Leake beat Charlie Roberts to the toss and the Green's played with the wind at their backs toward the Cricket Field End. It was clear that the players on both sides were struggling to stay on their feet, but Burnley seemed to cope with the conditions slightly better than United. Burnley won the first corner of the game only for Stacey to clear. Following some early action by Dawson, Burnley attacked through the centre with Dick Smith who headed a Smethams cross just over the United crossbar. Then Cretney had a goal chance that was dealt with by Moger. On 15 minutes, Smethams got a good centre into the United box, Ogden won the ball and his shot flew past Moger and into the United net! Burnley were in front and through no fluke. Ogden's goal had stunned Meredith's men. Straight after the re-start, Burnley won the ball in midfield and pressed forward again down the left. Moger was called on three times in succession. First an effort from Smith, and then Ogden twice, whose second attempt on 20 minutes should have put Burnley 2-0 ahead, his shot striking the inside of Mogers' post, the ball re-bounding to safety. Burnley won two successive corners and maintained the pressure, looking for that second goal.

Sportsman declared that, "play was pretty vigorous" and Ogden was badly fouled near the edge of the United penalty area. Shortly after, Dawson rushed out from his goal to stop an attack from Alec (Sandy) Turnbull. The two players collided, with Turnbull needing attention from the trainer. Dawson saved a Halse effort with a superb diving save, getting his fingers to the ball and sending it out for a corner and shortly after, referee Bamlett signalled for half-time, with Burnley leading 1-0.

United started the second half and now had the advantage of the wind and the snow behind them. Sportsman on the state of the weather at the start of the second half, "The snowfall was heavier now than before and in the course of a few minutes the fleecy flakes descended more copiously than ever and approached a blizzard." Play continued regardless. Ogden once again found himself fouled on the edge of the United penalty area – but where was the line? Bamlett rejected the Burnley forwards' appeal for a penalty. Burnley appeared the more confident, and on occasion showed neat footwork despite the falling snow and slippy surface. Shortly after, Barron and McLean were both injured. Barron limping away from a challenge while Mclean was winded in a tussle with Billy Meredith who had been fairly inconspicuous throughout the game. "Send him off" was shouted from the crowd. McLean got up and just got on with matters. "After attention he was as lively as ever for after defeating the Welshman once he intercepted him again, but in his rush he [Meredith] slid along the ground for half a dozen yards, 'barking' his shoulders in the process," said Sportsman. After this incident, the Burnley goal was under siege for about 15 minutes according to Sportsman. The intensity of the snowstorm increased. United were on the attack but the Burnley players stood fast. A frozen Jerry Dawson, his blue jersey crusted in snow, pulled off a series of fine saves which the crowd loudly cheered. The match had gone past the three-quarter mark when with eighteen minutes left, Mr Bamlett was approached by Charlie Roberts.

"The stubborn nature of the defence evidently broke the hearts of the besiegers and overtures were made by the United captain [Roberts] to the referee to stop the game. Burnley, getting relief, carried the war into the enemy's camp on two or three occasions. Referee Bamlett then sounded a cessation and consulted his linesmen re the abandonment of the game. Burnley were in the United half when the game was stopped and leading 1-0." (Burnley Express)

Result: Match Abandoned on 72 minutes (snowstorm) with Burnley leading Manchester United 1-0 (Ogden)
Attendance: 15,471 (Gate Receipts of £1,089 5s)

---xxx---

The home crowd were stunned at Bamlett's decision. To have allowed the match to first of all start but then to see it though to half time where he could have evaluated the situation, and then for the sides to appear again for the second period was unbelievable. It was clear that United captain Charlie Roberts had appealed to Bamlett for the game to be abandoned while Burnley's Alec Leake wanted to play on.

The Daily Mail's reporter at the match said,

"The Cup-tie at Turf Moor was abandoned with 18 minutes to go because of the blizzard which had raged from the previous midnight becoming worse than ever. The sleety storm was bad enough to have justified the referee in refusing to begin at all, and, curiously enough the weather improved ten minutes after the teams had retired to the extent which would have enabled the game to be played out in comparitive comfort... Mr Bamlett explained to a Daily Mail representative that the increase in the gales severity and the fact that officials and players were benumbed by the cold dictated his action. Burnley took the game to United and with the wind at their backs outplayed the League Champions in the first half. Young Dawson in the Burnley goal displayed a wonderful resource and was never in difficulties."

(Daily Mail 8/3/1909)

After Burnley scored and as the second half the conditions worsened, Charbel Boujaoude alleges in his book, *Manchester United - Legends of a Bygone Era*,

"Referee Bamlett was so cold he couldnt blow the whistle. So Manchester United captain Charlie Roberts felt in Bamlett's pocket, pulled out his whistle and blew it for him and abandoned the match!" Strangely, the local reporter at the Burnley Express, Sportsman makes no mention of this incident anywhere in his match report. Nor did the national papers.

After the match, the captains were interviewed by Press journalists. According to Sportsman, an aggrieved Burnley captain Alec Leake said, "I think it is hard lines for Burnley, and I should say the same even if we had not been a goal ahead. The weather was bad, but after playing so long we ought to have finished the match. I am absolutely confident we should have kept them out to the end – they would never have scored.

As for being fit, every man here was able and willing to see it out – weren't you boys?" A chorus of "YES" confirmed his opinion. "We should have beaten them on merits," he concluded, " as we shall do in the end." "We may have no 'class' players, as some critics say, but we are eleven triers, and don't you forget it!"

Roberts burst out: "I think it was a shame to take us out at all on a ground like that – just a sheet of ice. Men's lives were at stake, but nobody considers players as they ought to do when the elements are in question. It was not fit for a dog to be out, and all through the first half we could hardly see the ball for the snow in our eyes. I fancy Burnley players were just as thankful as we were to get off."

(Burnley Express 10/3/1909)

It was clear that this contest wasn't over by a long chalk. Burnley had led the League Champions for over an hour and were 18 minutes away from their first Cup Semi-Final. The match went down in Burnley F. C. folklore as the, "*Stop The Game It's Snowing*" match. Both clubs had managed to enter the semi-final draw that took place the following Monday. Due to the weather postponements, abandonments and two draws, the draw couldn't have been more complicated;

The FA Cup Semi-Final Draw

> **Burnley or Manchester United v Newcastle or Sunderland to be played at Bramall Lane**
> **Derby County or Nottingham Forest v Glossop or Bristol City to be played at Stamford Bridge.**

The two teams met up again on Wednesday for the resumption of hostilities. United having spent a few days at their Cup training retreat in Cuddington, Cheshire. The snow had melted but the players tempers had not.

Burnley v Manchester United FA Cup Quarter Final, Turf Moor Wednesday 10 March 1909 3:30 Kick-Off

Burnley were forced to make one team change from Saturday. Full-back Fred Barron was suffering a leg injury that he picked up on Saturday. He was replaced by Howarth. It was the first team change Spen Whittaker had made in the Cup run since the First Round at Bristol. For the superstitious among the Burnley supporters, it was a bad omen. The attendance for a mid-week match was one of the best Burnley had ever experienced. "The pitch was clear but had held onto most of the melted snow," as Sportsman saw the pitch he said it resembled, "a veritable quagmire."

The Teams lined up:
Burnley: Dawson, Haworth, McLean, Cretney, Leake(c), Moffatt, Morley, Ogden, Smith, Abbott, Smethams.
Manchester United: Moger, Stacey, Hayes, Duckworth, Roberts(c), Bell, Meredith, Halse, Turnbull J., Turnbull A., Wall.
Referee: Mr. H. S. Bamlett (Gateshead)

A stiff wind was blowing down Brunshaw Hill as Leake and Roberts met once again in the middle to decide the toss. The wind and the pitch would prove to play a big part in matters. Roberts won the toss and United kicked off playing toward the Cricket Field End. Against the wind, Burnley pushed forward and attacked the visitors. The Greens got off to a great start and on 15 minutes Ogden opened the scoring. Smethams got away and put in a good centre into United's goalmouth. The ball hit the crossbar and re-bounded into play finding Ogden whose shot gave Moger no chance. 1-0 and first blood to Burnley.

Sportsman noticed a change in Burnley's style of play from then on. "If Burnley had kept up their attacking style of play all might have been well, but instead of following the style they adopted all through the ties, they went in for the short-passing method."

A United attack from Sandy Turnbull saw his shot rattle Dawson's crossbar. Then Moger was called on two or three times to stop Burnley scoring a second goal. On 24 minutes a United attack saw Halse coming forward with the ball. Burnley's McLean slipped and fell on the wet ground. With only Dawson to beat, Halse bore down on the Burnley goal. Dawson came out of his goal but before he met the United forward it was too late and Halse made certain, chipping the ball over him. 1-1 and United attacked again. Three minutes later Meredith got away and crossed to Wall who centred, the ball coming to Sandy Turnbull who got his foot to it to steer the ball past Dawson. From the re-start Cretney dribbled his way into the United half and before he shot he was dispossessed by Hayes. Morley also had a good chance who should have shot when he had the opportunity. Like the first game there were a number of bad fouls, the worst of all committed by Sandy Turnbull on McLean who was cautioned by Mr Bamlett. Burnley continued to press for an equaliser and at the interval the teams went in for tea at Burnley 1, Manchester United, 2.

With the wind at their backs Burnley made several attempts to break through the United defence, the ball sticking in the mud more as the ground churned up and the game wore on. Two minutes in and Jerry Dawson pulled off a fine save from Wall, falling on the ball before getting it clear. He was the far busier goalkeeper and on 14 minutes the other Turnbull, Jimmy this time, received the ball in the centre and registered United's third goal. Things didn't look to be going Burnley's way and for the next ten minutes United had much the upper hand. Jerry Dawson kept Burnley in the game. The second half wore on and in the last ten minutes Burnley saw more of the ball sensing United had settled at 3-1. Five minutes from time, Ogden received the ball from Morley and placed it past Moger to reduce the deficit. 3-2 Could Burnley find an equaliser? A frantic final five minutes saw several attacks from The Greens against a packed Red defence. And after a gallant attempt the final whistle came. Burnley's Cup run had come to an end against a strong United side, losing 3-2 against the League Champions.

At Full Time: Burnley 2 (Ogden 2), Manchester United 3 (Halse, Turnbull A, Turnbull J.)
Attendance: 16,850 (Gate receipts, £1,036 6s 6d)

---xxx---

Jerry Dawson had made a name for himself in this match and was not responsible for any of United's goals. Burnley had done well and could feel proud of what they had achieved in reaching the last eight. Sportsman in the Express put Burnley's failure down to their change of game plan, adopting an unfamiliar short-passing game to which he had not seen them play to effect. "An over-indulgence in dribbling and sticking to the ball instead of sending it out to the wings," his comments concluded.

Mr Bamlett interviewed after the game said, "The game had been very strenuous and played amid great excitement and it had not been so pleasant as it might have been." He didn't say it was a dirty game but the number of fouls was excessive but commented that, "his lips were sore from too much whistle blowing."

The Burnley captain Alec Leake said, "the meaning of the result was that United got the most opportunities and accepted them. Burnley possibly had not played the best game on the mud, but they had done their best and had nothing to regret."

Manchester United went through to the Semi-Finals where they beat Newcastle United 1-0. In the Final at the Crystal Palace, United beat Bristol City 1-0 with a Sandy Turnbull goal. It was the first time the Cup had come to Old Trafford.

The 1909-10 Cup

In the First Round of the Cup the following season, as if by some twist of fate, Burnley were drawn against Manchester United again. Turf Moor would host a re-match of the previous years contest, Burnley taking on the Cup holders.

Apart from Green for Ogden, Burnley lined up with the same side that had played in the abandoned tie at Turf Moor the season previously. Dick Smith returned to the Burnley side after a three-month absence through injury, along with McLean who had also been out for six weeks.

It was election day in Burnley on the Saturday the match was played and the town was bristling with people in town to cast their votes. The weather on Saturday morning however was awful. The skies around Burnley were heavy and grey and from after lunchtime when Turf Moor opened for business, the clouds opened and a thin veil of drizzle fell, soaking those that ventured out to watch the 'rematch' of the previous year. As the teams appeared, it sounded as if they were in an unforgiving mood, certainly at the start.

"The hooting of a team [United] prior to the commencement of a match is just the kind of thing to make players lose their tempers." (Daily Dispatch) The same comment was picked up the Athletic News reporter who said that, "the conduct of the crowd was disgraceful and of a character that no fair-minded sportsman would uphold." The Turf Moor crowd would be influential and become Burnley's 12th man.

Burnley v Manchester United, FA Cup First Round, Turf Moor, 15 January 1910 Kick Off 3:00 pm

The teams lined up:
Burnley: Dawson, Barron, Mclean, Cretney, Leake, Moffatt, Morley, Green, Smith, Abbott, Smethams.
Manchester United: Moger, Stacey, Hayes, Duckworth, Roberts, Curry, Meredith, Picken, Halse, Turnbull A., Wall.
Referee: Mr T. Field (Mexborough,) Linesmen: Messrs., T. H. Chicken and Mr D. Dickinson.

Alec Leake beat Charlie Roberts to the toss and Burnley attacked the Cricket Field End. The Greens got off to a good start, passing the ball well and taking the fight to the visitors. There were only three minutes on the clock when Cretney started a clever move on the right wing. Smith passed to Smethams whose cross found Morley who beat a defender and placed it for Green. As the ball was going in, it looked as if Moger might prevent it going over the line, but Abbott rushed in and bundled the ball into the net. "A tremendous shout rent the air," said Sportsman, "the play was very fast, and considering the conditions, the exhibition of football by the Burnley men was wonderful."

Burnley never gave United a moments respite. They were at their heels the whole match. At the other end Dawson had very little to do it was so one-sided. Dick Smith was brought down in the United area but Mr Field waved away his appeal for a penalty. An injury to Turnbull forced him to leave the field and United were down to ten men for the last five minutes of the half. The only United chance of note was a Meredith effort which was given offside, after he had put the ball in the net. And at half time a spirited Burnley led the Cup holders 1-0.

At the start of the second half Sandy Turnbull returned but he was clearly not fit. Straight after the start a United defender mis-kicked giving Morley a good chance to score but he also swung at the ball and missed. Good defending at the back by

Barron and McLean kept Meredith and company at bay for a long period. Dick Smith once again was badly fouled in the United penalty area but again Mr Field turned down the penalty claim. The pitch was now quite slippy and first McLean skidded on his backside which was a source of amusement for the crowd. Then Roberts did the same when he was charged off the ball by Abbott. Roberts, clearly angered, grabbed a handful of mud and threw it in Abbott's face, but the United skipper later apologised. Smethams received rough treatment from a United defender but overall, Sportsman said the game was "very clean," apart from the mud-throwing incident.

Turnbull had the ball in the Burnley goal, but like Meredith's effort in the first period, he too was offside. With 14 minutes remaining and no signs of a blizzard coming anytime soon, Burnley scored their second. Smethams looked at first to be offside but one of the United full-backs had played him on. The Burnley winger ran in and hit a low shot past Moger to great cheers from around Turf Moor. With time running out, United suddenly woke up and pushed forward. The Burnley back line fought well to hold onto their advantage and at the end of an exciting afternoon, Burnley defeated the Cup holders 2-0 and avenged their defeat of the previous year.

At Full Time: Burnley 2 (Abbot, Smethams), Manchester United 0
Attendance: 16,625 (Gate Receipts of £871)

---xxx---

Burnley's result was the biggest shock of the First Round. C.E. Sutcliffe wrote in the Daily Mail, "The pleasure of the victory from the Burnley point of view lay in the fact that the triumph was no fluke. The boys in green played with pluck and spirit from the commencement to the finish." The week following Burnley's victory, Manchester United funeral cards, and postcards were doing the rounds in Burnley.

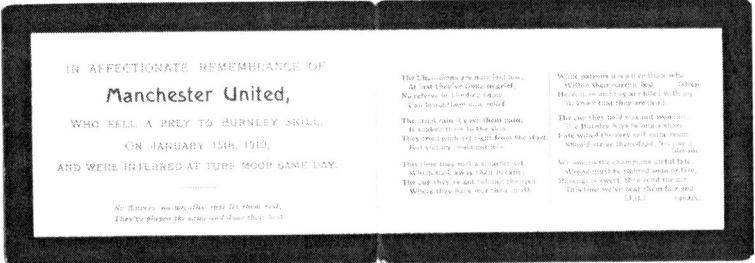

Figure 6

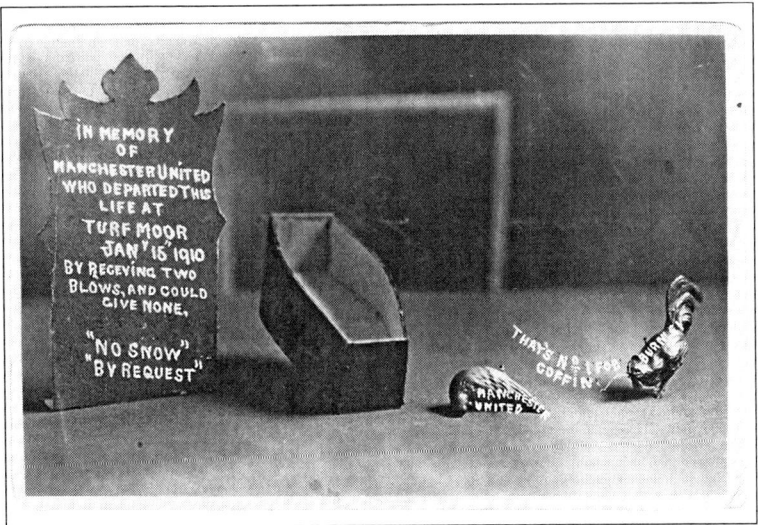

Figure 7

Round Two: Swindon Town v Burnley

In the Second Round, Burnley had been paired against Southern League side Swindon Town. After knocking out the Cup holders, Spen Whittaker's men were full of confidence as they set off early on Friday morning by train from Bank Top station for an overnight stay in Cheltenham.

Sportsman reported that around 450 Burnley supporters had made the journey to Wiltshire on a special train after setting off overnight. The party arrived before six o'clock to a deserted Swindon town centre. It was raining and the train back wouldn't leave Swindon until 11:00 pm, some six hours after the match had ended. Despite that, Sportsman noted, "they were a very jolly party and made themselves heard before the commencement of the game. They carried with them the flag that had been raised at other grounds with the words, '**SUCCESS TO GOOD OLD BURNLEY**.' Another travelling banner bore the words, '**STICK IT JERRY**,' in reference to Dawson's heroics in the Burnley goal.

Swindon Town v Burnley, FA Cup Round Two, County Ground, 5ᵗʰ February 1910 Kick-Off 3:00 pm

The teams lined up
Swindon Town: Skiller, Kay, Walker, Tout, Bannister, Silto, Jefferson, Fleming, Wheatcroft, Bown, Lavery.
Burnley: Dawson, Barron, McLean, Cretney, Leake, Moffatt, Morley, Green, Smith, Abbott, Smethams.
Referee: Mr J. W. Bailey (Leicester).

Alec Leake won the toss and Burnley in green shirts kicked off with the wind behind them. Swindon in red, were a good Southern League side and soon showed their skills on what was a heavy pitch. Not long after the kick-off the ball burst and another one called for. With the game re-started, the home side pressed forward and won a throw-in inside the Burnley half. The throw-in found Swindon's inside-forward Bown, who took a crack at goal from 30-yards out. The ball caught in the wind and curved in the air. It arced away from Dawson's outstretched arms and flew into the back of the Burnley net. Burnley were stunned by the goal. It was not until after 25 minutes that Burnley mounted their first attack. Green and Morley combining well but their joint effort was thwarted.

Five minutes before the tea interval, Moffatt got away from his marker and almost scored the equaliser, the ball kicked off Moffatt's toe at the final moment by a Swindon defender. At the interval, Swindon led 1-0.

Burnley started the better side in the second half. Apart from the Swindon goal, the best shot of the game came from Burnley's Smethams, who struck the ball on the volley, the fast ball cutting a parabola in the air and looking like it would land under Skiller's crossbar only for the Swindon keeper' to save. The game swung end-to-end. Abbott's chance 25 minutes into the second half led to a melee in the Swindon area. Several Burnley players had a swing at the ball and just couldn't put it over the line. Ten minutes later, Swindon's Bown and Lavery combined. Lavery's pass found Fleming who ran in and side-footed the ball past Dawson to put Swindon 2-0 up and win their place in the Third Round.

At Full Time: Swindon Town 2 (Bown, Fleming), Burnley 0
Attendance: 10,000 (Gate receipts of £503)

---xxx---

Swindon had played well and done their homework on Burnley Sportsman reported. '**WHACKED IN WILTS**' ran his column headline in the Express the following Wednesday. Burnley were out of the competition again. The impressive victory over United counted for nought and Swindon became the surprise side of the 1910 FA Cup, going all the way to the Semi-Final where they were knocked out by Newcastle United. Newcastle United went on to win the Cup that year, eventually beating Second Division Barnsley, captained by Tommy Boyle, 2-0, in a replay at Goodison Park. For the Burnley supporters leaving the County Ground it had been another long day and an even longer journey with only 'what-if's to ponder on as they made their slow way back to Lancashire.

Burnley's Great Loss

Two months after their exit from the Cup against Swindon, tragedy struck Burnley Football Club when the Burnley manager Spencer Whittaker, was killed in a train accident. On the night of 15 April 1910, Whittaker was travelling to London on the overnight express train to register a new player, Harry Swift so he could play for Burnley the following day. How Whittaker came to fall from the train carriage still remains a mystery. His body was found on the railway tracks near Crewe station. Whittaker suffered multiple injuries and died in the early hours of Saturday morning. He was just 38 years old and had a long career ahead of him. The inquest into Whittaker's death provided no hard evidence as to how his death had occurred. The death of the popular Burnley manager was a huge shock and the entire town mourned his passing. The tragedy led the Burnley board to seek a new manager. John Haworth, the manager of neighbouring club Accrington Stanley applied for the post and took over as the new Burnley secretary-manager in the Summer of 1910. Spencer Whittaker's death marked the end of an era at Burnley. With a new manager in place, a number of things would change.

Here's to the boys of Leake's brigade.
And the grand charge they made.
Oh when will their glory fade?
When the Emerald Green has lost its shade.

So drink to the health of Leake's brigade
And may their glory never fade
Till they have lifted the Cup,
Midst the cheers and shouts and the flags that wave.

N.H. Burnley Express 10/3/1909

On the 6th of May 1910 there was another death, this time at Buckingham Palace. Following a long illness, His Majesty King Edward VII passed away aged 69. At his bedside was his second eldest son, now first in-line to the throne, George, the Prince of Wales. The Prince informed his father that his horse, 'Witch of the Air,' had won at Kempton Park that afternoon and Edward's last words were, "Yes, I have heard of it. I am very glad."

At fifteen minutes to midnight, George Frederick Ernest Albert acceded the throne and became King George the Fifth. The coronation of the new king took place the following year in June 1911.

---xxx---

CHAPTER TWO

The Birth of the Clarets

Figure 8: Yorkshire Street Burnley, Looking Towards Turf Moor

One of John Haworth's first changes was to drop the green and white colours. The favoured choice was claret and blue, worn in the style of the 1909-10 League Champions, Aston Villa. The Green and Whites were no more. Of the Burnley players who had played in the historic Cup encounters against Manchester United in 1909 and 1910, only Jerry Dawson remained a first team player. Most of the others had either moved on to new clubs or had retired and been replaced by a new school of younger players. Within two seasons of Haworth taking charge, the Burnley team had changed completely.

In January 1911, Howarth mounted his first Cup campaign. Burnley did well in their new colours. The Clarets met Exeter City in Round One at Turf Moor and beat them 2-0. In Round Two, Burnley were again at home where they met Tommy Boyle's Barnsley and beat them by the same scoreline. In the Third Round, the Clarets trounced Coventry City 5-0 at Turf Moor to land a quarter-final tie away at First Division Bradford City. All was going well in the home Cup games but could the Clarets win away? 40,000 turned out at Valley Parade, but City beat Burnley 1-0. The Yorkshiremen went on to beat Blackburn Rovers in the Semi-Final. In the Final, they met Cup holders Newcastle United at The Crystal Palace. The game ended 0-0 and a replay took place the following Wednesday at Old Trafford. Bradford, with defender Dave Taylor having an outstanding game, won the replay 1-0 and took the Cup back to Yorkshire.

With the income from the Cup runs of 1908, 1909, 1910 and 1911, by the summer of 1911 and Windle's astute financial management, Second Division Burnley were starting to pay out big fees for players. In April 1911, Burnley paid Everton £550 for the England international and the First Divisions record goal-scorer, Bert Freeman. In September that year, Burnley paid its biggest ever transfer fee, £1,250 for Tommy Boyle the Barnsley centre-half. Shortly after Boyle's arrival, Howarth made him the team captain. The following year, Burnley spent another £2,000 for Bradford City's Dave Taylor and George Halley a half-back from Bradford Park Avenue. Burnley meant business and wanted success.

Burnley's 1911-12 League campaign was full of early promise but their Cup campaign that season was a short one. Burnley travelled to Fulham in Round One and were knocked out 2-1. Despite an early Cup exit, the team were making good progress in the League, but after leading the Second Division at Easter and promotion looking almost certain, the Clarets promotion bid faded and lost out in the last game of the season at Wolves. After spending thousands of pounds on players, it had to be promotion next year.

The Clarets got off to a great start in the first half of the 1912-13 season. By Christmas 1912, Burnley were top of the Second Division and were the divisions leading goal scorers. Come January it was time to mount a challenge in the Cup. Burnley were on an excellent run of form and a cartoon in the Burnley Express weighed up the Clarets options.

Figure 9

The 1912-13 FA Cup Campaign

In Round One, Burnley were drawn away against a fellow Second Division side, Leeds City. Going into the game, the Clarets had beaten Clapton Orient 5-0 at Turf Moor in the League the Saturday before to clock up their ninth successive League victory. The Monday before the Leeds tie, the Clarets took up residence by the seaside in Blackpool for Cup training. There was a lot of interest in the match as it wasn't far to travel and the local newspapers reported that as many as 10,000

Burnley supporters would travel to Leeds on 14 specially chartered trains. But the January weather had other plans. From early Friday morning snow began to fall which led to line blockages and the cancellation of the special trains.

Leeds City v Burnley FA Cup Round One, Elland Road, Saturday 11 January 1913 Kick-Off 2:30 pm
The teams lined up,
Leeds City: Scott, Law, Affleck, Allan, Lintott, Foley, Bainbridge, Robertson, McLeod, Spiers, Croot.
Burnley: Dawson, Bamford, Taylor, McLaren, Boyle, Watson, Mosscrop, Lindley, Freeman, Hodgson, Husband.
Referee: Mr E. P Squire (Newcastle) Linesmen: Mr Pritchard (Derby) and Mr Jones (Sheffield)

Sportsman in the Burnley Express estimated that at least half of the spectators at Elland Road were from Burnley but how they managed to get there without the trains wasn't clear. The gates opened at Elland Road at 1:30 pm around the same time as match referee Mr Squire was inspecting the pitch. There was some four inches of snow covering the pitch and the snow was still falling. Squire arranged for the sidelines to be swept clear and the game started on time at 2:30 pm.

The first half was a real end-to-end Cup tie with both sides going for the win. Teddy Hodgson put Burnley ahead after just four minutes before Leeds equalised straight away through McLeod. Two minutes later Tommy Boyle put Burnley back in front with a direct free kick from outside the penalty area. On twenty-four minutes, Foley equalised for Leeds to make it 2-2. Then Burnley's Bert Freeman got the better of the Leeds defenders and scored twice putting Burnley four-two ahead at the interval. Snow continued to fall during the break and the second half was only underway a few minutes when Mr Squire called a halt and went to consult with his linesmen. While the officials deliberated, the Burnley players engaged in a snowball fight on the pitch, much to the amusement of the crowd. Mr Squire and his officials agreed that due to the conditions, the match couldn't continue and the match was abandoned much to the disgust of the travelling spectators who had travelled through a snowstorm to get to Leeds.

Result: Match abandoned on 50 minutes with the score at Leeds City 2 (McLeod, Foley), Burnley 4 (Hodgson 2, Freeman 2) **Attendance:** 13,000 (Gate receipts of £505)

---xxx---

The following week it was reported that one group of Burnley supporters had set off from Nelson for Leeds at 10:00 am in a taxi. On reaching the Yorkshire border, the weather was so bad they had to turn back for a set of snow chains. They set off again, proceeding at a steady 7 mph in a raging blizzard. One frozen occupant fell out of the vehicle but they managed to haul the man back into the car and thaw him out. The group eventually reached Elland Road at 5:30pm only to find the stadium locked and in darkness.

Four days later with the snow all but gone, Burnley returned to Elland Road on the Wednesday afternoon. After the free-scoring first match, it was a much closer affair according to the Manchester Guardian.

Leeds City v Burnley FA Cup Round One, Elland Road, Wednesday 15 January 1913 2:3 Kick-Off 2:30 pm

The teams lined up unchanged from the abandoned first game, **Leeds City:** Scott, Law, Affleck, Allan, Lintott, Foley, Bainbridge, Robertson, McLeod, Spiers, Croot.
Burnley: Dawson, Bamford, Taylor, McLaren, Boyle, Watson, Mosscrop, Lindley, Freeman, Hodgson, Husband.
Referee: Mr E. P Squire (Newcastle) Linesmen: Mr Pritchard (Derby) and Mr Jones (Sheffield)

Burnley found it a lot more difficult to beat Leeds City than was shown during Saturday's match. During a large part of the game, Burnley were engaged in a tight struggle. Leeds scored first through McLeod on eight minutes, before Burnley replied with goals from a Boyle penalty kick, a direct free-kick from Dick Lindley and a third from Bert Freeman. Towards the end, Leeds City made great efforts to get back on level terms. Leeds hammered at the Burnley defence and Foley managed to pull a goal back for the home side just before the final whistle.

At Full Time: Leeds City 2(McLeod, Foley), Burnley 3 (Boyle, Lindley, Freeman).
Attendance: 13,200 (Gate receipts of £453)

---xxx---

In the Second Round, Burnley had been drawn at home against Lincolnshire side Gainsborough Trinity. Trinity had been voted out of the League at the end of the previous season to be replaced by their local rivals, Lincoln City. With Burnley continuing their fine League form and going for promotion, non-League Trinity were very much the Cup-tie underdogs. The bookies had high-spending Burnley the clear favourites and were expected to win comfortably. Around 500 Gainsborough supporters made the trip aboard a special train, most of them wearing the club colours, some of them The Express reported, 'forming a tin whistle marching band.' Burnley however were suffering with injuries to no fewer than nine players and a cartoon in the Saturday Express made light of the situation. What team would Burnley play in the Cup?

Figure 10

Burnley v Gainsborough Trinity, FA Cup Round Two, Turf Moor, 1st February 1913 Kick-Off 3:00 pm

The teams lined up,
Burnley: Dawson, Bamford, Taylor, McLaren, Boyle, Watson, Mosscrop, Lindley, Freeman, Hodgson, Husband.
Gainsborough Trinity: Sewell, Gunton, Jones, Verrill, Coe, Tellum, Lounds, Green, Ibbotson, Bolton, Parker.
Referee: Mr H. T. Yates (Bolton)

In the first half, the Burnley forwards were thwarted mainly due to the heroics of the Trinity goalkeeper, the 22 year old Ronnie Sewell, who was outstanding. Alongside him, full-backs Sam Gunton and Cliff Jones had also played brilliantly. After half an hour of Burnley pressure, completely against the run of play, Trinity broke away and Ibbotson scored on 33 minutes with a header from a Parker centre. The goal stunned the Burnley players for the remainder of the first half as the teams left the field at half-time with the non-League visitors 1-0 up.

Things must have been said in the Burnley dressing room at half time as the team's mood was more serious as the second half began. Five minutes after the restart, Bert Freeman levelled the scores. Another goal from Freeman, then a penalty from Tommy Boyle followed by a Teddy Hodgson goal, sealed the game at four-one. But the big talking point among Burnley supporters following the match wasn't Burnley's 4-1 victory. Trinity's defence must have certainly impressed during the match, as after game had ended and the Gainsborough team had already left for the Lincoln train, the Trinity club officials along with Sewell, Gunton and Jones were all called back for talks. "By 6.30pm, Burnley had signed all three players for a reputed fee of £2,400!" (Manchester Evening News)

At Full Time: Burnley 4 (Freeman 2, Boyle pen, Hodgson), Gainsborough Trinity 1 (Ibbotson)
Attendance: 18,092 (Gate receipts of £586)

---xxx---

In the next round the Clarets had been handed another home tie against Middlesbrough. For the Third Round the admission prices went up, doubling from the normal sixpence on the ground to a shilling and four shillings in the stand. Regardless of the prices, a big crowd was expected and the match was scheduled to kick off at 3:15 pm to enable all the special trains from the north-east to arrive. The Middlesbrough team train arrived at Bank Top station at 1:43 pm and a fleet of taxis were waiting to shuttle them to Turf Moor.

Burnley v. Middlesbrough, FA Cup Round Three, Turf Moor, Saturday 22 February 1913 Kick-Off 3:15 pm.

Burnley: Dawson, Bamford, Taylor, McLaren, Boyle, Watson, Mountford, Lindley, Freeman, Hodgson, Husband.
Middlesbrough: Williamson, Hisbent, Weir, Crosier, Jackson, Malcolm, Stirling, Carr, Elliott, Windridge, Eyre.
Referee: Mr I. Baker (Nantwich)

A clash of colours meant hosts Burnley played in an all-white strip. Dawson wearing 'a kind of blue' reported Sportsman, while the visitors appeared in their familiar red and white stripes. Tommy Boyle beat Williamson to the toss and Burnley played toward the Bee Hole End. "The pace was nearly as hot as the furnaces on Teesside," Sportsman noted. After four minutes, Boyle struck a thirty-yard shot to test Williamson the Boro' goalkeeper, which he managed to hold on to. It was a fast-flowing end-to-end game, the first half evenly matched. Sportsman noted that Boyle got in more shots on target than any other player on the field, letting fly whenever the chance arose. Jerry Dawson was tested a few times, but it was Williamson the much busier 'keeper, stopping efforts from Boyle, Dick Lindley (twice) Bert Freeman and Teddy Hodgson. At the interval the teams went in at 1-1, Hodgson scoring first for Burnley with Carr equalising for Middlesbrough shortly after.

Thirteen minutes into the second half Burnley won a throw-in. Dick Lindley took the ball down the wing. He cut inside Boro' defender Hisbent and crossed the ball to Freeman, who scored. Two-one to Burnley. With their tails up, 'The Whites' continued to attack, and Williamson in goal had to handle more long-range shots from Boyle. Ten minutes from time, Burnley were awarded a free-kick. It was taken by McLaren who found Teddy Hodgson. Hodgson passed the ball to an on-rushing Freeman, who had run a good thirty yards to dribble through the Boro' defence to score his second goal. Three-one and Burnley supporters were a bit more relieved. Moments later Freeman got away again, sensing the hat-tick. Burnley supporters around Turf Moor cheered him on as he skipped over tackles and closed on Williamson's goal before finally losing the ball. Middlesbrough made several attacks to get back into the game and Dawson pulled off two fine saves the first from Jackson and later Windridge before Mr Baker brought proceedings to a close.

Final Score: Burnley 3 (Hodgson, Freeman 2), Middlesbrough 1 (Carr)
Attendance: 27,824 (Gate receipts £1,679)

---xxx---

Boyle and Freeman for Burnley along with Williamson for Middlesbrough had been the best three players on the field. Sportsman praised the Clarets in his mid-week column, "it shows that the Turfites are worthy aspirants both for the First Division and The Cup, and that if they succeed in their ambition and win both trophies, they will be capable of holding their own in the best company."

The Quarter-Final draw was made the following Monday at FA Headquarters in Russell Square, London. It brought a mouth-watering tie for supporters of the two East Lancashire clubs.

Blackburn Rovers v Burnley
Sunderland v Newcastle United
Everton v Oldham Athletic
Bradford Park Avenue v Aston Villa

For Burnley supporters it was a dream tie. First Division Blackburn Rovers at Ewood Park for a place in the Semi-Final. Blackburn Rovers, mid-table in Division One and five times

Cup winners. Burnley who had never won the Cup, never even reached the Semi-Final. Second Division Burnley who were second in the table. Blackburn Rovers, with their Cup record, with home advantage and a team of internationals playing in the higher division were clear favourites. Rovers had reached the Semi-Finals in both 1911 and 1912. Surely they would do it again in 1913?

Saturday came and it was a glorious day in East Lancashire. Many Burnley supporters set off early in the morning, some walking the twelve miles to Ewood Park. Burnley collieries closed on the Friday evening and the local mills and foundries had worked overtime on Friday night so the workers could attend the match on Saturday. Sportsman in the Express reported it was the largest, noisiest assembly of people he had ever seen on a football ground, with a good half of the crowd travelling from Burnley to Ewood by a dozen special trains, organised by Abraham Altham's. Alternatively Eastwood's were running wagonette and charabanc return trips to Ewood Park for 2s 6d.

Sportsman, "When the whistle sounded one would be pardoned for thinking Burnley supporters outnumbered those of their rivals who certainly never got the opportunity to shout." Both sides had injury worries. Eddie Mosscrop who had been ill in bed all week was only passed fit on the morning of the match. Bill Husband was nursing a knock from the previous game while Rovers had five players doubtful. An array of Burnley banners were prominent in the ground. Officiating the match was the familiar Mr Herbert Sydney Bamlett, now one of the Football Associations top referees.

Blackburn Rovers v. Burnley, FA Cup Quarter Final, Ewood Park, 8 March 1913 Kick-Off 3:00 pm

Blackburn Rovers: Robinson, Crompton, Cowell, Walmsley, Smith, Bradshaw, Simpson, Shea, Aitkenhead, Latherton, Anthony.
Burnley: Dawson, Bamford, Taylor, McLaren, Boyle, Watson, Mosscrop, Lindley, Freeman, Hodgson and Husband.
Referee: Mr H. S. Bamlett (Gateshead)

Tommy Boyle beat the Blackburn captain Bob Crompton to the toss and Burnley played with the wind toward the Darwen End. The game began at a "cracking pace" according to Sportsman, the game swinging from end to end, with favourites Rovers making the early running. Jerry Dawson was in fine form, saving efforts first from Bradshaw, then Latherton and Aitkenhead. Burnley gradually got into their stride. Dawson throwing rather than kicking the ball out to Boyle, whose wide passes across Ewood began the attacks down both flanks through Eddie Mosscrop and Bill Husband. Mosscrop's pace caused Bob Crompton, the Rovers full-back problems all afternoon. Boyle fired in the occasional long-shots when the chance came as he had done against Middlesbrough. With just over half an hour gone, Burnley took the lead.

"When operations had been in progress for 33 minutes, Freeman got off splendidly and had the better of two Rovers defenders. Crompton prevented him giving possession to one of his colleagues, conceding a corner. The ball was placed by Mosscrop whose centre was met by Boyle full on his forehead, the ball soaring through Robinson's fingers and into the Rovers net." Sportsman had never heard a celebration like it: "An outburst of enthusiasm the like of which I have never seen on an opponent's ground in the course of my twenty-seven years following Burnley." Play resumed and shortly after another Burnley attack saw Dick Lindley 'floored.'

No foul said Mr Bamlett. Before the break Boyle tried another long-shot which Crompton allowed to roll between his legs and over the line, Robinson only clearing the danger in time. After 45 action-packed minutes, Mr Bamlett brought the first half to a close with Burnley leading 1-0.

In the second half, Rovers fought hard to pull their way back into the game. They had much more of the play. It was Dawson the busier goalkeeper who was called on several times to clear, finger-tipping the ball over the crossbar on more than one occasion. Boyle and Taylor were prominent at the back, in fact Taylor was the player of the second half for his work rate. Burnley had further chances to extend their lead with efforts from Freeman, Mosscrop and another fine effort from Boyle. Finally and after a hard-fought game, Mr. Bamlett blew his whistle with The Clarets winning 1-0. Burnley had reached the semi-finals of the FA Cup for the very first time.

At Full Time: Blackburn Rovers 0, Burnley 1 (Boyle)
Attendance: 43,000 (Gate receipts of £3,003)

---xxx---

ONE OF THE BURNLEY BANNERS.

Figure 11

Burnley supporters had never experienced anything quite like it. The underdogs had won. The result prompted Burnley's member of Parliament Phillip Morrell to send a telegram to Burnley chairman Harry Windle: "It is with great delight that I have read in today's papers of the magnificent victory won by our team yesterday at Blackburn. Please accept and convey to Captain Boyle and all members of the team my warmest congratulations."

Cup fever hit the town, prompting one Burnley supporter to take up his pen,

> It's a long way to Crystal Palace
> It's a long way to go,
> It's a long way to Crystal Palace,
> Leeds City told us so;
> Goodbye Middlesbrough,
> Poor old Rovers too,
> It's a long, long way to Crystal Palace
> But we're going there, that's true.
>   (Burnley Express 2/4/1913)

Following the great victory at Ewood Park, two more players arrived at Turf Moor to bolster the squad. Right-half George Halley arrived from Bradford Park Avenue, along with Tom Charlton, a centre-forward signed from Stockport County. There were rumours that Burnley had also wanted to bring Dickie Downs and Robert Glendenning to Turf Moor from Barnsley. Twenty-five-year old George Halley's fee was another outlay of around £1,200, and he had also been selected for the Scottish International trial game at Hampden Park later that month.

The draw for the Semi-Final of the Cup made the following week paired the following.

Burnley v Sunderland or Newcastle United at Bramall Lane.

Aston Villa v Oldham Athletic at Ewood Park.

Burnley would eventually play Sunderland following their victory over Newcastle after a replay. Sunderland were currently England's form team. They led the First Division and were going for the 'Double.' In previous rounds, Sunderland had beaten Clapton Orient 6-0, Manchester City 2-0, Swindon Town 4-2 and finally Newcastle United 3-0 after two replays. Their 3-0 win coming at St. James's Park, a brilliant result against their local rivals. The Wearsider's had scored 17 Cup goals with only 4 goals against. Sunderland were a team full of international stars, they were big, they were physical and they were a skilful. A well-drilled side managed by Bob Kyle. Burnley would most definitely be the underdogs.

The Athletics News lead-up to the match, gave spectators travelling to the match that it wouldn't be interrupted by any suffragist demonstrations, "Bramall Lane has been guarded day and night for fear of certain intruders."

Rail travel to Bramall Lane for the Semi-Final was 3s 6d return plus a shilling in the ground. A lot of money to watch football, but that didn't stop 33,655 turning out, Burnley bringing around 15,000 supporters to South Yorkshire. Twelve special trains began leaving Burnley railway stations for Sheffield from 9:30 am. It had rained in the county all the previous week, and after more overnight rain, the vast Sheffield pitch was like a swamp.

Burnley v Sunderland, FA Cup Semi-Final, Bramall Lane, 29 March 1913
Kick-Off 3:30 pm

The teams lined up
Burnley: Dawson, Bamford, Taylor, McLaren, Boyle Watson, Mosscrop, Lindley, Freeman, Hodgson, Husband.
Sunderland: Butler, Gladwin, Ness, Cuggy, Thomson, Low, Mordue, Buchan, Richardson, Holley, Martin.
Referee: Mr A. Adams (Nottingham) Linesmen: Mr A. Ansell and Mr P. Sant

Tommy Boyle beat Charlie Thomson to the toss and Burnley defended the Bramall Lane End in the first half. The game began in lashing rain with a gale force wind behind it that made any attempt at decent football impossible. Anyone not under cover was soon soaked to the skin. Even the pressmen under their oilskins on the touchline were drenched. Sportsman later reflected on his experience, "I was one of the small band of unfortunate pressmen who had to sit at temporary tables on the track side near the touchline and I had the worst experience of my life in reporting a match."

Sunderland managed the first attack of the match and Boyle, Watson and Taylor were called upon early on to clear the danger. The other flank of Burnley's defence was also kept busy from Buchan and Mordue. Burnley soon became accustomed to the Wearsider's game plan and adapted themselves well to cope with it. Boyle was in the thick of things, both in attack and defence performing a valuable pivotal role, mustering his forces. Freeman was well watched by Thomson and it was Husband who managed to get in Burnley's first shot on the Sunderland goal. Husband was Burnley's most dangerous player in the first period. One shot from him whistled across the Sunderland area but was cleared and so easily have gone into the net. As the rain continued to pour down, the players and officials took well-earned rest with the scores level at 0-0.

Early in the second half, Bill Husband was injured in a collision with Gladwin. He was alright again soon after attention and resumed his place. Jerry Dawson was called upon several times to save from Butler and a fine feature of the Burnley defence was Dave Taylor's excellent work. It was later learned that Taylor had received the doctor's attention in the dressing room at half-time. Fifteen minutes into the second half, Burnley claimed for a penalty for hand-ball by Gladwin. Mr Adams declared it was accidental. Sunderland then won several corners, but the Burnley defence was, "safe as the proverbial house," according to Sportsman. Sunderland adopted the short-passing game while Burnley's style was to swing the ball out to the wingers across the wide Bramall Lane pitch. Bert Freeman got away from Charlie Thomson and dribbled toward Butler's goal when he was knocked off the ball by Thomson inside the penalty area. The offence should have brought a penalty but Freeman's claim was ignored, by referee Adams, as a similar Sunderland claim in the Burnley area was also refused. The game was almost over when Freeman was tripped again just outside the Sunderland penalty area. Boyle's free-kick was passed out to Mosscrop whose centre was cleared but only to Dick Lindley whose header went just over the crossbar. Bearing in mind the poor weather conditions, both sides were happy to settle for a draw and a replay at St. Andrew's the following week.

At Full Time: Burnley 0, Sunderland 0
Attendance: 33,655 (Gate receipts £ 2,263)

---xxx---

The Burnley players went home to rest for the weekend before regrouping on Monday morning at their training base in Blackpool. They had played well against a very good Sunderland side. They had matched them in every department but could they repeat their performance and beat them? On Monday morning, eight of the Burnley team travelled over to Blackpool on the 8:51 train. As the train approached Kirkham and was steaming at full speed, the passengers heard a loud banging and clanking noise and saw huge pieces of iron flying past the carriage windows. A crankshaft on the train had broken and had almost led to the train's derailment. Tommy Bamford, joking to his colleagues, had said, "Hello lads, Sunderland are going to have themselves a walkover." All on-board were lucky that the train had not come off the rails and no one had been hit by the flying debris.

Sunderland had travelled down to Birmingham from the North-east the day before and stayed at a hotel in central Birmingham overnight while Burnley had made the unusual decision to travel on the morning of the match. It would prove to be a bad decision that would cost the Clarets dearly.

The big story in the morning newspapers was the start of the trial at the Old Bailey of leading suffragette, Mrs Pankhurst on the charge of attempting to blow up the house of Mr Lloyd George. In football news, the Football Association were investigating a claim brought by Fulham director, Mr H. G. Norris, that members of the Liverpool Football team were, "not trying their best" to win the match v. Chelsea held at Anfield Road on Easter Monday (the 24th of March). The FA's investigation would run for almost a year.

The Burnley train left Bank Top station at 8:40 and travelled via Manchester, zigzagging its way across the country to Birmingham. After several unscheduled delays, what should have been a 3½ half hour journey took almost five hours. The train finally pulled in to Birmingham New Street at 1:50 pm, well over an hour late. The players had managed to have their lunch on the packed train but had had no space to walk up and down to stretch their legs. With less than two hours to go before the kick-off, most of the Burnley players were nowhere near St. Andrews and by the time they had collected their kit and exited the station there were no taxis. It wasn't the best start to such an important game. "A Jading Journey," noted Sportsman who travelled with the team.

The players managed to reach St. Andrews in just enough time. Burnley made one enforced change. Winger Jimmy Bellamy came in for Eddie Mosscrop, who had not been given release from his teaching commitments.

Burnley v Sunderland FA Cup Semi-Final (Replay) St. Andrews, Wednesday April 2 1913 Kick-Off 3:30 pm

The teams lined up:
Burnley: Dawson, Bamford, Taylor, McLaren, Boyle, Watson, Bellamy, Lindley, Freeman, Hodgson, Husband.
Sunderland: Butler, Gladwin, Ness, Cuggy, Thomson, Low, Mordue, Buchan, Richardson, Holley and Martin.
Referee: Mr A. Adams (Nottingham)

It was a warm afternoon in the Midlands as Sunderland came out onto the pitch first, followed by Tommy Boyle leading out the Burnley team. Charlie Thomson won the toss and elected to kick off, with Burnley playing against the wind in the first half. Despite their exhausting journey, Burnley began the first half well and were, "the more aggressive side," said Sportsman. An early Billy Watson effort came close for Burnley. His shot going just wide of Butler's left post. Three minutes later Teddy Hodgson had the ball in the Sunderland net, only for the linesman to flag Hodgson for offside. From the resulting free kick, Sunderland broke up field. Martin crossed for Charlie Buchan who scored with a leaping header past Jerry Dawson. One-nil to Sunderland. A minute after that Buchan put the ball in the Burnley net again, only to be flagged offside. In the first half, apart from the two Sunderland goal attempts by Buchan, Burnley had seen most of the ball. A melee in the Sunderland area led to a deliberate handball by defender Gladwin. Mr Adams blew his whistle this time and pointed to the penalty spot. Tommy Boyle picked up the ball and placed it on the spot. He took his customary ten paces back, ran in and with his right foot drove the ball past Butler in the Sunderland goal to level the scores. Five minutes later, Burnley attacked again this time through Husband down the left. Husband played a one-two with Freeman, as Sportsman noted,

"Freeman sprinted with great speed and though the goalkeeper came out and ran full tilt into him, the Burnley centre had already skilfully guided the ball into the net."

Two-one to Burnley! The game had turned in Burnley's favour. The first half was just drawing to a close when Boyle was viscously kicked under the kneecap by Sunderland's Charlie Thomson. Boyle limped on until the end of the half, "but he was not the same after," said Sportsman in the Express.

Boyle did appear in the second half but he probably only made his knee much worse. The injury slowed him down but he soldiered on. In the second half Sunderland attacked and were awarded a dubious penalty, when Holley went down after Dawson had already collected the ball. The referee whistled and pointed to the penalty spot. Jackie Mordue stepped up for Sunderland and scored from the penalty to make it 2-2. Both sides fought tooth and claw for the next goal. Sunderland claimed for another penalty as Dave Taylor cleared the ball but it wasn't given. Two minutes later, Mordue collected the ball, chipped the ball over Dave Taylor's head and passed it to Holley, who shot past Dawson to make it three-two to Sunderland. The balance and momentum was now with Sunderland as Burnley tired on the heavy pitch and Boyle's knee injury got worse. The Clarets searched for an equaliser in the final minutes and had chances for Lindley and Husband, but the goal never came and the Clarets were out of the Cup.

At Full Time: Burnley 2 (Freeman, Boyle pen), Sunderland 3(Buchan, Mordue, Holley)
Attendance: 25,000 (Gate Receipts of £2,000)

---xxx---

The match had been a bruising, bloody and painful encounter as Tommy Boyle could testify. The mood in the dressing room would have been funereal, the players were done in, knackered, having given their all. They had come so far in the competition only to lose in the last phase of the game. Burnley had tired in the second half there was no question of that. The long train journey on the morning of the match must have been one factor, injuries to key players and tiredness another. The Clarets were out of the Cup and that was that for another year.

Burnley manager John Haworth needed to pick his team up quickly. Six important League games remained starting on Saturday with a trip to Bradford Park Avenue. There were twelve valuable promotion points at stake. Burnley had fallen to third in the table, one point behind second placed Birmingham but had two games in hand on them. The team would have to play all six games without Tommy Boyle who was ruled out for the rest of the season thanks to Charlie Thomson's boot. Eddie Mosscrop would also miss the two mid-week games in hand due to his teaching commitments.

Burnley got off to a good start in their promotion quest, beating Bradford Park Avenue (2-3). They then pulled off a fine 1-1 draw with League leaders Preston at Deepdale, where Burnley were also without the services of Billy Watson. The following Saturday, the Clarets produced another excellent performance beating Wolves 4-2 at Turf Moor. Three games down and three to go. Six points left. Two promotion points needed.

So much rested on the next match at Filbert Street against Leicester Fosse. Burnley travelled down to Leicester on Friday morning and stayed overnight. A win and two more points would be enough to secure the runners-up spot in Division Two. The match took place on Cup Final day, where Sunderland were playing Aston Villa at The Crystal Palace. Burnley's team were now relying on their reserve players. They had to re-organise at the back. Winger Jimmy Bellamy was brought in as a makeshift right-back! George Halley took over at centre-half and Ernie Bradshaw filled in at left-half. Leicester had three changes of their own which included the loss of their normal goalkeeper Mearns, with the youngster Harry Furr deputising.

Leicester Fosse v Burnley, Filbert Street, Saturday April 19 1913 Kick-off 3:00 pm

Leicester Fosse: Furr, Thompson, Currie, McWhirter, Hanger, King, Douglas, Mills, Sparrow, Osborne, Harrison.
Burnley: Dawson, Jones, Taylor, Bellamy, Halley, Bradshaw, Mosscrop, Lindley, Freeman, Hodgson, Husband.
Referee: Mr L. N. Fletcher (Bury)

Burnley kicked-off facing the sun, the wind in their faces. They began the better side and after half an hour of stalemate, on 36 minutes Teddy Hodgson opened the scoring, sending a 20-yard shot flying past Furr and into the net to give the Clarets a deserved lead. Hodgson's shot took Furr completely by surprise who saw it way too late and had no chance of stopping it. Three minutes later, Burnley attacked again forcing a corner on the left. From the cross, Furr fisted the ball out but it came straight back into the area and from the resulting melee, Hodgson scored his second goal. Burnley held on to their two-goal lead as Mr Fletcher blew his whistle for half-time.

The second half was a much different game. With Leicester also needing the points to avoid being sucked into the League re-election places they came out fighting. With nine minutes of the second half played, Leicester's Douglas found Osborn who scored to pull a goal back for the home side. The Foxes took the game to Burnley and five minutes later following more pressure saw the best move of the game. Leicester attacked in numbers to seek the equaliser. Jerry Dawson left his goal to meet their inside-left, Mills running toward him. Mills put the ball over to Harrison. Harrison's low strike went behind the Burnley keeper to find Sparrow running in to tap in. It was all square and at this point the game could have gone either way. The following weeks Athletics News describing it as a "ding-dong struggle for mastery." Fifteen minutes remained and it looked as if Burnley had thrown a precious point away, and that promotion would have to be secured the following week. Bert Freeman had the final say. With five minutes left, Freeman scored to restore Burnley's lead and see the Clarets out eventual winners 3-2.

At Full Time: Leicester Fosse 2 (Osborn, Sparrow), Burnley 3 (Hodgson 2, Freeman).
Attendance: unknown- not given in Sportsman's or the Athletics News reports.

---xxx---

When the results of the other matches were known, Burnley had something to celebrate at last. Sportsman's regular football column on Wednesday 23rd April, began with a simple headline that read,

BURNLEY BACK

It was a case of lucky thirteen according to Sportsman, "After thirteen years wandering in the wilderness of the Second Division, Burnley on Saturday, on their thirteenth visit to Leicester, won their way back to the First Division..."

A cartoon accompanied the match report showing the good ship 'Turf Moor', being waved into the 1st Division harbour by a collection of players from other 1st Division Clubs, With the line beneath ...

"Safe in Port at last. The good ship 'Turf Moor,' after 13 years buffeting by storms, adverse currents and the avoiding of dangerous rocks and shoals, returns safely to 'harbour' with a full crew, a full treasure chest, and an enhanced reputation."

Several telegrams of congratulation arrived at Turf Moor. Burnley's Member of Parliament, Philip Morrell, wrote, "Well done Burnley! Delighted to hear of your brilliant achievement in regaining once more your true place in First Division. Please accept my heartiest congratulations upon a great and well-deserved triumph."

The 1912-13 Cup Final

As Burnley were busy securing their First Division future at Leicester, the Cup Final at the Crystal Palace between Aston Villa and Sunderland was in full swing. It is worth mentioning this for a few reasons that would have a bearing on the following year's competition. With so much riding on the game between the top two sides in the Football League, massive numbers of spectators turned out to see the battle of the giants. It was the biggest attended Cup final in England with an official gate of nearly, 122,000. In trying to get the best view of the match, some spectators climbed onto one of the stand roofs. Their weight was too great and the roof collapsed, with people falling through the roof and on top of the seated fans below. The Daily Mirror showed a photograph of the wrecked stand. A number of people were hurt but fortunately none badly.

All around the stadium there was crushing on the terraces. People lost their footing and slid down the mud and grass banking. The Daily Express headline on Monday 21st April read, 'THE CUP FINAL SCANDAL' followed by 'THOUSANDS OF PEOPLE MAKE LONG RAILWAY JOURNEYS AND SEE NOTHING OF THE GAME,' as many who had paid for entry couldn't get in to see the match.

A protracted FA investigation followed. They demanded changes be made to the stadium and threatened to pull the next Cup Final out of The Palace. An argument over funding broke out over who should foot the bill and a war of words took place in the newspapers. On 21 November 1913, the football correspondent *Orion*, writing in a detailed article in the Daily Express said, "there does not appear to be the slightest chance of the Football Association and the Crystal Palace authorities coming to terms with regard to improvements to the Final Tie ground." Some £70,000, a massive sum, had been identified as the figure needed to improve the standard of the Palace if the problems of 1913 were not to be repeated. The arguments ran on into early 1914 and it looked highly likely that the 1914 Final would not take place at The Palace.

On the field, the 1913 Final lasted 18 minutes over the scheduled ninety, mainly for the foul temper in which the match was played. Hacking, injuries and fouls on both sides took place throughout. The worst of it was a running feud that took place between Sunderland's Charlie Thomson and the Villa centre-forward, Harry Hampton. Hampton had been kicked, punched, and knocked to the ground and had got up each time and smiled at his assailant. Hampton had clearly got the better of Thomson who didn't like it. The referee told Thomson to cool it, his Sunderland teammates told him, but it was only after Tommy Barber had scored for Villa twelve minutes from time did he quit. The personal battle led to both players being suspended for a month at the start of the 1913-14 season. The same Thomson who had crippled Tommy Boyle in the semi-final and had put him out of the last six games of Burnley's season. The Cup Final referee, Mr Adams, was suspended by the Football Association for lack of control. He never officiated again. Villa playing in claret and blue won. They carried away the Cup, the gold medals and the glory back to the Midlands. Charlie Buchan's Sunderland lost. They would win the League Championship a week later but that achievement got small mention in the newspapers by comparison. Cup winners Villa were all over the front pages of every national paper. If Burnley were ever going to win the Cup they would need to take on and beat the likes of these two sides. These two were among the best teams in England. Burnley would have to raise their game next season that was without question as they played among the big boys.

Burnley's Final Match of the Season

With promotion secure, two games remained of Burnley's season. The Clarets eased off in the next game, losing at home to their promotion rivals Barnsley 1-0 in front of a crowd of over 18,000 on Wednesday 23rd April. The final match of the 1912-13 season was against Stockport County the following Saturday. Burnley were without the services of four players. Tommy Boyle was still nursing his injured knee and Billy Watson, Dave Taylor and Cliff Jones were all injured. Bert Freeman captained the Clarets for their final League game in Division Two against Stockport County.

Burnley v Stockport County, Turf Moor Saturday 26 April 1913 Kick Off 3:00pm

The teams lined up
Burnley: Dawson, McLaren, Bamford, Bellamy, Halley, Bradshaw, Mosscrop, Lindley, Freeman, Hodgson, Husband.
Stockport County: Birds, Froehlich, Fagan, Tattersall, Garrett, Chivers, Crossthwaite, Rodgers, Cook, Smith, O'Brien.
Referee: Mr A. Briggs (Blackburn)

The weather was 'wretched' according to the match reporter in the Athletics News with rain falling continually throughout the match which also affected the attendance which turned out to be the smallest gate of the season. Burnley kicked off with the advantage of the wind and after a dull start, the Clarets scored twice, just a few minutes from half-time, firstly through Dick Lindley and two minutes after by Teddy Hodgson. The two-goal margin 'flattered Burnley' according to the Athletics News reporter. The match was a much more even affair in the second half. County attacked and Rogers pulled a goal back for the visitors. Thirty minutes into the half, from an Eddie Mosscrop centre, Bert Freeman restored Burnley's two-goal advantage. County came more into the game after Freeman's goal and they scored a second through Garret from a fine shot which struck the inside of Dawson's post and deflected into the net. At the end of a damp April afternoon, the Clarets signed off their excellent season with a 3-2 victory and cheers from the small crowd.

At Full Time: Burnley 3 (Lindley, Hodgson, Freeman), Stockport County 2 (Rogers, Garret).
Attendance: 5,000 (The Burnley Express gave the gate receipts of £128 the lowest of the season which would equate to around only 5,000 people.)

---xxx---

The final top four places in Division Two for the 1912-13 season were now complete;

Preston North End,	53 points, Champions
Burnley,	50 points, Runners-Up
Birmingham City,	46 points,
Barnsley,	45 points.

The high-scoring Clarets had netted 88 League goals and another 13 goals in the FA Cup to make it over a hundred for the season. In recognition of their achievement, on Thursday the 1st of May, a celebration dinner was hosted by Philip Morrell MP at Burnley's Mechanics Institute. During the evening the Mayor of Burnley presented Burnley's Billy Watson with a gold watch, chain and medal in recognition for his services in having played in a hundred consecutive matches for the football club. The dinner was attended by several noted guests and dignitaries and speeches given by Mr J. McKenna and Mr C. E. Sutcliffe representing The Football League. They were followed by Philip Morrell's vote of thanks and lastly Burnley captain Tommy Boyle who toasted the Burnley team and gave these words,

"On behalf of the members of the team I beg to thank you most heartily for the toast which has been so ably proposed by Alderman Whitehead, and which you have drunk with such enthusiasm. As captain of the Burnley team I feel proud to have the honour of responding to it. (Hear, Hear) Since I first joined the Burnley club, it has been my ambition to see the team back again in the First Division, and I need scarcely to say that it was a most bitter dissapointment – especially to the players when we failed to win out last match at Wolverhampton last season. But we have made amends this season. (Hear, Hear and applause) Our task has not been an easy one by any means, for we have had many difficulties to face. Especially in regard to injuries, but the players have shown a skill and determination which have brought us through successfully (Hear, Hear). We also gave a good account of ourselves in the English Cup Competition, and the form we displayed in those matches should fill us with confidence for our fight in the First Division next season. I should like to say how much we appreciate the kindness of Mr. Morrell in entertaining us to dinner and for the great interest he has always taken in the team, especially when we have visited London (Loud applause)."

By the end of May, the 1913-14 League fixtures were published. Burnley would begin the season against Everton at Goodison Park before travelling to The Hawthorns for a meeting with West Bromwich Albion. The Clarets first home game would take place on the Bank Holiday Monday against the old enemy, Blackburn Rovers.

The biggest news of summer 1913 came on the 4th of June at Epsom racecourse. Those in attendance for the 1913 Derby were King George V and Queen Mary to see their horse, Anmer, run in the Royal colours. Among the thousands present were a contingent of suffragettes, many who had travelled together to raise the profile of their campaign at important and well known sporting events. Knowing they faced arrest on entering the grounds if wearing their WSPU colours, the group of women kept the colours hidden until they were safely inside. One of the suffragettes present was Emily Wilding Davison. She was a known militant who had been arrested two years previously for planting a bomb. Davison had been imprisoned and was force-fed in Strangeways prison after going on hunger-strike. As the afternoons programme began, Davison was waiting by the rails at Tattenham Corner. On hearing the horses approaching Davison slipped under the rails and strode onto the course. She spotted the distinctive scarlet and blue colours worn by Anmer's rider, Herbert Jones. The King's horse was going flat out as Davison attempted to pin the WSPU colours to Anmer's reins.

"The horse struck the woman with its chest, knocking her down among the flying hooves...blood rushed from her mouth and nose. Anmer turned a complete somersault and fell upon his jockey who was seriously injured." (Daily Mirror, 5/6/13)

Davison never recovered from the injuries she received and died four days later. Queen Mary was a well-known anti-suffragette and though it has always been thought that Davison did not intend to commit suicide, she did want to make a point of protest before the Royals. What made Davison's act more prominent was that it was captured on moving film and shown to cinema audiences across Britain.

A week later, over six thousand women marched behind Davison's funeral cortege while some 50,000 lined the funeral route from St. George's church in Bloomsbury to Kings Cross railway station where her body was taken home to Morpeth in Northumberland for burial in the family grave. Following Davison's death, the Suffragette's protests intensi-fied. Racecourse stands were burned down, golf courses were dug up, shop windows smashed, buildings fire-bombed and politicians targetted for stonings. In the wake of Davison's death, all manner of mayhem took place across the country. Security around The Royal Family was tightened as they attended the summer seasons events at Ascot, Wimbledon and Henley. To date football matches had not been targetted, but would that change in the coming season?

---xxx---

CHAPTER THREE

Burnley Are Back

Not in the clamour of the crowded street,
Not in the shouts and plaudits of the throng,
But in ourselves are triumph and defeat.

– Henry Longfellow 1876

The New Boys

After the long hot summer, September arrived and Burnley
Football Club was ready to begin a new football season in the
First Division. John Haworth's team would now compete
amongst the biggest and the best. Teams including Billy
Meredith's Manchester United, Newcastle United and
Liverpool. League Champions Sunderland and FA Cup winners,
Aston Villa. But the matches Burnley supporters were keenly
looking forward to were against rivals Blackburn Rovers, who
would arrive at Turf Moor in just one week's time.

It had been a busy close season behind the scenes at Turf
Moor. Work on the new Brunshaw Road stand had been
completed. The huge stand with a walled enclosure in front
had new dressing rooms for the players and boasted a, 'nice
little tea-room on the first floor' according to the Burnley
Express. The top-priced season tickets at 25 shillings in the
new stand had all sold out. The old Star stand on the opposite
side had been demolished and replaced by high, sloped

cinder banking, increasing Turf Moor's ground capacity to 40,000.

Despite promotion, the cost of watching Burnley from the terraces in the 1913-14 season were held at last seasons prices. Sixpence for adults (2.5p) and threepence for ladies and children. A match programme cost one penny (1d) and a pre-match pint of Massey's best bitter threepence - a full afternoon's entertainment for under a shilling (5p). (See appendix for prices of watching football in 1914.)

Burnley head groundsman Abel Hudson had prepared a fine playing surface over the summer that was ready for the visit of Rovers, but before that encounter, Burnley faced a trip to Goodison Park for the opening fixture of the new season. For three shillings, Burnley supporters could travel to Goodison Park with the Burnley team in luxury on a special chartered train, departing from Burnley after lunchtime and returning at 8:55 pm after the match. It would be a welcome return to Goodison Park for Burnley centre-forward Bert Freeman, who had joined Burnley from Everton for the sum of £550 only two years before. Before the match Everton and Burnley had agreed to pool the income and share the proceeds of both League games at the end of the season. (See Appendix - Calculating Burnley's Income from Gate Receipts.)

Everton v Burnley, Goodison Park, Monday 1st September 1913, Kick-Off 5:45 pm

The teams lined up at Goodison Park:
Everton: Mitchell, Stevenson, Maconachie, Harris, Wareing, Grenyer, Beare, Jefferis, Browell, Bradshaw, Palmer.
Burnley: Dawson, Bamford, Taylor, Halley, Boyle Watson, Bellamy, Lindley, Freeman, Hodgson, Husband.
Referee: Mr T. P. Campbell (Blackburn)

Burnley began the game the more positive side with Bert Freeman having two good runs on goal, one effort skimming the crossbar. After a goalless first period where both sides had played not to lose, it was Burnley who took the lead with Jimmy Bellamy's low drive past an outstretched Mitchell on 71 minutes. Two minutes later Freeman should have doubled Burnley's tally. With Mitchell beaten, Freeman's shot hit the post and re-bounded to safety. Heroics from Jerry Dawson in the Burnley goal kept the Clarets on course for a Burnley victory, but with seven minutes remaining Everton equalised. Dawson managed to grab hold of the ball on the floor after a long-range effort from Jefferis. The Everton centre-forward Browell ran in to pick up any prospect of a loose ball. There wasn't one as Dawson had shielded the ball under his body, so Browell tried to kick the ball out from under him. A free-for-all in the Burnley penalty area ensued. Full-back Dave Taylor, who was standing in front of Dawson, was knocked into the Burnley net. Up to a dozen players were involved in the melee. Mr Campbell eventually stepped in to call a halt to the fracas but rather than award Burnley a free-kick, he gave a drop-ball in the Burnley goalmouth. Burnley managed to clear but the ball came out to Browell, who probably shouldn't have been on the field after his foul on Dawson, to strike the Everton equaliser.

At Full Time: Everton 1 (Browell), Burnley 1 (Bellamy).
Attendance: 35,000 (Gate receipts of £974 7s).

---xxx---

What the Papers said:

The Manchester Guardian – "Burnley thoroughly deserved the draw they made with Everton and a continuation of the same form will give them a high place. Dawson was as sound as ever in the Burnley goal with Freeman repeatedly dangerous. There was not a weak spot in the team."

The Daily Mirror – "Burnley were a little unlucky not to beat Everton. It was a great contest up to the last kick."

The Burnley Express's Football correspondent Brunhilde said simply – "Burnley were splendid!"

Burnley supporters travelling home on the train that evening must have wondered how their side had not won the match. The Clarets had certainly made an impressive start on their return to the First Division and won their first point.

A Hard Time at the Hawthorns

Following their impressive start at Everton, The Clarets were on their travels again, this time to the Midlands to play West Bromwich Albion. Burnley soon discovered what life was like in the top division and were given a lesson in goal scoring from Albion centre-forward Alf Bentley, making his debut following his £500 summer transfer from Bolton Wanderers.

West Bromwich Albion v Burnley, The Hawthorns, Saturday 6 September 1913, K.O. 3:30 pm

The teams lined up:
Albion: Pearson, Smith, Pennington, Waterhouse, Buck, McNeal, Jephcott, Morris, Bentley, Lewis, Shearman.
Burnley: Dawson, Bamford, Taylor, Halley, Boyle, Watson, Bellamy, Lindley, Freeman, Hodgson, Husband.
Referee: Mr T. Kirkham (Burslem)

A warm, sunny afternoon greeted the travelling Burnley supporters and the game was only five minutes old when Albion took the lead with a goal by the debut-making Bentley who beat Jerry Dawson with a fine shot. Burnley rallied and from the re-start a good shot from Billy Watson went just wide of the Albion post. Albion countered, and on nine minutes

Tom Bamford failed to clear the ball. Bentley robbed him and slid the ball past Dawson to score his second goal. Straight from the re-start Burnley lost possession and Albion stormed forward again. Jephcott heading the ball at Dawson who caught the ball cleanly. But before Dawson could clear up-field he was charged into the net along with the ball by Bentley to make it three-nil and give the newcomer his hat-trick after only eleven minutes! At three down, Burnley gradually came into the game. A Bert Freeman shot rattled the Albion crossbar. But just before the interval, it got worse for Burnley when winger Jimmy Bellamy was hurt in a collision and had to be carried off the field.

Ten-man Burnley pulled a goal back early in the second half with a fine goal from Freeman. Running at the Albion defence, Freeman beat several defenders to score with a neat chip over the goalkeepers head. It was a great goal, but it was always going to be Albion's day after such a bad start. As Tommy Boyle pushed his men forward to try and reduce the arrears, six minutes from time, Boyle and George Halley joined the Burnley attack leaving the defence exposed. Pearson the Albion keeper lobbed the ball out to Shearman lurking in the Burnley half. Burnley full-back Tom Bamford protested to the referee that Shearman was offside, but Mr Kirkham waved his arms for them to play on. Shearman centred, Dawson rose to catch the ball and missed it, the ball falling straight to who-else but Bentley to score his fourth goal against a now shell-shocked Burnley.

At Full Time: West Bromwich Albion 4 (Bentley 4), Burnley 1 (Freeman).
Attendance: 25,000

---xxx---

The Albion defeat hurt and the team only had Sunday off before opening their home campaign with the eagerly antici-pated visit of local rivals, Blackburn Rovers.

The Rovers Return

Monday 8th September and a Bank Holiday for the return of the local derby against Rovers and a match that would draw a record crowd to Turf Moor. It would be the first League encounter between Burnley and Blackburn Rovers this century, the last League contest way back in 1899. With the mills and factories closed for the holiday, the Burnley Express reported that an hour before kick-off, huge crowds were seen making their way towards Turf Moor. The crowds must have delayed the Rovers team who arrived at Turf Moor late, only just in time to change into their kit. There was one team change for The Clarets. Local youngster Billy Nesbitt came into the Burnley side for the injured Jimmy Bellamy.

Burnley v Blackburn Rovers, Turf Moor, Monday 8 September 1913. Kick-Off 3.30pm

The teams lined up:

Burnley: Dawson, Bamford, Taylor, Halley, Boyle, Watson, Nesbitt, Lindley, Freeman, Hodgson, Husband.

Blackburn Rovers: Robinson, Crompton, Cowell, Walmsley, Smith, Bradshaw, Simpson, Shea, Chapman, Latherton, Hodkinson.

Referee: Mr W. J. Heath (Burslem)

Tommy Boyle led out the Burnley team to a bumper crowd at Turf Moor and the Clarets attacked the Cricket Field End in the first half. Jerry Dawson was in action shortly after the kick-off saving first from Chapman and then Shea. With only four minutes gone, Burnley attacked down the right, Boyle feeding the ball to Billy Nesbitt. Nesbitt put in a good centre for Teddy Hodgson who took the ball around Cowell and rolled it into the path of Bert Freeman. Freeman picked his spot and with a hard shot volleyed home to give Burnley the lead. Turf Moor erupted! Burnley held their own for the best part of half an hour before the visitors gained three corners in succession at the Bee Hole End. It was from the third corner that Smith scored the Rovers equaliser. Jerry Dawson found himself in the wars shortly after as did Dave Taylor, who got a nasty gash to his knee which forced him out of the game until the second half. The score at the interval was 1-1.

Burnley attacked strongly again in the second half. A lively Billy Nesbitt supplying Bert Freeman who came close, his shot striking the crossbar. Five minutes into the second half, Rovers won a direct free kick inside the Burnley penalty area. Chapman took the kick and struck it straight through a packed Burnley defence beyond Dawson to give Rovers the lead. Burnley had two chances through Bill Husband but he failed to put them away. Then Freeman was unlucky not to equalise for Burnley. He had a golden opportunity to score and was pulled back by a Rovers defender. Freeman appealed but Mr Heath waved play-on, no foul. After a gutsy performance, the Clarets went down fighting to a 2-1 defeat. Rovers went top of the League while John Haworth's men were left nursing more injuries.

At Full Time: Burnley 1 (Freeman), Blackburn Rovers 2 (Smith, Chapman)
Attendance: 38,000 (Record gate receipts for a League match at Turf Moor of £940 8s 1d)

---xxx---

What the Papers said,

Burnley Express: "It is a long time since I witnessed a game with Rovers in which the trainers services were so frequently required. Taylor needed three stitches in a knee and Halley received a blow to the jaw from an opponents elbow."

Wednesday on a Saturday

With only one point from their first three games, Burnley were fourth from the bottom of the First Division and desperate to find their first victory. On the back of two straight defeats, Burnley secretary John Haworth rang the changes. Eddie Mosscrop was available for selection and he replaced Billy Nesbitt despite the local youngster having a good game against Blackburn. Harry Mountford came in for Bill Husband on the right and Cliff Jones replaced injured full back Dave Taylor.

Burnley v The Wednesday, Turf Moor, Saturday 13 September 1913 Kick-Off 3:30 pm

The Teams lined up at Turf Moor:
Burnley: Dawson, Bamford, Jones, Halley, Boyle, Watson, Mosscrop, Lindley, Freeman, Hodgson, Mountford.
The Wednesday: Davison, Worrall, Spoors, Brittleton, McSkimming, Campbell, Kirkman, Glennon, Burkinshaw (J), Wilson, Robertson.
Referee: Mr J. E. Hall (Olton)

It had rained overnight but the pitch was in good order and a light breeze blew from the Bee Hole End toward the town. The visitors started the more positive and had several chances to take the lead. Jerry Dawson was the busier of the two goalkeepers and punched clear two dangerous Wednesday crosses from corner kicks. Cliff Jones settled well in defence alongside Tom Bamford, and both full-backs were kept busy. After thirty minutes, Burnley settled down and came more into the game. Teddy Hodgson had a goal ruled offside. Then Eddie Mosscrop came close to scoring for the Clarets just before the interval but skewed his shot wide of the post at the last moment and at half-time the scores were level, 0-0.

The visitors started the better side in the second half and saw more of the ball. With 20 minutes of the second half gone, the game had a goalless draw written all over it. On 68 minutes, a breakthrough came for Burnley. Tommy Boyle placed a good pass out to winger Harry Mountford. Mountford passed inside to Teddy Hodgson. Hodgson was thirty yards from goal, he swivelled, beat the Wednesday full-back and headed on toward goal. Wednesday's goalkeeper Teddy Davison, at five feet seven inches, the smallest goalkeeper in the League, came off his line to meet Hodgson. Hodgson spotted a small gap between Davison and his post and hit a low shot along the floor that found the bottom corner of the Wednesday net. It was a good goal from Hodgson and won great cheers from all around Turf Moor. The game suddenly came to life as Wednesday pressed forward. Wednesday found the back of the Burnley net only for Mr Hall to rule their effort offside. Six minutes later Burnley attacked again. After shots on goal from several Burnley players the ball came to winger Harry Mountford to score Burnley's second with a good shot.

Ten minutes from time, Burnley went 3-0 up when Billy Watson and Mountford combined. Mountford sent a through ball to Freeman for the centre-forward to score his third goal in three games. It was a brilliant goal by Freeman, described by Sportsman in the Burnley Express, "Freeman got the ball and dribbling on in his best style, got in between the backs and hooked the ball over Davison's head." The Clarets left the field to rapturous applause after an excellent second half performance.

At Full Time: Burnley 3 (Hodgson, Mountford, Freeman), The Wednesday 0
Attendance: 23,000 (Gate receipts £509)

---xxx---

What the Papers said:

Daily Mail: "Burnley played like a team inspired and their forwards in the last quarter did pretty much as they liked."

Daily Dispatch: "Burnley gained their first victory without the services of key players but the material the Turf Moor executive has to work upon is good enough to hold its own with the majority in first-class company."

Another Lancashire Derby

Next was a short journey to Burnden Park and another Lancashire derby against a Bolton Wanderers side going well in the League. John Haworth fielded the same team that had played so well against The Wednesday.

Bolton Wanderers v Burnley, Burnden Park, Saturday 20 September 1913, Kick-Off 3:00 pm

The Teams lined up:
Burnley: Dawson, Bamford, Taylor, Halley, Boyle, Watson, Mosscrop, Lindley, Freeman, Hodgson, Mountford.
Bolton Wanderers: Edmonson, Baversock, Feebury, Gimblett, Rowley, Thomas, Donaldson, Jones, Lillycrop, Smith and Vizard.
Referee: Mr R. Eccles (Darwen)

Burnley kicked off on what was a dull, cloudy, afternoon with their opponents in a determined mood having beaten Manchester United at Old Trafford the previous weekend. George Lillycrop, Tommy Boyle's former team mate at Barnsley and now Bolton's centre-forward, was in the Wanderers team. Lillycrop sent a good ball out to Vizard the Wanderers outside-left. The Welsh international was tackled well by Mosscrop who stole the ball off him and made his way into the Bolton half. With no other Burnley forwards nearby, Mosscrop let fly from thirty yards with a shot that skimmed the Bolton crossbar. After Mosscrop's effort, Bolton took command and had a number of attempts on goal, Jerry Dawson pulling off several fine saves from Donaldson, Smith and Jones. Once when saving from Lillycrop, Dawson was unfairly bundled into the net and was awarded a free-kick.

It was a rough game. Burnley's trainer, Ernie Edwards, was kept busy throughout the first half, attending to Boyle, Lindley, Bamford, Halley and finally Dawson. Shortly before half-time, Burnley won their first corner. Mosscrop centred and found Billy Watson ten yards out whose drive rattled Edmondson's right post. At the interval it remained goalless.

The second half featured mostly Bolton pressure but their attacks were thwarted by heroics from Dawson in the Burnley goal. With an hour gone, there was a moment of controversy when a Bolton claim for a penalty was turned down by Mr Eccles. Donaldson's cross had bounced up and struck Dave Taylors arm who was stood on the edge of the penalty area. The Bolton players appealed and after consulting with his linesman, Mr Eccles only awarded a free-kick outside the penalty area. The Bolton players were incensed and remonstrated strongly with Mr Eccles, who would have none of it. Sportsman in the Burnley Express, reckoned Taylor was inside the penalty area when he handled, but that it had not been intentional.

Jerry Dawson pulled off a series of flying saves in the latter stages of the game to deny the home side. The game suffered from the high number of fouls from both sides that ruined the run of play. In one tackle, Sportsman described that Halley was 'laid-out.' An 'ankle-tap' on Freeman should have led to a sending off and then, 'a retaliatory kick at Donaldson by Taylor' brought boos from the home crowd. Finally, Burnley's best player of the contest, Jerry Dawson, was knocked into the back of his net for the second time in the match after saving from a corner, just before the final whistle.

At Full Time: Bolton Wanderers 0, Burnley 0
Attendance: 33,000

---xxx---

England Call-ups for Watson and Freeman

After their performances in the previous matches, it was announced on the 24th September that Billy Watson and Bert Freeman had both been selected to play in the English League side to play the Irish League, in Belfast on 1st October.

Brilliant Burnley

After two good team performances against Wednesday and Bolton Wanderers, Burnley returned to Turf Moor. It was a golden, end-of-summer afternoon at Turf Moor with mid-table Chelsea the visitors. This was a match where everything came together for John Haworth's men who put on a performance that would live long in the memory of the Burnley supporters that witnessed it. Haworth again had replacements to find for injuries. McLaren came in at centre-half for an injured Tommy Boyle and Tom Charlton replaced Harry Mountford (thigh).

Burnley v Chelsea, Turf Moor, Saturday 27 September 1913, Kick-Off 3:30 pm

The Teams lined up:
Burnley: Dawson, Bamford, D. Taylor, Halley, McLaren, Watson, Mosscrop, Lindley, Freeman, Hodgson, Charlton.
Chelsea: Molyneaux, Whittingham, Sharp, F. Taylor, Logan, Calderhead, Ford, MacFarlane, Turnbull, V. J. Woodward, Fairgay.
Referee: Mr J. Fowler (Sunderland)

Chelsea began the better team and Jerry Dawson's services were required early on from a corner kick. From Dawson's clearance, Eddie Mosscrop was put through and his shot on the Chelsea goal on five minutes led to Burnley's first corner. Mosscrop's in-swinger corner found Teddy Hodgson totally unmarked at the far post to head in and put the Clarets a goal up. Chelsea attacked but the Burnley defence held firm. George Halley setting up quick counter-attacks for Bert Freeman and then Dick Lindley who both had good chances to score. On fourteen minutes, Freeman found Mosscrop, who centred to find George Halley just inside the Chelsea penalty area to score with a hard shot that Molyneaux never saw until he picked it out of the net. It was a rare goal from the Burnley centre-back to double Burnley's lead. A Chelsea attack found Ford in the Burnley penalty area who was fouled by Tommy Bamford. Mr Fowler awarded Chelsea the penalty from which Whittingham stepped up to score and make it 2-1. Chelsea surged forward looking for the equaliser but it was the quick breaking runs from Mosscrop, the most dangerous man on the field, who gave Chelsea's defence problems all afternoon. A shot by McLaren on 30 minutes led to another Burnley corner. It was quickly taken by Mosscrop who's accurate centre found Bert Freeman's head this time to score Burnley's third, making it Freeman's fourth goal in five games for the Clarets. And at half time Burnley led Chelsea, 3-1.

Chelsea fought to get back in the match right from the whistle. A Woodward shot pulling off a good save from Dawson. Chelsea had much of the early play but their attacks simply couldn't breech Burnley's defence. On sixty-eight minutes, Lindley and Mosscrop combined. Lindley's pass inside finding an unmarked Hodgson who finished brilliantly, to score his second goal of the afternoon. Chelsea pushed forward and were left exposed at the back. Tom Charlton punished them with a fast dribbling run and an excellent finish on his own to make it 5-1 to The Clarets. To cap a fine afternoon, five minutes from time, Eddie Mosscrop won another corner. Mosscrop floated the ball across, Hodgson snuck between two confused Chelsea defenders and headed in to complete his hat-trick and score Burnley's sixth!

At Full Time: Burnley 6 (Hodgson 3, Halley, Freeman, Charlton), Chelsea 1 (Whittingham pen.)
Attendance: 24,000 (Gate receipts of £555)

---xxx---

It had been a brilliant afternoon for the Clarets who gave Chelsea a lesson in finishing. It was difficult to pick out an individual Burnley player for special praise, they had all played so well. Teddy Hodgson's hat-trick gained much praise from Sportsman in the Burnley Express but it was winger Eddie Mosscrop's all-round performance that made him the Clarets stand-out player.

"Mosscrop has never played a better game for Burnley. He was on the top of his form in speed, command of the ball, centring and placing corners."

After a shaky start, Burnley were gradually finding their feet and climbing the League table. After six games, the Clarets were now up to ninth place in the Table.

MP Philip Morrell and Lady Ottoline's visit

Burnley's Member of Parliament, Philip Morrell and his wife, Lady Ottoline were holidaying in Burnley, staying for a month in Upper Brunshaw with Lady O'Hagan. The couple had watched two of Burnley's home matches against Sheffield Wednesday and Chelsea.

In Other News

The Government announced they were considering proposals for a joint project with the French to construct a tunnel under the English Channel that would allow trains to run directly between London and Paris.

A Drab Afternoon in Oldham

Burnley's next match was a short trip to Boundary Park to play Oldham. After Burnley's recent form, a large number of their supporters made the trip. Kestrel, the Burnley News reporter, wasn't too impressed with Oldham. His match report complained about the weather, the midges and the mud in Sheepfoot Lane. "Sheepfoot Lane bears an appropriate name for it is more fitted for a sheep track than for an approach or exit to or from a football ground." His verbal attack went on, "Just as Oldham under a muggy sky was a study in mono-chrome – dirty brick houses, dirty children and slatternly women – so the game itself was a study in one colour – drab." The referee also came in for a scathing attack as Kestrel thought the Clarets were "again deprived of both points." The match featured the Burnley Cricket Club professional Billy Cook playing in defence for Oldham. Tommy Boyle was back at the heart of defence for the Clarets.

Oldham Athletic v Burnley, Boundary Park, Saturday 4 October 1913, Kick-Off 3:30 pm

The Teams lined up:
Burnley: Dawson, Bamford, Jones, Halley, Boyle, Watson, Mosscrop, Lindley, Freeman, Hodgson, Charlton.
Oldham Athletic: Matthews, Hodson, Cook, Moffat, Roberts, Wilson, Tummon, Walters, Toward, Woodyer, Donnachie.
Referee: Mr S. D. Peers (Liverpool)

After a slow start, the game came to life when Oldham took an early lead on 17 minutes. Billy Cook scoring for Oldham from a penalty, given away by Tommy Boyle for, "fisting out a goal-bound header by Walters." The Burnley skipper was stood on the goal-line at the time and had little choice, the ball too high to reach with his head. Boyle wasn't cautioned, booked or even spoken to by the referee. On twenty three minutes, the Burnley captain made amends. Dick Lindley found Tom Charlton with a return pass who tore down the wing and beat Hodson the Oldham full-back. The ball came inside to Teddy Hodgson, who passed to Bert Freeman. Freemans shot cannoned off a defender straight into the path of Boyle. The Burnley skipper let rip from 25 yards with a screamer. Matthews in the Oldham goal sighted the ball coming his way, coming at pace, heading straight for his top right-hand corner. Kestrel – "the custodian sprang for the ball and reached it but so great was the speed the ball, tumbled him back into the net." At half-time the sides remained at 1-1.

The second half featured very little football. It became more of a kicking contest, the play littered with nasty, niggling fouls between the players. Roberts the Oldham centre-half, according to Kestrel, "was particularly offensive to Freeman, who had to protest about his tactics" and who was later kicked for his complaining. Moffat lost his temper after an incident when he and Charlton were going for the ball. Moffat deliberately kicking Charlton on the shin when the ball was out of play. No record was given of any bookings or sending's off by the referee. In the match summary, Kestrel reported that Oldham had most of the play in the first twenty minutes but after that Burnley dominated for well over an hour.

At Full Time: Oldham 1 (Cook pen), Burnley 1 (Boyle)
Attendance: 16,000.

---xxx---

Victory over Rovers in the Lancashire Cup

The second round of the Lancashire Cup took place at Turf Moor on Monday the 6th of October. Both sides played their first teams and Burnley knocked Blackburn Rovers out in front of a small crowd of around 6,000. The match featured the return of Billy Nesbitt in place of Eddie Mosscrop who was teaching. The Clarets won comfortably, 3-0 with goals from Dick Lindley, a Tommy Boyle penalty and Bert Freeman.

Burnley's Walking Wounded

With the season less than a month old, the team were picking up results but injuries were mounting. Jimmy Bellamy was still ruled out. Tommy Boyle had missed the Chelsea game "through slight concussion, the result of hard knocks in the Bolton and Blackburn matches." Dave Taylor's knee had been stitched up, he was sporting a head injury and had torn a ligament in his left ankle in the first half during the Chelsea game but had played on. Harry Mountford had a damaged thigh muscle. In the reserve team, goalkeeper Ronnie Sewell had received such a bad kick on the thigh it required the trainer to be called out at midnight. Bill Husband had influenza and reserve full-back Bob Reid was in bed suffering from 'quinsy' (tonsillitis).

New Burnley Stand Proposal

The Club directors had asked Mr Arthur Bell, the club's architect, to cost the provision of a shelter on the side of the ground where the 'Star' stand was located (The Longside). The directors were keen on something similar to what was being completed at Ewood Park, a 'semi-double-decker.' This would consist of a stand overhead with seating accommodation and rising terraces underneath. The designs and proposals were currently under discussion by the Burnley board.

The Return of the Welsh Wizard

Burnley's next encounter was against Manchester United. Between two and three thousand United supporters arrived in Burnley by train early on Saturday morning. It was the first return to Turf Moor of United since their 2-0 defeat at the hands of Spen Whittaker's Burnley in the 1910 FA Cup. United's Billy Meredith had celebrated his 39th birthday earlier in July but was still up to his old tricks. The Clarets were unchanged from the previous week's game at Oldham.

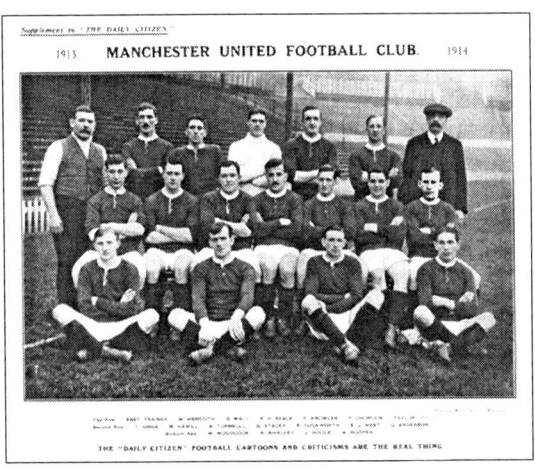

Figure 12: Manchester United 1913-14

Burnley v Manchester United, Turf Moor, Saturday 11 October 1913 Kick-Off 3:00 pm

The Teams lined up:
Burnley: Dawson, Bamford, Taylor, Halley, Boyle, Watson, Mosscrop, Lindley, Freeman, Hodgson, Charlton.
Manchester United: Beale, Chorlton, Stacey, Duckworth, Whalley, Hamill, Meredith, Turnbull, Anderson, West, Wall.
Referee: Mr J. T. Hornby (London)

Manchester United appeared in dark blue shirts to avoid the colour clash. Burnley captain Tommy Boyle won the toss and elected to play with the wind behind the Clarets, toward the Cricket Field End. Right from the kick-off, United pressed forward. Billy Meredith gave Dave Taylor a torrid time and the

Burnley defence was severely tested. On 23 minutes, a long ball from United sailed over the heads of the Burnley full-backs. Jerry Dawson ran out to claim the ball but was beaten to it by United's centre-forward George Anderson, who opened the scoring. Tommy Boyle called to his wingers to get forward and on 36 minutes Burnley won a deserved equaliser. Full-back Tom Bamford sent a long ball up-field. Teddy Hodgson held the ball up in the United half and passed inside to Bert Freeman who fired into the United goal. Freeman's strike generated enthusiastic applause from the home crowd. The Clarets had their best spell of the game and efforts from Dick Lindley, Teddy Hodgson and a long-distance blast from the skipper completed the first half with the teams going in for tea at 1-1.

Burnley began the second half strongly and Beale in the United goal was kept busy by Tom Charlton, but a mix-up at the back cost Burnley on 49 minutes. The ball was received on the right by Wall who centred and found and unmarked Anderson to score his second goal. Dawson's view was blocked by a Burnley defender and Dawson couldn't stop the ball going in. Burnley poured forward and a claim for a penalty was turned down when a shot from Bert Freeman hit a United defenders hand, but Mr Hornby waved play-on. Burnley had another good chance through Eddie Mosscrop with a run on goal, only he was pulled back by a United defender. No foul and play on said Mr Hornby. United were more dangerous in the closing ten minutes after Burnley first lost Teddy Hodgson to injury and then Tommy Boyle. Burnley finishing the match with only nine players. United left Turf Moor with the points while the Clarets were left nursing more injuries.

At Full Time: Burnley 1 (Freeman), Manchester United 2 (Anderson 2)
Attendance: 30,000 (Gate receipts of £730 14s 9d)

---xxx---

Burnley's Best

According to Sportsman in the Burnley Express, "Bamford was the better of the defenders, Boyle in the intermediate line while Hodgson and Mosscrop were perhaps the pick of the forwards with Freeman running them close."

Death of Old Burnley Groundsman

The death was announced by the Club on October 15th of Mr Onias Pickles, aged 71 who for a number of years was the head groundsman at Turf Moor. As a mark of respect the flag was lowered to half-mast.

Burnley Win Their Spurs

Burnley had played five out of the top six sides when sixth placed Tottenham Hotspur arrived at Turf Moor. It had been five years since Burnley had last played the London side who had started the season well with only one defeat in eight games.

Burnley v Tottenham Hotspur, Turf Moor, Saturday 18 October 1913, Kick-Off 3:15 pm

The Teams lined up:
Burnley: Dawson, Bamford, Jones, Halley, Boyle, Watson, Mosscrop, Charlton, Freeman, Hodgson, Husband.
Tottenham Hotspur: King, Collins, Webster, Weir, Steel, Grimsdell, Fleming, Minter, Cantrell, Bliss, Middlemiss.
Referee: Mr J. E. Hall (Olton)

Tottenham had more of the play in the first period with Jerry Dawson the busier of the two goalkeepers. On fifteen minutes Burnley won a free kick. Tom Bamford placed the ball and struck the ball toward goal. The ball bounced higher than King in the Spurs goal expected and though he managed to get a finger to it, the ball slipped from King's fingers. The ball rolled towards goal and winger Tom Charlton ran in and knocked it over the line to give Burnley the lead. Following Spurs pressure, ten minutes later an attack led to Fleming centring for Cantrell to score for the visitors with a fine header to level the scores. Before the interval, Bert Freeman had a good chance to put Burnley back in front but his effort went just wide of King's post.

Seven minutes into the second half, Freeman was causing problems among the Spurs defenders. He held up the ball and released it to Tommy Boyle who was brought down in the penalty area. Mr Hall pointed to the spot and Boyle stepped up to score and put the Clarets back in front. Burnley maintained the pressure and from an Eddie Mosscrop centre, Teddy Hodgson put the ball in the net but it was flagged offside, which was met by derision by the home crowd.

On 78 minutes Boyle found Mosscrop on the wing with one of his long swinging passes. Mosscrop set off down the line on one of his hare-like runs, leaping over flying tackles. Taking the ball into the corner, Mosscrop beat the Spurs defender, pushed the ball along the dead-ball line and then got his cross in. The ball landed in front of the oncoming Tommy Charlton to score his second of the afternoon and Burnley's third. Spurs showed some clever combinational play in the latter stages of the game but never really threatened to score while Burnley held firm right up to the final whistle.

At Full Time: Burnley 3 (Charlton 2, Boyle pen), Tottenham Hotspur 1 (Cantrell)
Attendance: 23,000 (Gate receipts of £545)

---xxx---

That evening as Burnley supporters celebrated their team going 7th in the Table, Doc Hodges, the Burnley club physician was the busiest man at Turf Moor. Bill Husband had wrenched both his calf and thigh muscles in his right leg. George Halley had tendon trouble in his right knee and Jimmy Bellamy was still two weeks from being fit again. With the nights drawing in and winter approaching, the Burnley squad was getting ever thinner.

Who'll be Outside-Left?

With injuries to his two regular wingers, Jimmy Bellamy and Bill Husband, the big problem for John Haworth was who could play in the outside left position. The other ten positions more or less picked themselves but in the first nine league games, three players had filled the outside-left berth. The previous Monday during a Lancashire Cup-tie against Manchester City at Turf Moor, Haworth had even tried out full-back Dave Taylor in the outside-left berth. Taylor was a keen sprinter but after City won the tie 2-1, Sportsman in the Burnley Express wrote, "Taylor was clearly out of his element, though his head came in useful on occasions." Local youngster Billy Nesbitt had provided cover for Eddie Mosscrop on the right and was a regular outside-right in the reserves, but could he make the step-up to the first team and switch to play on the left?

Next, a short trip to Deepdale. George Halley's knee kept him out and Willie McLaren came in to cover at right back. Billy Nesbitt came back into the team at outside-left for Bill Husband and Tom Charlton kept his place after his two goals against Spurs. (Burnley captain Tommy Boyle would switch Nesbitt and Mosscrop over from right to left several times during a game.) Sportsman commented on the travelling support, a large number of Burnley supporters making the trip via four special trains, numerous hire cars and charabancs, "there appeared to be as many Burnley shouters as Prestonians."

Preston North End v Burnley, Deepdale, Saturday 25 October 1913 Kick-Off 3:00 pm

The Teams lined up:
Burnley: Dawson, Bamford, Taylor, McLaren, Boyle, Watson, Mosscrop, Charlton, Freeman, Hodgson, Nesbitt.
Preston North End: Taylor, MacFadyen, Broadhurst, Johnstone, McCall, Henderson, Morley, Common, Toward, Osborn, Barlow.
Referee: Mr L. N. Fletcher (Bury)

With a quarter of the season gone, Preston North End had yet to chalk up their first victory in the First Division. Burnley got off to a good start. With only 90 seconds on the clock, Teddy Hodgson fired in to give Burnley the lead from Billy Nesbitt's cross. The goal delighted Burnley's travelling army of supporters. Preston attacked, sending passes out to the wings, Jerry Dawson managing to clear efforts first from Barlow, and then Toward. On twelve minutes, Bert Freeman set off from the half-way line in a straight-line for goal. Two North-End defenders, MacFadyen and Broadhurst raced toward Freeman to intercept him from left and right. Freeman saw them coming and his clever timing slipped the ball between the two full-backs at just the right instant, before the pair of defenders crashed into each other, which the crowd loved, but Freeman failed with his goal effort. Preston grabbed an equaliser on 36 minutes after sustained pressure on Dawson's goal. McCall kicked the ball long up-field for Toward to chase who wrestled that ball away from Boyle and when it seemed he would pass it out to the wing, he did the complete opposite. He swivelled and shot on the turn past an outstretched Dawson. It was an excellent goal and Preston were in the ascendency. More Preston pressure and three minutes before the interval, Dawson saved a penalty, fisting the ball high over the crossbar to send the teams in at one goal each after an exciting first half.

In the second period, Tommy Boyle switched Eddie Mosscrop and Billy Nesbitt over on the wings. Teddy Hodgson rattled the Preston crossbar with a header and then another Hodgson effort skimmed past the post. At the other end, Jerry Dawson saved Burnley on a number of occasions. Sportsman's views on the Burnley keeper', "Dawson was brilliancy itself. He fisted away, gathered the ball, dodged eager opponents, kicked away and for one, flung himself full length to push a shot by Morley just round the upright." The game looked to have a 1-1 draw stamped all over it but on 83 minutes, North End grabbed a late winner with a fierce, low shot from Barlow, which found the net through a crowd of players.

At Full Time: Preston North End 2 (Toward, Barlow), Burnley 1 (Hodgson)
Attendance: 27,000 (Gate receipts of £640)

---xxx---

The Return of the Geordies

It had been thirteen years since Burnley had played Newcastle United at Turf Moor and another big crowd turned out at Turf Moor to see the match. Burnley's new signing from Blackpool, Levi Thorpe, came into the defence in place of the still injured George Halley.

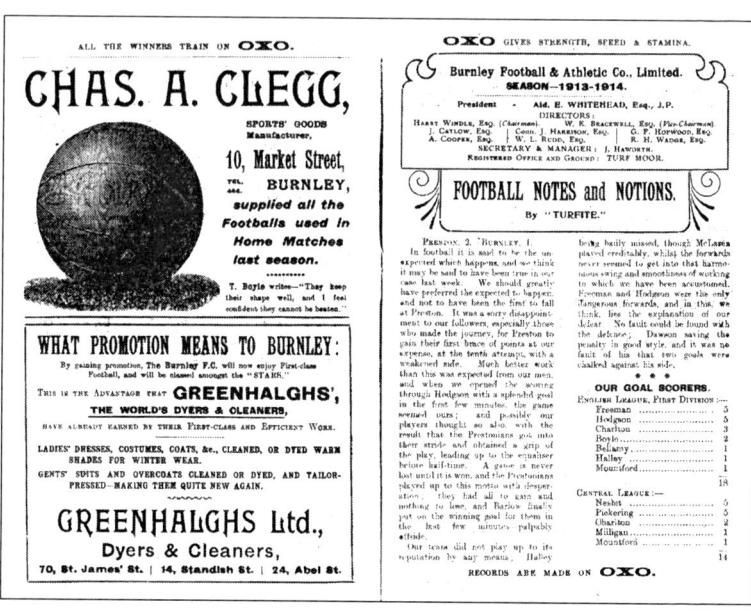

Figure 13: Burnley v Newcastle Programme

Figure 14

Figure 15

Burnley v Newcastle United, Turf Moor, Saturday 1st November 1913 Kick-Off 2:45 pm

The Teams lined up:
Burnley: Dawson, Bamford, Taylor, Thorpe, Boyle, Watson, Mosscrop, Lindley, Freeman, Hodgson, Nesbitt.
Newcastle United: Lawrence, McCracken, Hudspeth, Hay, Low, Finlay, Douglas, Hall, Sheperd, Hibbert, Wilson.
Referee: Mr L. Baker (Nantwich)

Tommy Boyle won the toss and Burnley played toward the Cricket Field End in the first half. Sportsman in the Burnley Express reported that the game was played at a fast pace. The first real chance of the game fell to Burnley on 22 minutes. Eddie Mosscrop got away from his marker and put in a good centre for Bert Freeman to flick the ball on with his head to Teddy Hodgson whose shot was saved low down by Lawrence. At the other end, Shepherd missed an opportunity to score from a Wilson cross. Burnley countered and a good shot from Billy Watson struck the Newcastle post. With 35 minutes gone, Burnley had the ball in the Newcastle half on the right. Freeman slipped the ball between two defenders to Dick Lindley's shot beat Lawrence. "To a scene of wild enthusiasm. The shout was heard quite plainly about two miles away," according to Sportsman.

In the second half Newcastle went with five up front. Dave Taylor was Burnley's saviour on a number of occasions according to Sportsman. With gaps at the back, Burnley's Teddy Hodgson and Dick Lindley had further chances to increase Burnley's lead. Towards the end of the half, a Lindley shot cracked the paint off Lawrence's post before going out for a goal kick. Burnley's defence were tested before the end which overall had been a fine all-round performance by the Clarets and two more precious points.

At Full Time: Burnley 1 (Lindley), Newcastle United 0
Attendance: 30,000 (Gate receipts of £712)

---xxx---

A Star Is Born

Figure 16: Robert Kelly

Burnley were still finding their feet in the First Division but it was only two months into the season and they were already suffering a number of injuries. Jimmy Bellamy and now George Halley were on the long-term injured list and several other regulars were carrying knocks but playing. Following the 2-1 defeat at Deepdale a fortnight before, John Haworth had been on the hunt for new players. The Burnley manager had missed the Clarets home victory over Tottenham. Along with a number of other managers, Howarth was in St. Helens, watching a talented eighteen year-old amateur playing in the Lancashire Combination. The youngster had played well and at the end of the match, Haworth approached Robert Kelly and his father, and made him an offer ahead of a number of other First Division clubs. Howarth convinced Kelly he had a great future at Burnley Football Club and the youngster signed professional forms and became a Burnley player later that evening.

And so to Anfield Road. Home of Liverpool Football Club and a rain-drenched afternoon on Merseyside. Burnley were unchanged from their 1-0 victory over Newcastle United.

Liverpool v Burnley, Anfield Road, Saturday 8th November 1913 Kick Off 2.45pm

The Teams lined up:
Burnley: Dawson, Bamford, Taylor, Thorpe, Boyle, Watson, Mosscrop, Lindley, Freeman, Hodgson, Nesbitt.
Liverpool: Campbell, Longworth, Pursell, Fairfoul, Lowe, Ferguson, Goddard, Lacey, Miller, Dawson, McKinlay.
Referee: Mr G. W. Drewery (Hull)

With only a minute on the referees watch, Dave Taylor was hit square in the face by the sodden, heavy ball that felled him like a tree. After a whiff of smelling salts and a dousing from Ernie Edwards cold sponge, Taylor was dazed but soon back on his feet. Five minutes later, Burnley had their first break when Billy Nesbitt won Burnley's first corner. Watson's corner floated over the Liverpool defence to the far post where an unmarked Bert Freeman found the top corner of the Liverpool net with a close-range header. The ball struck the iron stanchion of the goals and stuck there. From the re-start Liverpool attacked. Jerry Dawson was kept busy several times. On twenty minutes, a Liverpool attack saw a Goddard centre loop over the Burnley defenders to reach Bill Lacey who scored to make it 1-1.

Burnley began more aggressively in the second half and took the game to Liverpool.

Bert Freeman found himself in a good scoring position, only for Campbell, coming off his line, to block a good shot. The ball came straight out to Billy Watson who had pushed forward, whose shot flew across the goal and out for a goal-kick. One of the best chances of the game fell to Teddy Hodgson who after rounding Fairfoul, sent the ball over the crossbar from an oblique angle. On two occasions Freeman was 'bowled over' according to Sportsman in the Burnley Express, when he had certain goal-scoring opportunities that could have won the match for Burnley. The game ending with honours even at Anfield and the points shared.

At Full time: Liverpool 1 (Lacey), Burnley 1 (Freeman)
Attendance: 20,000

---xxx---

Meanwhile Back At Turf Moor.

Burnley Reserves were playing Liverpool Reserves in a Central League fixture. New signing Bob Kelly was in the Burnley side wearing a claret and blue shirt for the first time. In front of a crowd of around 5,000, three players were making their Burnley debuts, Shaw, Bell and Kelly. Burnley Reserves beat the visitors 2-0. One goal coming from George Milligan's boot, the other from the debut making Kelly with a fine header. "Kelly was the star artiste," reported the Burnley Express the following week.

Kelly's performance must have impressed the watching Burnley directors who selected the eighteen year-old for the next first team fixture against Aston Villa the following week. Villa had won the FA Cup in April and had finished runners up in the League to Sunderland last season. On paper, visitors Villa were the strongest side Burnley had faced in the League so far. Another good home crowd turned out to witness a brilliant team performance from Burnley. Again injuries had forced changes. Bob Kelly was making his debut in place of the injured Teddy Hodgson. Cliff Jones was deputising for Dave Taylor and Bill Husband came in for Billy Nesbitt.

Aston Astonished

Burnley v Aston Villa, Turf Moor, Saturday 15 November 1913 Kick-Off 2:45 pm

The Teams lined up:
Burnley: Dawson, Bamford, Jones, Thorpe, Boyle, Watson, Mosscrop, Lindley, Freeman, Kelly, Husband.
Aston Villa: Anstey, Lyons, Weston, Tranter, Harrop, Barber, Wallace, Whittaker, Slade, Stephenson, Hall.
Referee: Mr H. Swift (Sheffield)

With the colour clashes, Villa turned out in white shirts with red shoulder flashes. The pitch was in excellent condition for November according to Sportsman in the Burnley Express. Tommy Boyle won the toss and elected to play toward the Bee-Hole End, profiting from the strong easterly wind. Villa began well, the centre-forward Whittaker testing Jerry Dawson in the Burnley goal, who finger-tipped his effort over the crossbar. Following the corner-kick, Burnley cleared and attacked. Bob Kelly's run on goal and shot winning Burnley a corner. From Eddie Mosscrop's corner kick, the ball found Dick Lindley who rose above the defence to head in and give Burnley the lead with only five minutes played.

Burnley were the more settled in midfield and more dangerous in front of goal. Anstey was much the busier of the two goalkeepers. On 23 minutes, Kelly won the ball in midfield and found Eddie Mosscrop. Mosscrop's run and centre found Billy Watson who had pushed forward to run in and score Burnley's second. Burnley were in command and nine minutes later, a lovely one-two combination between Kelly and Freeman, led to Kelly on his debut, making it three-nil with a fine shot. After more sustained Burnley pressure, Mr Swift brought the game to a close and at the interval, Burnley led Aston Villa, three goals to nil.

Villa came out a different side in the second half and exerted early pressure on Dawson's goal. The Burnley goalkeeper making three or four good saves, one Villa effort hitting the upright. Kelly and Freeman were working well as a pair and continued to cause havoc among the Villa defence with their neat combination play. Burnley's defence was solid and managed to keep Villa out following a number of attacks. Three minutes from time, Lyons, the Villa full-back, failed to clear a Burnley cross from Husband and let Bert Freeman in to net Burnley's fourth goal of the afternoon. Burnley running out comfortable winners, 4-0.

At Full Time: Burnley 4 (Lindley, Watson, Kelly, and Freeman), Aston Villa 0
Attendance: 25,000 (Gate receipts of £599)

---xxx---

It had been a wonderful performance from Burnley and no-one in the crowd would have expected such an overwhelming performance or predicted a 4-0 scoreline. Burnley had shown that they could compete with the very best at this level. Bob Kelly came in for praise in the papers and the Athletics News sang his praises in this poem to the youngster that was printed on their front page.

Robert Kelly

Has anyone seen Kelly!
To whom I strike the lyre;
The Burnley 'find,'
Swift as the wind -
The talk of Lancashire?
Why, Burnley folk acclaim him
A jewel, by the mass;
A diamond rare
Beyond compare
Raised in the town of glass.

Has anyone seen Kelly?
The newest rising star
Who scintillates
To cheering gates
With brilliance regular
At Burnley you may find him
If you will use your eyes
And Kelly will
With Polished skill
Inspire your mild surprise.

Has anyone seen Kelly?
His years are but eighteen,
A stripling slim
But dour and grim
In League campaigns, I weep
An old head on young shoulder
With cunning, twinkling feet
At inside right
As bold as wight
A sturdy back may meet.

A younger generation
Are knocking at the door
So Ibsen says
In may way
The fact I much deplore
And ardent souls like Kelly
Are apt to make a din
Importunate
At Fortune's gate
Twere best to let him in.

Athletics News 29 December 1914.

It's Grim up North (East)

After the stunning victory over Villa, Burnley were brimming with confidence. The Clarets travelled north on a long train journey to Redcar early on the Friday morning where they stayed overnight in preparation for the match against Middlesbrough. George Halley returned after injury for the Clarets and after his stunning debut against Villa, Bob Kelly kept his place in the Burnley attack. Middlesbrough featured the famous Carr brothers, Jackie and Walter.

Middlesbrough v Burnley, Ayresome Park, Saturday 22nd November 1913 Kick-Off 2:45 pm

The Teams lined up:
Middlesbrough: Davies, Hisbent, Walker, Davidson, Carr (W), Cook, Stirling, Carr (J), Elliott, Windridge, Nicholl
Burnley: Dawson, Bamford, Jones, Halley, Boyle, Watson, Mosscrop, Lindley, Freeman, Kelly, Husband.
Referee: Mr T. Garner (Barnsley)

Tommy Boyle won the toss and elected to play with the sun behind his team on a blustery, but dry afternoon in the north-east. Middlesbrough won several of the early scraps in midfield and Jerry Dawson was tested early on by Jackie Carr, punching his shot over the crossbar. George Elliott then had a good chance to give Boro' the lead with an open goal, but missed his chance. A Jimmy Windridge effort brought another fine save from Jerry Dawson.

On ten minutes a solo run from Jackie Carr found Windridge lurking in the Burnley penalty area. Windridge was unmarked and scored with a diving header that gave Dawson no chance. The goal woke Burnley up who retaliated with a three-man forward attack involving Bob Kelly, Bill Husband and Bert

Freeman. On a follow-up attack, Freeman got on the end of an Eddie Mosscrop centre, the ball landing straight to his feet for the Burnley centre-forward to smash the ball past Davies giving him no chance. All square, and as the half drew to a close, Burnley came close through a Bill Husband run on goal which was thwarted by the other Carr brother, Walter in the Boro' defence. The ball going out for a Burnley corner. From the corner-kick, the ball was handled by a Burnley player just outside the Boro' penalty area. From the free-kick, Elliott struck a long shot at Dawson who only just managed to parry the ball and turn it around the post for a Middlesbrough corner. Carr's short corner found Windridge to tee up the ball for Elliott who struck the ball past Dawson and gave Boro' a 2-1 lead at half-time.

Burnley began the second half with attacks down both wings, first through Eddie Mosscrop who beat Walker and then Husband who beat Hisbent on the other wing but both of their efforts were dealt with. Sportsman in the Burnley Express noted that the exchanges in the match were, "fast and interesting". Both sides mounted quick attacks that were halted by the opposing half-backs. Mid-way through the second half, Burnley won a corner. Davies in the Boro' goal managed to scramble the ball out after Bert Freeman's goal-bound effort. With only five minutes remaining, Freeman had another good chance, but put the ball wide of the Boro' post. Just before the final whistle, Billy Watson picked up a bad knee injury and had to go off the field. Burnley had come close in salvaging a point, with several chances for the forwards but Middlesbrough saw the game out and ran out winners, 2-1.

The following week's Athletic News picked up on the better exchanges of the contest, "the tussles between Walker the sturdy Scot and Mosscrop, the outside-right of Burnley were a frequent source of delight."

At Full Time: Middlesbrough 2 (Windridge, Elliott), Burnley 1 (Freeman)
Attendance: 16,000 (Gate Receipts of £534)

---xxx---

Mountford and Charlton moving on

Prior to the next match it was announced by Burnley that Harry Mountford had been sold to Third Lanark and Tom Charlton, scorer of three goals in seven appearances, had signed for Blackpool, his third club in a year after his signing from Stockport County. The football club announced no new signings to replace the two outgoing players.

Burnley made two changes for the visit of Sheffield United that included the return of Dave Taylor in defence and Levi Thorpe came in for Billy Watson who was nursing the leg injury he picked up at Middlesbrough. For Tommy Boyle, it was a day for renewing old acquaintances. George Utley, his old midfield partner at Barnsley, was now captain of United, the Sheffield club breaking the £2,000 transfer record in the summer.

Burnley v Sheffield United, Turf Moor, Saturday 29th November 1913 Kick-Off 2:30 pm

The Teams lined up:
Burnley: Dawson, Bamford, Taylor, Halley, Boyle(c), Thorpe, Mosscrop, Lindley, Freeman, Kelly, Husband.
Sheffield United: Gough, Cook, English, Brelsford, Hawley, Utley(c), Simmons, Gillespie, Kitchen, Fazackerley, Revill
Referee: Mr H. H. Taylor (Altringham)

Tommy Boyle beat George Utley to the toss and the Clarets played with the breeze toward the Bee Hole End. Burnley had the better of the opening chances and won the first corner.

United took up the attack and Billy Gillespie's shot narrowly missed the target, shooting across Dawson's goal. Gough, the Sheffield goalkeeper, repelled several Burnley attacks, saving first from Boyle, and then from Dick Lindley whose header hit the crossbar. In the struggles that followed, the visitors defence was kept busy. Levi Thorpe fired in a long shot which Gough saved low down. Then the United keeper' saved a follow-up effort from Bob Kelly. At the other end, Tommy Boyle saved a dangerous situation, clearing the ball as Gillespie was about to pounce. Burnley were the more aggressive side and Bert Freeman received a good delivery from Husband the left which Cook managed to head away. Just before the interval Jerry Dawson saved The Clarets as a close-range United effort struck the Burnley upright.

In the second half the wind increased and drizzling rain made the pitch heavy. The light was also fading on a murky afternoon, both teams struggling to pick out their players in the darkness. Sheffield pressed forward and Boyle, Thorpe and Taylor were all kept busy. The Burnley defence according to Sportsman were "outstanding all afternoon." Burnley's best opportunity came on 75 minutes. Bert Freeman won the ball in the Sheffield half and set off on a solo run. With only the goalkeeper to beat, Gough ran out of his penalty area and according to Sportsman, "successfully tackled him with both feet, and managed to clear the ball." As the game drew to a close, it was Gough again who saved the day for United. In was an awful day for football and in the end both sides settled for a share of the spoils.

At Full Time: Burnley 0, Sheffield United 0
Attendance: 23,000 (gate receipts of £500)

---xxx---

In Other News

In other Burnley news this week, Eddie Mosscrop had secured a permanent teaching position at a boy's school in his home town of Southport, and was shortly transferring from the school in Salford where he was currently teaching. Burnley's inside-forward, Dick Lindley got married on December 3rd and Burnley FC reported that all the stand tickets for the match on Christmas Day against League Champions, Sunderland had sold out. In local politics, Burnley pork butcher, Mr. George Haffner, had been elected to serve as councillor for Burnley's Fulledge Ward.

The Long Month of December.

Three months had passed since the start of the season. The dark nights had drawn in and the month of December had arrived. From the footballers point of view it was the worst month of the year. They would be away from their wives and families over Christmas, spending the festive period sleeping in strange hotels with games one after another.

Burnley's previous two games against Middlesbrough and Sheffield United had been dour affairs which had won just one point. John Haworth decided to change things. Bob Kelly and Bill Husband were dropped. A fit again Teddy Hodgson returned to his place in the forward line and Billy Nesbitt came back into the team, replacing Bill Husband. It was the first time that the same forward line had played together since November 8th when the team had drawn against Liverpool at Anfield. Burnley's defence would have to be alert toady. They were up against Derby County forward Horace Barnes who had cost the princely sum of £10 in 1908 and was the current First Division's leading scorer with twelve goals. Burnley travelled to Derbyshire on the Friday prior to the game.

Figure 17: The Baseball Ground, Derby

Derby County v Burnley, The Baseball Ground, 6th December 1913 Kick-Off 2:30 pm

The Teams lined up:
Derby County: Scattergood, Atkin, Barbour, Bagshaw, Buckley, Richards, Grimes, Moore, Leonard, Barnes, Neve.
Burnley: Dawson, Bamford, Taylor, Halley, Boyle(c), Thorpe, Mosscrop, Lindley, Freeman, Hodgson, Nesbitt.
Referee: Mr A. Hargreaves (Blackpool)

Burnley started well on the Baseball Ground's mud covered surface. Straight from the kick-off, Eddie Mosscrop won the ball on the wing, ran and centred for Teddy Hodgson whose shot was hit straight at Scattergood. Dick Lindley and then Bert Freeman both had good chances. Scattergood saving what should have been a certain goal from Freeman off the line at the last moment. Further Burnley pressure was applied from two ouoooooivo oornor liiolto, tho oooond of whioh tho ball wao again cleared off the goal-line, by defender Atkin. On 20 minutes, Tommy Boyle had a crack at goal from range which went just over the Derby crossbar. With half an hour gone, County won a corner after Dawson had tipped the ball over the crossbar following a shot by Buckley. From the corner, the ball was cleared and eventually came to Henry Leonard whose strike through a crowd of players, gave Derby the lead against the run of play. From the re-start, Burnley attacked with efforts from Mosscrop and then Hodgson that kept Scattergood busy. Then Lindley and Freeman had chances that were foiled by the Derby custodian. It was all Burnley as Freeman charged Scattergood who dropped the ball in the Derby area, but he managed to gather it in time. Five minutes from the break, an attempt by George Halley led to Scattergood clearing the ball, only for Buckley to charge at a Burnley player. That offence led Mr Hargreaves to award Burnley a penalty. Tommy Boyle stepped up and put it past Scattergood and the teams went in for tea all square at 1-1.

Burnley again dominated the play at the start of the second half. The tempo of the game picked up and tempers rose. Hodgson, Halley and Bamford were all in the wars and Barbour was struck on the nose with the ball. A goal-line clearance from a Freeman effort, should have given Burnley the lead, the ball chested off the line by Buckley. From the clearance, Teddy Hodgson blasted his shot wide. A Dick Lindley header then went just wide from a Mosscrop centre. The game looked to be ending in a draw, but with ten minutes remaining Leonard beat the Burnley offside trap to score his second of the game with a low shot to beat Jerry Dawson. Tommy Boyle pushed his men forward to find an equaliser. Derby had the ball in Burnley's half and won a free-kick. Grimes free-kick found the head of Horace Barnes, who headed down and past Dawson to make it 3-1 and secure the points for County. It had been a game of missed opportunities for the Clarets who had had plenty of goal-scoring chances but just couldn't put the ball in the net.

At Full Time: Derby 3 (Leonard 2, Barnes), Burnley 1 (Boyle (pen))
Attendance: (Unofficial gate of 12,000)

---xxx---

The Other Freeman

At Turf Moor the same Saturday that Burnley played Derby, Burnley Reserves were playing hosts to Stalybridge Celtic at Turf Moor in the Central League. In a bad-tempered match, in front of around 5,000 spectators, Burnley beat The Celtic, 2-0, with both goals scored by the Clarets promising young Scottish centre-forward, Billy Pickering. The match was notable for the appearance of the other Freeman brother, Bert's elder brother, Walter, playing at outside-left for the visitors. The match itself was quite a violent affair. "There was more or less unpleasantness for the greater part of the game," according to the Burnley Express reporter. Immediately after Pickering's second goal, two players (Lockett and Husband) were both sent off for 'kicking each other.'

It was back to Turf Moor the following Saturday for the first team and the visit of Manchester City. Despite defeat at Derby, John Haworth kept faith with the same team. Billy Watson was still unfit, so Levi Thorpe kept his place in central defence. The Clarets had met City at Turf Moor earlier in the season in the Lancashire Cup and had lost 2-1 so Tommy Boyle's men were out to make amends.

Burnley v Manchester City, Turf Moor, Saturday 13th December 1913 Kick-Off 2:45 pm

The Teams lined up:
Burnley: Dawson, Bamford, Taylor, Halley, Boyle (c), Thorpe, Mosscrop, Lindley, Freeman, Hodgson, Nesbitt.
Manchester City: Smith, McGuire, Fletcher, Hughes, Hanney, Hindmarsh, Dorsett, Taylor, Howard, Browell, Wallace.
Referee: Mr J. T. Howcroft (Bolton)

The weather was pretty awful as Sportsman's report began, "The weather was cold and threatening and a strong wind blew across Turf Moor toward the Bee Hole End which in my opinion completely spoiled the game." City won the toss and elected to play with the wind. Burnley began the match with only ten men. Tom Bamford had broken a boot stud coming onto the field and could only watch from the touchline as it was repaired. Tommy Boyle put George Halley temporarily at full-back. As a consequence, City took advantage and Jerry Dawson was the busier goalkeeper saving efforts first from Browell, then Taylor and Howard. With Bamford's boot now fixed, and the Clarets at full-strength, Burnley re-shaped and went on the attack. Burnley's first attempt came from a Dick Lindley, his header going just wide of City's post. With a City attack ruled out for offside, Burnley had a free-kick. From the kick Burnley pressed forward again. On sixteen minutes, Levi Thorpe ran through and was fouled just outside the City penalty area by Hanney. Tommy Boyle stepped up to take the free-kick. "A shot with terrific force" according to Sportsman, that went straight to Smith in the City goal who palmed it out for a corner. Billy Nesbitt took the corner and his cross picked out Dick Lindley whose bullet header gave Smith no chance and Burnley went a goal in front. City pushed forward and Jerry Dawson made a fine save from Dorsett, when a City goal looked certain. After winning the ball fairly, Teddy Hodgson was ruled offside by Mr Howcroft who, "was soundly hooted" by the Burnley crowd. Eddie Mosscrop's centres from the right were causing City problems and with Mr Howcroft's whistle, the teams went in for the interval with Burnley on top, leading 1-0 at half time.

With the wind at their backs, Burnley attacked the Bee Hole End in the second half. The wind swirling around Turf Moor made good football difficult. The forwards on both sides taking every opportunity to shoot at goal in the hope the wind would assist the ball into the net. The two goalkeepers were the busiest players on the field. Sportsman reported on an incident regarding a Billy Nesbitt corner. "From a corner placed by

Nesbitt, the ball curved and blew straight into the net, evidently without touching a second player." (No goal was awarded*). With ten minutes to go, Dawson made a good save from Howard, tipping the ball around the post for a City corner. From the corner, George Halley cleared the ball up-field, the ball going out for a throw-in close to the Bee-Hole End. Dick Lindley took the throw long, the ball finding Hodgson, who got in a low header, the ball rolling past Smith over the line and into the net. Eddie Mosscrop's last shot of the game almost brought a third goal for the Clarets but the ball scuffed the crossbar and went out to safety before Mr Howcroft brought the game to an end.

At Full Time: Burnley 2 (Lindley, Hodgson), Manchester City, 0
Attendance: 20,000 (gate receipts £437) Burnley's lowest gate of the League season so far.

---XXX---

Football Association Headquarters, Russell Square

The draw for the First Round of the FA Cup was made on Monday the 15th of December at the Football Association headquarters in Russell Square. Burnley had been given a home draw and would play the winners of the 5th Qualifying round drawn match between Luton Town or South Shields, that match being replayed at South Shields ground on the 17th December.

Christmas with the Clarets

December rolled on and the start of four League games packed together over eight days, with three of those played on consecutive days. These matches would test already bruised

---

* *Goals scored directly from corners were not allowed until 1924.*

and tired legs with no time to recover. Football played on cold, dark-early, winter afternoons, on rock-hard unforgiving pitches. Pitches that barely showed a blade of grass, covered in tonnes of sand and goalmouths covered in straw. Pitches that would occasionally burst the ball if it hit a frozen jagged rut that could also finish a player's career. As protection, knees and elbows would be swathed in bandages to protect the players exposed joints. But that would offer little protection against half a dozen wooden boot-studs that would easily rake the flesh from a players shin. The footballers played in all conditions over the winter of 1913-14 but it wasn't that bad a winter weather-wise. Only a handful of matches were called off, none of which involved Burnley's programme. Despite a mild winter, only the strongest and fittest players would survive all the games played through December. The players needed to keep fit, stay alert for the wild challenges. There would be no drink, no turkey and very little in the way of Christmas cheer for them. There would be hardly any family time over Christmas as the players would either training, playing at Turf Moor or playing away somewhere.

The Burnley players now knew that they would face South Shields at Turf Moor in the First Round of the Cup. But before that match arrived, the first of the four Christmas games involved a short trip to Bradford City with Burnley still looking for their first away win. The Clarets were without the services of Tommy Boyle, the skipper suffering from a chest infection. Levi Thorpe took over at centre-half and Billy Watson returned to the side from injury.

Bradford City v Burnley, Valley Parade, Saturday 20 December 1913 Kick-Off 2:15 pm

The Teams lined up:
Burnley: Dawson, Bamford, Taylor(c), Halley, Thorpe, Watson, Mosscrop, Lindley, Freeman, Hodgson, Nesbitt.

Bradford City: Ewart, Potts, Boocock, Robinson, Torrance, Gane, Bond, McIlvenny, Storer, Fox, Currie.
Referee: Mr J. H. Palmer (Hucknall Torkard)

Despite the earlier kick-off, Sportsman in the Burnley Express noted that the light was quite poor on a really grey afternoon. Dave Taylor took over as the Burnley captain and the Clarets began well, attacking Bradford's, Spion Kop End. An early Burnley corner was taken by Eddie Mosscrop whose centre was headed just wide by Teddy Hodgson. Billy Watson was enjoying his return to the Burnley defence and it was Watson who began the move that led to the first goal on eight minutes. Watson challenged for the ball and won it in midfield. Seeing Billy Nesbitt free on the left, Nesbitt set off into the Bradford half, passing inside to Teddy Hodgson. Hodgson beat Torrance and then evaded Boocock before passing to Bert Freeman. Freeman hit the ball hard and low to Ewart's right who had come too far off his line to put Burnley a goal up. It was a well-worked goal from the Clarets. With few threats from City, Burnley defended well for the remainder of the first half and took their 1-0 lead into the tea interval.

From the start of the second period, Burnley protected their lead and pulled men back, with only occasional forays up field. But the plan didn't work. Successive Bradford attacks led to their equalising goal. A corner to City resulted in a melee in the Burnley penalty area. The ball was crossed and Dawson grabbed for it. He only half held on to it and was charged into the net, the ball slipping from his grasp, and put over the line by McIlvenny. Sportsman spoke of Burnley's ill-luck and once again the Clarets had been a goal up only to be pegged back to come away with only a point. Worse for the team was at the end of the match, Burnley were suffering injuries to no fewer than five players; Taylor, Halley, Thorpe, Freeman and Hodgson all picking up knocks.

At Full Time: Bradford 1 (McIlvenny), Burnley 1 (Freeman)
Attendance: 20,000

---xxx---

In the middle of the week there was an early Christmas dinner organised for the players by the football club and then it was down to business and training for the visit of Sunderland on Christmas Day. It was the first time Burnley had met the Wearsider's since their exit from the FA Cup last season. Sunderland, the reigning League Champions. Sunderland and their all-international star-line-up. Sunderland and their uncompromising captain Charlie Thomson who had kicked Boyle out of the Semi-Final replay and ended his season. Burnley would play them twice in two days. Burnley would have to be on their mettle for their two toughest games of the season. It was a match that saw the return of Tommy Boyle and Jimmy Bellamy was fit again who replaced Billy Nesbitt on the left wing.

Burnley v Sunderland, Turf Moor, Christmas Day, Thursday 25 December 1913 Kick-Off 2:15 pm

The Teams lined up:
Burnley: Dawson, Bamford, Taylor, Halley, Boyle (c), Watson, Bellamy, Lindley, Freeman, Hodgson, Mosscrop.
Sunderland: Butler, Hobson, Ness, Cuggy, Thomson (c), Low, Best, Buchan, Richardson, Holley, Martin.
Referee: Mr P. Sant (Barnsley)

The frost of the previous night had given place to rain and the game was played in an almost continuous downpour. Tommy Boyle returned as captain and the Clarets played with the wind toward the Bee Hole End. "Burnley played brilliantly in the first half, Mosscrop being the most conspicuous forward, and it is no exaggeration to pronounce him the best outside-left of the season," said Sportsman. Burnley outplayed their opponents for two-thirds of the game but as in recent games, Burnley simply could not score. Butler was the much busier goalkeeper, with Dawson playing a minor role in the first half an hour. After an uneventful first half, the players went in for tea at 0-0 at half time.

With the wind at their backs, Sunderland came more out of their shell in the second half and did more attacking as rain continued to pour down. With twenty-four minutes of the second half gone, and against the run of play, a long range shot from Cuggy flew like a rocket with the wind behind it, straight into the top corner of Dawson's net. It had been Sunderland's only real shot on target and it stunned Burnley. The Clarets eventually rallied and with three minutes remaining and following a melee in the Sunderland penalty box, Burnley had the ball in the Sunderland net from the boot of either Lindley or Hodgson, but the goal was disallowed by Mr Sant who whistled for an offside player. In the end it had been a fairly uneventful game regards Christmas entertainment. Burnley again simply couldn't put the ball in the net and the Wearsider's punished them for it.

At Full Time: Burnley 0, Sunderland 1 (Cuggy)
Attendance: 25,000 (Gate receipts of £700)

---xxx---

Within half an hour of the end of the match, both teams travelled up to Sunderland on the same train. From Towneley Station, the party (including the match referee, Mr Sant) travelled to York, before changing trains to reach Sunderland late on Christmas Day arriving at 10:30 pm, with another match to play the following day. Bert Freeman was ruled out with a bad cold and Jimmy Bellamy with a recurrence of the same leg injury that had plagued him all season. Levi Thorpe, Bob Reid and Bob Kelly all travelled with the Burnley party as reserves.

With Bert Freeman ruled out and John Haworth struggling to pick a side, the manager made some surprising team changes. Centre-half Tommy Boyle became centre-forward Tommy Boyle. Levi Thorpe replacing Boyle at centre-half. Injured outside-right Jimmy Bellamy was replaced by Bob Kelly now a winger, switching wings with Eddie Mosscrop. Tommy Bamford and Dick Lindley were both suffering heavy colds but played regardless. Boyle and Teddy Hodgson were also carrying knocks but played. Sunderland also made two changes of their own from Christmas Day.

Sunderland v Burnley, Roker Park, Boxing Day, Friday 26 December 1913. Kick-Off 2:15 pm

The Teams lined up:
Sunderland: Butler, Hobson, Ness, Cuggy, Thomson (c), Cringan, Best, Buchan, Low, Holley, Martin.
Burnley: Dawson, Bamford, Taylor, Halley, Thorpe, Watson, Mosscrop, Lindley, Boyle (c), Hodgson, Kelly.
Referee: Mr P. Sant (Barnsley)

The ground was soft and the weather fine on a dull afternoon in the north-east. Burnley were the first to attack before Sunderland broke forward and gave Dawson work to do, saving first from Best then Charlie Buchan. Levi Thorpe adapted well to his new role as did Tommy Boyle. Boyle's first opportunity was, "a lovely rising shot" according to Sportsman in the Burnley Express that Butler the Sunderland goalkeeper tipped over his crossbar.

Bob Kelly took the corner but the home side cleared. With fourteen minutes gone, Burnley took up the running. The ball found Mosscrop who beat Cringan to cross for Hodgson who headed home past Butler to give the Clarets a well-deserved lead. 1-0 to Burnley. Hodgson was hurt in scoring his goal, winded by Cuggy's knee, but was alright again after some attention from Ernie Edwards. Dick Lindley had an opportunity not long after the Burnley goal but for the rest of the half the Burnley defence held strong and were kept busy with Billy Watson clearing up, first from Buchan and then Holley. Sunderland pushed forward just before the interval and Mosscrop was on the receiving end of a few "unfair charges as at Burnley" according to Sportsman, "...once Cringan banged him into the rails when the ball was out of play." Buchan later claimed for a penalty after he was brought down, and then made another appeal when it seemed Bamford had handled. Mr Sant consulting with his linesman but waving away both of Buchan's appeals. The referee was roundly hooted by the Roker Park crowd as the teams left the field at the interval with Burnley leading 1-0.

Burnley began the second period with long ball up-field from Levi Thorpe which found Teddy Hodgson. Hodgson's effort was cleared only to Dick Lindley who was brought down by Charlie Thomson in the penalty area, Lindley needing attention from the Burnley trainer after that challenge. No penalty said Mr Sant. Sunderland's Charlie Buchan then went forward and tripped Dave Taylor before centring the ball for Low to head past Dawson but the goal wasn't awarded. Burnley given a free-kick instead.

On sixty minutes Sunderland scored a carbon copy of the goal they scored the day before at Turf Moor. Sunderland broke down the right, Best centred and as the ball came down, half a dozen Burnley and Sunderland players took a swing at the ball. Holley nipping in to place the ball into Dawson's net. Burnley bounced straight back. Mosscrop swung the ball across the field having spotted Bob Kelly free. Mosscrop's long pass was just a yard too long for the youngster to reach. At the other end Jerry Dawson pulled off a fine save from Best. A Buchan shot struck Billy Watsons hand in the Burnley area and the former again remonstrated with the referee without success. (Buchan seemed to make a habit of claiming for penalties at every opportunity according to press reports.). Once again he was turned down by Mr Sant. It was at this point that an "excited" spectator according to Sportsman, "ran onto the field toward the referee and the game had to be stopped. Charlie Thomson prevented the man from approaching the referee, and a policeman, the Sunderland secretary and both team trainers hurried to the spot, the policeman escorting the intruder off." Shortly after that incident Mr Sant blew his whistle with the teams sharing the points and a score of 1-1.

At Full Time: Sunderland 1 (Holley), Burnley 1 (Hodgson)
Attendance: 35,000

---xxx---

Regardless of the score, it had been an excellent performance at Roker Park to go to the League Champions and take a point off them. The performance began a run of form that carried the team well into 1914. Straight after the match the Burnley party caught the 5:00 pm train from Sunderland for a five-hour train journey back to Lancashire. At Turf Moor the following afternoon the Clarets opponents were West Bromwich Albion. The players had only twelve hours rest before another bruising encounter. Burnley had played West Brom already, losing that game at The Hawthorns 4-1 in September with Albion's' goals all scored by Alf Bentley. Luckily, Burnley had not picked any additional injuries at Roker Park. With Bert Freeman still ruled out, Tommy Boyle kept his position as centre-forward, leading the line for Burnley's final game of 1913.

Burnley v West Bromwich Albion, Turf Moor, Saturday 27th December Kick-Off 2:15 pm

The Teams lined up:
Burnley: Dawson, Bamford, Taylor, Halley, Thorpe, Watson, Mosscrop, Lindley, Boyle (c), Hodgson, Kelly.

West Bromwich Albion: Pearson, Cook, Pennington, Waterhouse, Deacey, McNeal, Jephcott, Edwards, Bentley, Morris, Nicholls.
Referee: Mr T. Kirkham (Burslem)

Sportsman reported that the weather at Turf Moor was, "unfavourable" and noted that fewer supporters than the Christmas Day match had turned out because of it. Tommy Boyle won the toss and the Clarets kicked off in their third game in three days.

Burnley were soon busy, attacking down the right and from a throw-in by Dick Lindley, Tommy Boyle had a good chance to score, his shot glancing off the Albion post. Pearson saved Albion on a couple of occasions before they got in their first attack. Five minutes later, Dick Lindley tested Pearson with shots that he blocked while at the other end, Jephcott brought off a good save from Jerry Dawson. In the closing minutes of the first half, Lindley was forward when he was fouled close to the penalty spot by Cook. Boyle claimed for the penalty but Mr Kirkham ignored him and waved play on only for the ball to be cleared by Pearson.

In the second half, Teddy Hodgson brought off the save of the match from Pearson, while Dawson diverted a shot from Jephcott's 'specials' that was going under the bar. Burnley struggled to penetrate the Albion defence and the game was all played out in the middle of the pitch. Commenting on the passing, "both teams lacked accuracy more than usual" reported Sportsman in the Burnley Express. Twenty minutes into the second half, Tommy Boyle and Levi Thorpe changed places, the Burnley skipper clearly tired. Thorpe, the reserve centre-half, now first team centre-forward, combined well with Dick Lindley. It was Thorpe who got in one of the best shots of the game which Pearson only just dealt with. The final 15 minutes was more of an end-to-end scrap. Dawson made a magnificent save in a goalmouth in the dying moments, before his long throw found Mosscrop, whose run and centre came to nought. And at the end of a lack-lustre performance from both teams, Burnley had to settle for the share of the points.

At Full Time: Burnley 0, West Bromwich Albion 0.
Attendance: 20,000 (Gate Receipts £477)

---xxx---

Burnley had clearly missed the services of Bert Freeman over Christmas and had scored just one goal in three games. Doc Hodges, the team doctor, had worked his magic and Freeman would be fit for the visit to Ewood Park on New Years Day.

Fire in Stand at Turf Moor

Over Christmas, a rumour gained currency to the effect that an attempt had been made, presumably by the suffragettes, to burn down the grandstand at Turf Moor by setting it alight in several places. This proved to be unfounded, but it was discovered that a slight fire had occurred in the boiler house, where some woodwork and a small cupboard had been destroyed.

Cup Ticket News - Burnley v South Shields

The Burnley directors announced that they had fixed the prices for the Cup-tie with South Shields. They would be the same as for League matches, (sixpence for adults) and the booking of Stand 'A' seats was now proceeding.

---xxx---

CHAPTER FOUR

January 1914

Figure 18: The Burnley Team at the Start of 1914.

Left to Right
George Halley, Billy Watson, Dick Lindley, Tommy Boyle
(Captain), Tom Bamford, Bert Freeman, Dave Taylor, Jerry
Dawson, Billy Nesbitt, Teddy Hodgson, Eddie Mosscrop.

January 1914

After the busy December, the new year of 1914 began with two
away games for Burnley. First, the return derby fixture with
Blackburn Rovers at Ewood Park, followed by a trip over the
Pennines to Hillsborough to meet The Wednesday. New Years
Day was a cold start. Overnight frost had led to the Blackburn
pitch being covered in tons of sand, so much that the pitch
resembled Blackpool beach. Despite the freezing temperatures,
the match went ahead.

Blackburn Rovers were two points clear at the top of the First Division. They were unbeaten at home and were a strong side away. Burnley were ninth in the table, still looking for that elusive first away victory. Nine football special trains brought an army of Burnley supporters over to Blackburn. Newspaper reports vary on the actual attendance at Ewood. The Athletics News said 30,000 were present at the start of the match and by the interval the crowd had risen to 40,000. The gate receipts suggest a higher figure of, 49,000. "It was the biggest crowd ever seen at Ewood," according to the brief report in a post match photographic souvenir (cost 1d) that was published the following week. Changes to the Burnley team saw Bert Freeman's return at centre-forward, Tommy Boyle returning to the centre-half position and Billy Nesbitt coming in for Bob Kelly on the left. Rovers were missing their charismatic captain, Bob Crompton, suffering a bad toe; the Rovers regular replaced by Walter Aitkenhead.

General View of Crowd from Press Box.

Figure 19: The Crowd at Ewood Park New Years Day 1914

Blackburn Rovers v Burnley, Ewood Park, Thursday 1st January 1914. Kick-Off 2:30 pm

The teams lined up:
Blackburn Rovers: Robinson, Aitkenhead, Cowell, Walmsley, Smith, Bradshaw, Simpson, Shea, Chapman, Latheron, Hodkinson.
Burnley: Dawson, Bamford, Taylor, Halley, Boyle (c), Watson, Nesbitt, Lindley, Freeman, Hodgson, Mosscrop.
Referee: Mr W. J. Heath (Burslem)

The Clarets got off to a good start at Ewood and took the game to the League leaders. On six minutes, Dick Lindley struck a shot that went just wide of the Rovers post. Burnley pressed again, through Lindley and Bert Freeman who did most of the Burnley attacking in the first half hour, with Freeman having no fewer than three good chances. Teddy Hodgson and Bert Freeman both put the ball in the Rovers net only for both of their efforts to be ruled offside by Mr Heath. One good attack by Rovers saw Jerry Dawson pull off a fine save.

In the second half, Rovers came more into the game. Teddy Hodgson had another good opportunity to give the Clarets the lead but missed his chance, volleying the ball over the crossbar. "It was only by reason of their failure to make use of their chances in this match that Burnley failed to bring away two points instead of one", said Sportsman in the Burnley Express, "Burnley only had themselves to blame, for it was a game of missed chances."

At Full Time: Blackburn Rovers 0, Burnley 0
Attendance: 49,000. Record League gate receipts at Ewood Park of £1,685.

A Thriller at Hillsborough

Things just were not going right in the Burnley goal-scoring department. Burnley had gone eleven First Division away games, half a season, without an away victory. They had also suffered a goal drought, the previous four games had seen only a single goal scored. The Clarets had come close to winning at Everton, Oldham and Blackburn and the team only needed a bit of luck to notch up their first away victory. The Clarets travelled over the border to Yorkshire for their first visit to Hillsborough in fifteen years. The Clarets were unchanged from New Years Day, while Wednesday had no fewer than six enforced changes due to injuries.

The Wednesday v Burnley, Hillsborough, Saturday January 3 1914. Kick-Off 2:30 pm

The teams lined up:
The Wednesday: Streets, Worrall, Spoors, Brittleton, McSkimming, Nicholson, Burkinshaw (L), Burkinshaw (J.D.) McGregor, Miller, Wright.
Burnley: Dawson, Bamford, Taylor, Halley, Boyle, Watson, Nesbitt, Lindley, Freeman, Hodgson, Mosscrop.
Referee: Mr J.E. Hall (Olton)

Burnley lost the toss and played against the wind in the first half. Despite the wind in their faces, the Clarets started positively. With ten minutes on the clock, Burnley won a free-kick for a foul on a Bert Freeman just outside the Wednesday penalty area. Tommy Boyle took the free-kick, the ball coming out to Eddie Mosscrop whose centre found George Halley well up field. Halley, dribbling toward goal, looked up and drove a hard shot that Streets could only parry into his own net to give the Clarets the lead. From the restart, Wednesday attacked and Jerry Dawson saved a good shot from J.D. Burkinshaw. On 17 minutes, Burnley went two goals in front when Mosscrop whipped in a fast centre and Dick Lindley hit the ball sweetly on the volley. Streets went down to save and parried the ball out only to Teddy Hodgson who steered the ball into the Wednesday net. Wednesday had the odd attack but Burnley coped with their forwards. The Clarets should have increased their lead further before half time with good chances for Bert Freeman and another for Teddy Hodgson. At half-time the score was The Wednesday 0, Burnley 2.

The second-half kicked off and Burnley broke quickly, Mosscrop was on the left and crossed for Freeman whose header missed the target, but the ball came back out for a follow-up from Lindley whose shot was also blocked. The ball came out to Teddy Hodgson and behind him, running in, was Billy Nesbitt who scored with a low shot. 3-0 to Burnley. Thirteen minutes into the second half, Wednesday pulled a goal back. L. Burkinshaw's pass finding Brittleton who got the better of Dave Taylor to beat Dawson. Lindley and Bamford were off the field for the trainer's attention for a short time, putting pressure on the nine remaining players and shortly after the pair returned, Burnley increased their lead. A Mosscrop shot struck the Wednesday woodwork. From the rebound, Lindley spotted Freeman and the centre-forward dribbled forward before hitting the ball past Streets with a good low shot to make it 4-1 to Burnley. The pressure continued. A Tommy Boyle free-kick just feet outside the Wednesday penalty area rattled the crossbar before being cleared. The final six minutes of the game saw three goals. By this stage the light was fading. First, McGregor pulled a goal back for the Yorkshiremen to make it 4-2. Burnley kicked-off and from an Eddie Mosscrop centre the ball came to Teddy Hodgson. Streets saved Hodgson's effort, but Lindley goal-poaching in the goal-mouth, scored goal number five. Finally another Mosscrop race down the flank and cross enabled Lindley to score his second and Burnley's sixth to make the final score 6-2 to the Clarets and notch up that first away League win.

At Full Time: Sheffield Wednesday 2, (Brittleton, McGregor), Burnley 6 (Halley, Hodgson, Nesbitt, Freeman and Lindley (2))
Attendance: 25,000

---xxx---

The result was just the tonic going into the following weeks FA Cup match. Eddie Mosscrop was picked out by Sportsman as Burnley's stand-out player, "It was a wonder that the delighted spectators did not invade the ground and carry him off shoulder high at the end of the game."

This result and all-round performance of the team, set the tempo for the following match, against South Shields. The Clarets had now gone four matches unbeaten and since Saturday, the goals were flowing again. Compared with the first half of the season, player injuries were slight. Morale was high after the Clarets best away performance of the season. After a good start to 1914, could the Clarets keep the momentum going?

Football Attendances

"It is announced that since the beginning of the 1913-14 season, over nine million people have watched football in England in the first four months of the season. The figures included the First and Second divisions and the first division of the Southern league. Over 5 million spectators attended first division games. Burnley's average home attendance for the first half of the 1913-14 season was given as 26,800." (Manchester Guardian 6/1/1914)

Burnley's European Tour?

Burnley have received a letter of invitation dated January 5th from the Deutscher Football Club in Prague to play six matches in Prague from the middle of May to June. The club are to consider the invitation before making their reply.

The FA Cup First Round

Burnley v South Shields

Following their emphatic win at Sheffield Wednesday the Burnley directors gave the players a few days leave. There was no special training arranged for the First Round Cup-tie. Burnley were back at Turf Moor for their first match of 1914 and the start of their FA Cup campaign against their opponents South Shields.

South Shields currently headed the North Eastern League and had beaten Luton Town in the 5th and final qualifying round and Hartlepool United the round before that. They were a tough semi-professional outfit, player-managed by Arthur Bridgett, the former England international winger. Bridgett made two team changes from The Shields previous match while Burnley fielded the same eleven that beat Wednesday. Around three hundred Shields supporters made the journey south by special train to Turf Moor.

Burnley v South Shields, FA Cup Round One: Turf Moor, Saturday 10th January 1914 Kick-Off 2:30 pm.

The teams lined up:
Burnley: Dawson, Bamford, Taylor, Halley, Boyle (c), Watson, Nesbitt, Lindley, Freeman, Hodgson, Mosscrop.
South Shields: Naisby, Smith, Johnson, Hall (B), Hall (E), Brookes, Keenlyside, Portlock, Thornley, Anderson, Bridgett.
Referee: Mr H. Swift (Sheffield) Linesmen: Mr C. Quinian (Barrow) Mr R. E. Kenyon (Hindley)

The weather had improved over the last two days and the ground at Turf Moor was in 'capital condition' according to Sportsman in the Burnley Express. The team mascots dressed in their respective South Shields and Burnley colours led the teams out. Arthur Bridgett won the toss and South Shields kicked off defending the Bee Hole End. The match began at a brisk pace. Shields began the brighter and had two early chances which were cleared away by Dave Taylor and Tom Bamford. The Clarets attacked down the right and from the centre, the Shields' right-back, Hall deliberately handled inside the penalty area. Mr Swift had no hesitation and pointed to the spot. Tommy Boyle stepped up to take the penalty that would give Burnley the lead. Boyle's penalty kick hit the crossbar, his first penalty miss of the season and the ball was cleared! Not the best of starts to Burnley's Cup campaign. At the other end, Shields won a corner and Dave Taylor headed out while Dawson in dealing with a follow-up shot from Smith, made the save of the game. Keenlyside 'sent the ball along the Burnley crossbar' before Anderson had another chance for Shields, showing that Burnley couldn't underestimate the team from the north-east. With 14 minutes gone, Eddie Mosscrop was giving the Shield's full-back, Johnson, a hard time and his centre found Dick Lindley to head Burnley in front and settle the player's nerves. A Billy Nesbitt corner found Boyle but his header ball hit the crossbar. The ball came out to George Halley who found Freeman. Freeman held off a Shields defender to head the ball into the path of Dick Lindley who scored his second only two minutes after the first. In the final five minutes of the first half, both sides had chances to score but it was Burnley who led 2-0 at the interval.

Straight from the kick-off Freeman had a chance to score, then Lindley and Bridgett of South Shields had chances at either end. A long-range shot from the Shields centre-forward Thornley went close. Seven minutes into the half, Lindley found Freeman and a typical Bert dribble toward goal, followed by a shot, gave Naisby no chance and put the Clarets 3-0 to the good.

Keenlyside had troubled the Burnley defence on a number of occasions but his efforts were cleared. Naisby then had to save well from a Freeman shot ten minutes from time. With five minutes remaining Shields scored. Arthur Bridgett was the supplier and when his initial shot struck Dawson who went down, the ball rebounded to Keenlyside whose shot went into the net off the upright. Two late Jerry Dawson saves, one from Bridgett and then another from Taylor, saved Burnley's blushes and Mr Swift brought the game to an end to put Burnley into the Second Round with a 3-1 victory.

At Full Time: Burnley 3 (Lindley 2, Freeman), South Shields 1 (Keenlyside)
Attendance: 18,000 (Gate receipts of £598 10s 3d)

A good solid performance from Burnley had seen them safely through the Round against a good side from a lower division. South Shields went on to become North Eastern League champions in 1913-14 and retained their title the following season. They were admitted to the enlarged Football League after the First World War in 1919-20, joining the Third Division (North).

---xxx---

Manchester United and Everton Go Out!

The big upsets of the First Round came at Southern League side, Swindon Town where the home side knocked out former Cup winners Manchester United, 1-0. There was a similar giant killing at Glossop Town who beat Everton 2-1. Blackburn Rovers beat Middlesbrough 3-0 at Ewood Park in front of 35,000, the biggest crowd of the day. Liverpool will have to replay at Oakwell after Second Division Barnsley earned a 1-1 draw at Anfield. FA Cup holders Aston Villa beat Stoke City 4-0, while Sunderland beat Southern League side Chatham Town 9-0 in the highest score of the day. Jimmy Richardson scoring four goals for the Black Cats at Roker Park. Leicester Fosse and Tottenham shared ten goals in an exciting 5-5 draw at Filbert Street and will replay. The best away result was by

Sheffield United who beat Newcastle United in a controversial match at St. James's Park. In a 'rough-house' game according to the newspapers, Newcastle were first reduced to ten men, then nine through injuries before going two-goals behind. They then lost their goalkeeper and 'played on manfully' with only eight men as Sheffield scored three more goals to finish the match 5-0 winners.

Clarets News

Newcastle United were rumoured to have offered £1,500 for the services of Ronnie Sewell, the Burnley reserve goalkeeper but this was not confirmed by the club.

Messrs Simpson Brothers who are erecting the new covered stand are making excellent progress with the foundations (at the Cricket-Field End). A hundred tons of stone have been laid in forming the foundations and progress has been made on the walling.

Eddie Mosscrop and Billy Watson had been selected for England who faced 'The North' in the trial match at Roker Park on Wednesday the 21st January.

In Other News

Eight Months' Clitheroe Bobbin Workers Strike Settled

"After lasting eight months, a strike at the Albion Bobbin Works, Clitheroe, has ended in a victory for the men. All their demands have been conceded, including a 10 per cent advance for those in receipt of less than £1 per week, 5 percent for those receiving over £1 and 2½ per cent for those engaged on piece-work. The refusal of the owner of the works to recognise the Woodturners Union was one of the reasons which determined the employees to strike."
(Manchester Guardian 7/1/1914)

FA CUP First Round Results
Matches Played Saturday 10th January 1914

	Home Team	Away Team	Gate	Receipts (£)
1	**Aston Villa 4**	**Stoke City 0**	18,000	563
2	Birmingham City 2	Southend 1	20,000	542
3	Blackburn Rovers 3	Middlesbrough 0	35,354	909
4	Bolton Wanderers 3	Burslem Port Vale 0	18,975	576
5	Bradford Park Avenue 5	Reading 1	12,000	325
6	Bradford City 2	Woolwich Arsenal 0	16,000	566
7	**Burnley 3**	**South Shields 1**	18,000	580
8	Clapton Orient 2	Nottingham Forest 2	15,161	478
9	Crystal Palace 2	Norwich City 1	20,000	470
10	Derby County 1	Northampton Town 0	12,000	493
11	Gillingham 1	Blackpool 0	10,581	323
12	**Glossop Town 2**	**Everton 1**	4,800	138
13	Huddersfield Town 3	London Caledonians 0	6,900	195
14	Hull City 0	Bury 0	12,000	399
15	Leeds City 4	Gainsborough Trinity 2	14,000	520
16	**Leicester Fosse 5**	**Tottenham Hotspur 5**	10,000	525
17	**Liverpool 1**	**Barnsley 1**	32,500	876
18	Manchester City 2	Fulham 0	25,345	814
19	Millwall Athletic 0	Chelsea 0	24,500	1,555
20	**Newcastle United 0**	**Sheffield United 5**	28,000	1,032
21	Oldham Athletic 1	Brighton & Hove Albion 1	14,392	421
22	Plymouth Argyle 4	Lincoln City 1	17,836	675
23	**Portsmouth 0**	**Exeter City 4**	18,379	712
24	Preston North End 5	Bristol Rovers 2	13,500	445
25	QPR 2	Bristol City 2	20,000	605
26	The Wednesday 3	Notts County 2	27,579	1,080
27	**Sunderland 9**	**Chatham Town 0**	14,000	428
28	Swansea 2	Merthyr 0	16,000	425

	Home Team	Away Team	Gate	Receipts (£)
29	Swindon Town 1	Manchester United 0	18,107	1,185
30	West Bromwich Albion 2	Grimsby Town 0	13,976	387
31	West Ham United 3	Chesterfield 1	18,000	508
32	Wolverhampton Wand. 3	Southampton 0	20,495	745

Figures supplied from The Times.

Replays
Barnsley 0, Liverpool 1 played on the 15th January at Oakwell.

After the Cup it was back to the business of the League and the return of Bolton Wanderers to Turf Moor for the first time in thirteen years. Burnley were unchanged from the South Shields game and Bolton were also unchanged. A good crowd turned out for the match despite the awful weather.

Burnley v Bolton Wanderers, Turf Moor, Saturday 17 January 1914 Kick-Off 2:30 pm.

The teams lined up:
Burnley: Dawson, Bamford, Taylor, Halley, Boyle (c), Watson, Nesbitt, Lindley, Freeman, Hodgson, Mosscrop.
Bolton Wanderers: Edmondson, Baverstock, Feebury, Glendinning, Fay, Rowley, Donaldson, Jones, Lillycrop, Smith, Vizard.
Referee: Mr R. Eccles (Darwen)

It had rained heavily on Saturday morning and the pitch had been well sanded but the weather had cleared by the kick-off time. Tommy Boyle won the toss and Burnley played toward the Cricket Field End with the wind advantage. In summary, Burnley took the lead through Teddy Hodgson on eight minutes from an Eddie Mosscrop centre. A Bolton free-kick led to a goal by Joe Smith beating Jerry Dawson to equalise for Wanderers on 23 minutes. The match was 1-1 at half-time.

In the second half Wanderers took an early lead, two minutes into the second period. Donaldson scoring after causing Dave Taylor no end of problems. Sustained Burnley pressure gained a well deserved equaliser with seven minutes remaining. A Burnley free-kick taken by George Halley, found Teddy Hodgson unmarked who made no mistake to level the scores.

At Full Time: Burnley 2 (Hodgson 2), Bolton 2 (Smith, Donaldson)
Attendance: 25,000 (gate receipts of £660)

---xxx---

Mosscrop, Boyle and Watson
Three Clarets play for England

The following Wednesday, Eddie Mosscrop and Billy Watson had been called up to play in the England trial side that played against The North at Roker Park on the 21st January 1914. Tommy Boyle travelled with the party as centre-half cover for McCall of Preston North End. With England leading 2-1 in the first half, McCall pulled up with an ankle injury with only thirty minutes gone. He limped on until the interval but in the second half, Tommy Boyle came onto the field in McCall's place to make it three Burnley players all playing in the same England side. (HT score 2-1) In the second half, Shea scored twice for The North until Vivian Woodward levelled the scores. Eddie Mosscrop then scored the winning goal in the 4-3 victory for England.

England: Hardy (Aston Villa), Crompton (Blackburn Rovers) Pennington (West Bromwich Albion) Brittleton (Sheffield Wednesday), McCall (Preston North End), Watson (Burnley), Walden (Tottenham Hotspur), Fleming (Swindon),

V J Woodward (Chelsea) Holley (Sunderland), Mosscrop (Burnley). (Boyle (Burnley) came on for McCall for the second half)

The North: Beale (Manchester United), Hudspeth (Newcastle United), English (Sheffield United), Cuggy (Sunderland) Buckley (Derby County) Whalley (Manchester United), Wallace (Aston Villa) Shea (Blackburn Rovers), Elliott (Middlesbrough) Latherton (Blackburn Rovers), Martin (Sunderland).

At Full Time: England 4 (Fleming, Holley, Woodward, Mosscrop), The North 3 (Elliott, Shea (2))
Attendance 18,000

---xxx---

Burnley travelled down to London on the Friday morning from Bank Top station for their match With Chelsea, Burnley again unchanged. Clarets supporters making the journey to London were all hoping for a repeat of the 6-1 demolition of the Pensioners earlier in the season.

Chelsea v Burnley, Stamford Bridge, Saturday 24 January 1914 Kick-Off 3:00 pm

The teams lined up:
Chelsea: Molyneaux, Bettridge, Harrow, Ormiston, Logan, Hunter, Ford, Halse, V.J.Woodward, Freeman and Bridgeman.
Burnley: Dawson, Bamford, Taylor, Halley, Boyle (c), Watson, Nesbitt, Lindley, Freeman, Hodgson, Mosscrop.
Referee: Mr J.W.D. Fowler (Sunderland)

In summary, the 0-0 scoreline reflected very few goal opportunities in the match. In the first half, Bert Freeman had a shot that struck the post and Chelsea were awarded a penalty after Bridgeman's shot had accidentally hit George Halley's elbow. Hunter took the penalty sending in a fast, rising shot but

Jerry Dawson went the right way to meet the ball and turned it over the crossbar.

Boyle's marking of V.J.Woodward the England centre-forward was picked up by the Daily Express, "Boyle sees his duty clear, and goes straight for it. His job on Saturday was obviously to look after Vivian Woodward and he accomplished it splendidly. For the whole of the first half and a large part of the second the famous amateur was held as in a vice!"

At Full Time: Chelsea 0, Burnley 0
Attendance: 35,000

---xxx---

Dick Lindley and Dave Taylor were injured in the Chelsea match, Lindley picking up a thigh injury and Taylor had both of his ankles badly kicked. Both were expected to be fit for the next match in the FA Cup Second Round against Derby County at Turf Moor.

The FA Cup Second Round

Burnley v Derby County

The Second Round of the FA Cup had paired Burnley with Derby County. The last time the sides had met in the League in December 1913, Burnley had lost 3-1 at the Baseball Ground. Former England international Steve Bloomer had celebrated his 40th birthday the previous week and came into the team as replacement centre-forward for Derby's leading scorer, Harry Leonard who was suffering from an ulcer. Edwin Neve was also injured so Walker came in at outside-right. The Burnley team were unchanged once more, Lindley and Taylor having recovered over the week. Despite the rain, another big crowd turned out at Turf Moor and enjoyed the

East Lancashire Regiment band playing a selection of popular tunes before the match began.

Burnley v Derby County FA Cup Second Round, Turf Moor, Saturday 31 January 1914 Kick-Off 3:00 pm

The teams lined up:
Burnley: Dawson, Bamford, Taylor, Halley, Boyle (c), Watson, Nesbitt, Lindley, Freeman, Hodgson, Mosscrop.
Derby County: Lawrence, Atkin, Waugh, Barbour, Buckley, Bagshaw, Grimes, Moore, Bloomer, Banes, Walker
Referee: Mr H. H. Taylor (Altringham) Linesmen: Mr T.E. Robinson (Hull) Mr W Dickinson (Barrow)

Derby took to the field playing in all white, their keeper Lawrence wearing a blue jersey, while Burnley were in their usual claret and blue shirts. Tommy Boyle beat Steve Bloomer in the toss for ends and Burnley kicked off attacking the Bee Hole End, taking advantage of the strong wind blowing across the pitch. The rain was light at the start but gradually worsened, Sportsman noting there was, 'a sudden very heavy downpour, making the conditions anything but agreeable'. After a number of Burnley attacks, the breakthrough came on thirteen minutes. Billy Nesbitt's quick run and looping centre caught in the wind surprising the two Derby full backs. Teddy Hodgson got in between them and as the ball fell to earth inside the penalty area, Hodgson met the ball with his forehead, the ball flying past Lawrence and into the Derby goal. "It was one of the finest goals ever scored anywhere," said Sportsman in the Burnley Express. Tommy Boyle got in two splendid shots, one effort hitting the crossbar, the other saved by Lawrence, before George Halley had a shot which also hit the crossbar. It had been all Burnley in the first half, with the scoreline 1-0 to the Clarets at the interval.

The second half saw a spirited fight-back by Derby. After a relatively foul-free first half, the tackles started flying in as Derby went in search of an equaliser. Dick Lindley was the first victim. After beating Derby's full-back Waugh and sending the ball up field, Waugh, "ran into him at full force knocking the Burnley player out, leading to a good deal of adverse comment." Waugh had already been spoken to for fouling Lindley before and Mr Taylor hadn't seen this incident which had happened off the ball.

Waugh was moved to the outside left position by Bloomer to avoid being sent off. Billy Nesbitt was the next victim. He was 'sandwiched' between two players so severely the little winger appeared at first to be quite badly hurt. The next incident took place in the Burnley goalmouth. The players nearly got to fighting, tempers only being calmed down by the referee, Mr Taylor. Twenty-two minutes into the second half came the second goal of the game when Horace Barnes equalised for the visitors from a right-wing cross.

With ten minutes left it looked as if both sides would settle for a draw and a replay.

"For a time the game deteriorated and just when people were becoming reconciled to a replay at Derby, Burnley suddenly revived," said Sportsman. Eight minutes remained when Bert Freeman was fouled just outside the Derby penalty area. George Halley took the free-kick and after the ball had cleared it came to Teddy Hodgson to tap in for his second goal. The cheers of the Burnley supporters had barely died down when Derby suddenly equalised. A minute after Hodgson's goal, Steve Bloomer put in a long dropping shot straight at Dawson who could only parry the ball away. The ball came out to Waugh (the full-back now turned inside-right) to run in and score to make the scoreline 2-2.

Again it looked that a replay was on the cards. Only five minutes remained. Burnley had the ball with Eddie Mosscrop on the wing. He ran forward at pace toward the Derby goal. Lawrence came off his goal line and Mosscrop's shot won Burnley a corner. From the corner-kick. Dick Lindley's header was parried over the crossbar by Lawrence for a second corner.

With the clock ticking down, Mosscrop placed the ball for the corner. Boyle brought Halley and Taylor forward into the box. Mosscrop's corner reached Taylor, his header goal-bound. Lawrence half-cleared the ball but it only came to Teddy Hodgson who steered the ball through the crowded penalty area to score and complete his hat-trick. There were anxious minutes later as pocket-watches were checked around the stadium with only seconds remaining. Burnley wound down the clock with Mosscrop in the corner and Burnley ended the match the winners in what was a tight contest.

At Full Time: Burnley 3 (Hodgson 3), Derby County 2 (Barnes, Waugh)
Attendance: 29,992

---xxx---

More Walking Wounded

Ernie Edwards the Burnley trainer and Doc Hodges were the busiest men at Turf Moor after the Derby Cup-tie. Dave Taylor, George Halley, Billy Watson, Bert Freeman, Eddie Mosscrop, Billy Nesbitt and Teddy Hodgson were all suffering knocks and bruises. The worst victim was Dick Lindley who had played the remainder of the second half in a daze after being knocked unconscious in the viscous challenge by Waugh. But there was no doubt who the hero of the match was, Burnley's hat-trick-hero and man-of-the-match, Teddy Hodgson. With injuries and the veteran Bloomer standing in for their star forward, Leonard, Burnley had squeezed past Derby and into the Third Round. When the draw was made the following week, Burnley had been handed a home tie with Bolton Wanderers.

Manchester Guardian: "Bloomer who played centre for Derby at Burnley has had 21 years experience of this type of football but it was quite evident his day had passed as he was mastered by Boyle."

Cup Final to Move Home?

The Football Association and The Crystal Palace Company are still arguing over the venue for the Cup Final. After the events of the last final, the FA was not confirming the venue until further work had been done at the Palace. (Daily Express 28/1/1914)

FA CUP Second Round Results
Matches Played Saturday 31st January 1914

Match	Home Team	Away Team	Gate	Receipts £)
1	Bolton Wanderers 4	Swindon Town 2	50,000	1,586
2	Blackburn Rovers 2	Bury 0	30,000	1,037
3	Birmingham 1	Huddersfield Town 0	60,000	1,125
4	Brighton & Hove Albion 3	Clapton Orient 1	15,776	996
5	Burnley 3	Derby County 2	29,992	1,025
6	Exeter City 1	Aston Villa 2	10,000	910
7	Glossop 0	Preston North End 1	10,736	310
8	Leeds City 0	West Bromwich Albion 2	29,000	1,566
9	Liverpool 2	Gillingham 0	40,000	1,317
10	Manchester City 2	Tottenham Hotspur 1	36,258	1,174
11	Millwall 1	Bradford City 0	20,755	1,217
12	Sheffield United 3	Bradford Park Avenue 1	51,000	1,595
13	Swansea 1	Queens Park Rangers 2	15,000	770
14	Sunderland 2	Plymouth Argyle 1	57,150	1,329
15	West Ham United 2	Crystal Palace 0	18,000	1,048
16	Wolverhampton Wanderers 1	The Wednesday 1	33,000	1,531

Figures supplied by The Times.

FA CUP Second Round News

In the Second Round matches, there were victories for all four Lancashire sides. Burnley, Bolton and Blackburn winning at home and a good away win for Preston North End. The biggest crowd of the day was at St. Andrews, Birmingham where 60,000 saw the home side beat Huddersfield 1-0, while a crowd of 51,000 saw Sheffield United beat Bradford Park Avenue 3-1 at Bramall Lane. Liverpool beat Gillingham 2-0 at Anfield and Cup holders Aston Villa won away at Exeter City, 2-1. Last years Cup finalists Sunderland, enjoyed a 2-1 home win over Plymouth Argyle.

Rovers Made Cup Favourites

After their victories over Middlesbrough and Bury so far in the Cup, The Daily Mirror made Blackburn Rovers their favourites to win the Cup.

In the FA Cup Second Round, some 480,000 people had attended the sixteen matches.

Seventy Spectators injured at Hillsborough in Replay

In the Sheffield Wednesday v Wolves replay played at Hillsborough, with only minutes from the end of the game, seventy spectators were injured when a wall collapsed and fell on top of them from a stand above. The game was halted for 20 minutes while spectators were attended to. The players helped get the injured into the pavilion. Eleven people were detained in the infirmary and three fans remained in a critical condition overnight in Sheffield Infirmary. The Wolverhampton Wanderers goalkeeper was so affected by the incident he could not continue.

There were 45,000 spectators at the match. (5/2/1914, Daily Mirror)

It was back to League business for Burnley the following week at Turf Moor against visitors Oldham Athletic. Burnley were unchanged and were unbeaten in their last eight games.

Burnley v Oldham Athletic, Turf Moor, Saturday 7th February 1914 Kick-Off 3:15 pm

The teams lined up:
Burnley: Dawson, Bamford, Taylor, Halley, Boyle (c), Watson, Nesbitt, Lindley, Freeman, Hodgson, Mosscrop.
Oldham Athletic: Matthews, Hodson, Cook, Dixon, Roberts, Wilson, Tummon, Walters, Kemp, Woodger, Donnachie.
Referee: Mr S.D. Peers (Liverpool)

The match was played on a grey afternoon with a light drizzle, the pitch soft. Oldham won the toss and defended the Bee Hole End. Burnley began at pace and from their first attack down the right Eddie Mosscrop fed the ball to Bert Freeman whose shot was cleared by the Athletic defence. With five minutes gone, Jerry Dawson threw the ball out to Billy Watson who set Mosscrop off down the wing. Mosscrop had almost reached the corner flag, then looked up and cut infield, his pass finding Teddy Hodgson lurking in the penalty box. Hodgson, his back to goal, swivelled and shot to make it one-nil to Burnley. Oldham had opportunities to equalise but their efforts went wide. For a brief period in the middle of the half Oldham had more of the play and in one attack with Dawson out of his area, Bamford saved a dangerous situation on Burnley's goal-line. Eddie Mosscrop was causing the Oldham defence numerous problems and in the last ten minutes, his centre was only parried by Matthews in the Oldham goal, the ball coming out to Nesbitt whose shot sailed over the Oldham crossbar.

With the half drawing to a close, Dave Taylor took a free-kick on the half-way line which found Mosscrop, his pass inside to Hodgson found Dick Lindley in space to head Burnley's second goal just before the half-time whistle.

In the second half, Oldham changed their players around. Kemp and Walters exchanged places and Woodger and Donnachie also. Sportsman in the Burnley Express reported that Oldham had the better of the play for much of the second half, Dawson bringing off fine saves from Woodger and Walters, Dawson running out and taking the ball from their toes. The best Burnley attempt of the second half fell to Dave Taylor whose long shot flew a few inches over the Oldham bar. The Clarets held on to their first half lead, the match ending with another two valuable League points to lift the Clarets to fourth in the League table.

At Full Time: Burnley 2 (Hodgson, Lindley), Oldham 0
Attendance: 18,000 (gate Receipts of £437)

---xxx---

Burnley Beat Meredith's Men

Burnley's next encounter was away to Manchester United. It was Burnley's first visit to Old Trafford for a League match and after the 2-1 defeat suffered at Turf Moor back in October, the Burnley players were keen to make amends. Boosted by their progress in the Cup, the Clarets, now nine games undefeated since Christmas, arrived at Old Trafford bursting with confidence to play Billy Meredith and his men.

Manchester United v Burnley, Old Trafford, Saturday 14th February 1914 Kick-Off 3:00 pm

The teams lined up:
Manchester United: Beale, Hodge, Stacey, Haywood, West, Wall, Meredith, Woodcock, Anderson, Travers, Norton.
Burnley: Dawson, Bamford, Taylor, Halley, Boyle (c), Thorpe, Nesbitt, Lindley, Freeman, Hodgson, Mosscrop.
Referee: Mr J. T. Hornby (London)

Billy Watson was away on England International duty at Middlesbrough and his place was filled by Levi Thorpe. Burnley played in all white shirts to avoid the clash of colours. Several hundred Burnley spectators had made the journey by train to Old Trafford to see the Clarets attack the City End in the first half. Tommy Boyle won the toss and Burnley began the game at a high tempo. With only two minutes on the clock, Sportsman in the Burnley Express takes up the commentary; "Burnley attacked and Stacey had to clear following a neat pass by Boyle. Meredith in attempting to gather a hanging ball, lifted it the wrong way and Hodgson gave it to Mosscrop. West went across to tackle him but Mosscrop, dribbling with splendid skill, utterly bewildered his opponent and racing to the goal-line finished with a fine centre. The United defenders were soon at sea. Freeman at once pounced on the ball and coolly worked to within five yards of Beale before he drove the ball hard and low into the net."

Burnley had much the better of the play, "the Burnley forwards were delightfully quick on the ball" described Sportsman. Mosscrop and Hodgson went close to scoring Burnley's second, but Enoch West saved the day. Stacey was struck full in the face with the ball and had to leave the field giving Burnley the advantage. Following a United attack which was put out of play by Dave Taylor, Burnley bombarded the United goal. Freeman had the ball and dribbling toward goal was pursued by Hodge who tackled Freeman, "the pair of them, tumbling down the embankment," said Sportsman. The Clarets mounted another attack. Beale was at full stretch, pulling off a great save from Dick Lindley. The ball came back off the United goalpost but was cleared to safety and at the end of the first half Burnley led United 1-0.

Stacey returned in the second half but it was Burnley again who had the better of the play. The Burnley defence proved too much for United's attackers whose efforts were beaten away by

Halley, Boyle and Watson. According to Sportsman, Burnley fully deserved their lead and were unfortunate not to extend it in the second half and with fewer goal attempts than the first period, Burnley ended the game winners by courtesy of Bert Freeman's goal on two minutes.

At Full Time: Manchester United 0, Burnley 1 (Freeman)
Attendance: 30,000

---xxx---

After this superb performance at Old Trafford, unbeaten Burnley were now 4th in Division One. In the Third Round of the Cup, Burnley had been drawn against Bolton Wanderers at Turf Moor, a place in the FA Cup Quarter-Finals at stake.

In Local News

Nelson Suffragettes Disrupt Ramsay MacDonald

In a Burnley Express article dated February 18th, titled "**Lively Scenes at Nelson,**" Ramsay MacDonald leader of the opposition Labour Party was a guest speaker at the Nelson Grand Theatre. Mr Macdonald had only been speaking a few minutes when a lady rose in the pit, shouting "We women demand this," while holding up a bundle of Suffragette literature. Amid considerable uproar, the chairman shouted that she would be given an opportunity for asking questions. There were cries of, "Chuck her out" but the woman continued to shout, "We demand votes for women." The lady was then approached by the stewards and escorted off the premises. Macdonald continued his speech but after a few minutes another woman rose from another part of the theatre shouting, "VOTES FOR WOMEN." She was treated with hostility by the audience around her and she threw Suffragette literature at them. She was led off the premises also. MacDonald tried to laugh off the incident, but again later in his address he was heckled by Suffragette supporters from different parts of the theatre.

Nellie Wallace Live

Packing in audiences all week at the Burnley Empire, direct from London's West End, was music hall sensation Nellie Wallace. Wallace, whose frustrated spinster act featured songs such as *Three Times a Day, Bang! Bang! Bang and Let's Have a Tiddley at the Milk* Bar, was a huge hit with audiences.

---xxx---

CHAPTER FIVE

The Third Round

Figure 20: The Burnley Bulldog cartoon.

The FA Cup Third Round

Despite being unbeaten since Christmas Day and after the recent victory over Manchester United at Old Trafford, not everyone was happy. In the week prior to the big Third Round Cup-tie, there had been local demonstrations about the Turf Moor admission price increases held during the Reserve teams last game at Turf Moor, aimed at the Burnley directors. There was a good deal of bad-feeling among some supporters over the decision to double the ground admission prices from sixpence to a shilling (5p). (Supporters knew this had happened in previous years whenever Burnley had reached the same stage of the competition.)

Several letters were published in the Burnley newspapers. One irate Burnley supporter wrote to the editor of the Burnley Express,

> "May I be allowed to express my contempt at the scurrilous treatment of the football public by Burnley Football Club. It is nothing but a most dirty attempt to exploit the workers to the last farthing."

Turf Moor would only be open on three sides as construction work on the terracing on the Cricket Field End had been delayed due to the winter weather. The Burnley team meanwhile had spent the week in Cup-tie preparation training at Lytham. The players were all reported fit and would return from the seaside on Saturday morning and have a light lunch at their local headquarters, Cronkshaw's Hotel in Burnley before the game.

The Manchester Evening Chronicle had reported that several Bolton players were suffering from injuries though they would be at full strength. Bolton were third in the League table, one place above the Clarets. Following the 0-0 and 2-2 draws in the League at Turf Moor the form book suggested this would be a tight game.

Ticket News

After a big gate in the previous round against Derby County, an even bigger attendance was predicted at Turf Moor, despite the price increases. The tickets were even advertised in the national papers.

FA CUP THIRD ROUND TIE
BURNLEY v BOLTON WANDERERS
Gates Open 12:45 pm. Kick-Off at 3:15 pm.
Tickets: 1 shilling Adults, Boys 6d.
Enclosure 2 shillings, Stand C 3s, Stand B 4s.

(Manchester Guardian 20/2/1914)

"At Turf Moor the game between Burnley and Bolton is arousing more interest than any cup tie ever played in Burnley. Applications for tickets have poured in from a very wide area – from Nottingham, in the Midlands, to Carlisle. Over 2,000 reserved seats at 4s and apart from 180 these had all been disposed of. There are 2000 seats at 3s on the unreserved portion of the stand but these along with tickets for the enclosure which holds 6,000 people will only be sold on the day of the match. Officials are confident it will hold 50,000 people. (The Times)

Figure 21: The Burnley and Bolton Mascots

Overnight rain in Burnley continued into the morning making the ground soft but by noon the rain ceased and the sun came out. The Turf Moor turnstiles opened at 12:45 pm and from then onwards a steady stream of spectators flowed into the ground, paying their shillings right up to kick-off time.

Sportsman reported on the crowds heading to the stadium, "The streets leading to Turf Moor were thronged, club favours were extensively worn and a few rattles and a bugle or two heard. Greeting the teams, the Burnley mascot for the day, was a man dressed as a dog, wearing claret and blue and carrying a matching umbrella, advertising a well known brand of dog biscuits. The Bolton mascot was a small boy on a bicycle who seemed by all accounts, to be terrified of the dog-man."

In Bolton the mills had closed at 11:00 am to give the locals time to travel over to Burnley. Ten thousand Bolton supporters were said to have made the journey by fourteen special trains, plus charabancs, motor-buses, taxis, horse-drawn vehicles and some even walking it.

Brunbank in the Express reported that, "sheep's feet were tied to vehicles and another evidence of the 'Trotters' invasion was the raid made on local tripe shops for pig's trotters." The sound of concertinas could be heard around Turf Moor, wheezing out the latest tunes like '*I didn't want to do it*', as spectators headed down Brunshaw Road to the ground. All around Turf Moor, vendors were selling all manner of coloured favours of both teams. Brunbank noting that, "one of the favourite decorations was a metal cup with the Burnley colours attached, the stall-holder shouting, "*Ere y'are, the winners colours.*"

Burnley v Bolton Wanderers FA Cup 3rd Round, Turf Moor, Saturday 21 February 1914 Kick-Off 3:15 pm

The Teams lined up:
Burnley: Dawson, Bamford, Taylor, Halley, Boyle, Watson, Nesbitt, Lindley, Freeman, Hodgson, Mosscrop.
Bolton Wanderers: Edmondson, Baverstock, Feebury, Glendenning, Fay, Rowley, Donaldson, Jones, Lillycrop, Smith, Vizard.
Referee: Mr T. P. Campbell (Blackburn)

At just before 3:15 pm, the teams took to the field from under the Brunshaw Road stand. Bolton appeared first wearing their white shirts and dark blue shorts, followed by Burnley in claret and blue shirts and white shorts. Tommy Boyle lost the toss and the Bolton captain, Bert Baverstock, played with the wind as Wanderers kicked off attacking the Bee Hole End. The first attack on goal was made by the visitors, Dawson saving a low shot from George Lillycrop, Tommy Boyle's old team mate from Barnsley. Then, a solo run by Bert Freeman, some three-quarters the length of the field, resulted in his shot just clearing the Bolton crossbar. At the other end, Jerry Dawson pulled off a fine save from a Joe Smith effort. The deadlock was broken on twenty-nine minutes. It began with a run by Billy Nesbitt into the Bolton half. Nesbitt was tackled by Rowley but he got up quickly and won the ball back. Nesbitt continued his run, this time beating Feebury before releasing the ball to Freeman who bore down on the Bolton goal. Freeman dribbled, left, right, left and finally veering to his right. Edmondson in the Bolton goal came off his line and ran toward Freeman thinking the Burnley centre-forward was about to shoot low to his left. Edmondson went down too early. Freeman saw the keepers' move and chipped the ball over the outstretched goalkeeper's body and into the Wanderers net! It was a cheeky goal but a superb finish by Freeman.

Shortly before the interval, a Ted Vizard shot struck the middle of the Burnley crossbar, the ball bouncing safely on top of the net and going clear. And at half-time in the Cup tie, the Clarets led 1-0.

Burnley were quickly on the attack as the second half got underway. Bolton's captain, Baverstock, was hit in the stomach and winded by the ball while blocking a Teddy Hodgson effort which put the visitors down to ten men temporarily. With sixteen minutes of the second half gone, Dick Lindley had the ball in the centre-circle. Lindley fed Nesbitt on the wing.

Nesbitt's cross found Hodgson who timed his run perfectly, got past Baverstock to beat Edmondson with a low hard shot. Two-nil to Burnley! There were great cheers from all around the packed terraces and you could have heard the noise all over the town. Time and again the Burnley forward line attacked in numbers overwhelming the Bolton defence. Boyle switching his team's tactics from one wing to the other to confuse the Bolton backs. "The Bolton defenders were run off their legs" wrote the Manchester Courier correspondent. Eddie Mosscrop then had the ball in the net only for it to be ruled offside. Thirty four minutes into the second half, Jerry Dawson took a goal-kick. Dick Lindley won the ball and dribbled toward the Bolton goal but his final effort missed the target. The ball came out to Nesbitt and he had a shot that was cleared before Mosscrop on the other wing had a similar chance. Boyle pushed his half-backs forward and a Billy Watson strike was saved by Edmondson. Edmondson's clearance found George Halley still forward. Then Halley by clever, cool, calculating work got the ball and dribbling close in, sent the ball past several players and into the net. At 3-0, the game was safe now and Burnley eased off a little. Bolton had two good opportunities of their own in the last ten minutes of the game but they were saved by Jerry Dawson, one a fine save from under his crossbar. And with no further action Mr Campbell from Blackburn brought the game to an end, Burnley winning 3-0 and progressing into the Fourth Round.

At Full Time: Burnley 3 (Freeman, Hodgson, Halley), Bolton 0
Attendance: 32,734 (Gate receipts £2,153,10s)

---xxx---

FA CUP Third Round Results
Matches played Saturday 21st February 1914

Match	Home Team	Away Team	Gate
1	Aston Villa 2	West Bromwich Albion 1	65,000
2	Blackburn 1	Manchester City 2	41,000
3	Birmingham 1	Queens Park Rangers 2	33,000
4	Burnley 3	Bolton Wanderers 0	32,734
5	Millwall 0	Sheffield United 4	18,500
6	The Wednesday 3	Brighton & Hove Albion 0	39,000
7	Sunderland 2	Preston North End 0	34,000
8	West Ham United 1	Liverpool 1	16,000

Third Round News

Burnley were now the only Lancashire side left in the Cup. Bolton, Blackburn and Preston all losing and going out. The biggest crowd of the day, 65,000, was at Villa Park to see the Cup holders beat local rivals West Bromwich Albion 2-1. Sheffield United had the best away victory of the day, winning 4-1 away at The Den. Last years finalists Sunderland reached the Fourth Round again at the expense of Preston. Liverpool drew at West Ham to force a replay at Anfield to be played later this week.

In Other News

Pickpockets were busy at some grounds in Cup day. At Burnley, a man who was unwise enough to attend with 20 sovereigns in his purse paid the penalty." (Manchester Guardian 23/2/1914)

The draw for the Quarter-Finals paired the following teams,

Manchester City v Sheffield United
Sheffield Wednesday v Aston Villa
Liverpool v Queens Park Rangers
Sunderland v Burnley

Punished in the Capital

The Burnley team set off by train on the Sunday morning after the Cup match from Burnley Bank Top station to London for their re-arranged League fixture against Tottenham Hotspur. The Clarets, unbeaten now in 11 games, were without the services of George Halley (injured in the Cup-tie) and Eddie Mosscrop (teaching). Levi Thorpe and Jimmy Bellamy came in as replacements.

Tottenham Hotspur v Burnley, White Hart Lane, Monday 23 February 1914 Kick-Off 3:15 pm

The teams lined up:
Tottenham Hotspur: Joyce, Clay, Cartwright, Weir, Steel, Grimsdell, Walden, Minter, Cantrell, Bliss, Middlemiss.
Burnley: Dawson, Bamford, Taylor, Thorpe, Boyle, Watson, Nesbitt, Lindley, Freeman, Hodgson, Bellamy.
Referee: Mr D. H. Asson (West Bromwich)

Spurs won the toss and kicked off. Cantrell had the first opportunity to score but his shot was cleared away by Dave Taylor. Burnley's first attack saw Bert Freeman go close but his effort was cleared by Clay. The first half was a fairly mediocre affair with only odd goal attempts from either side. The most amusing incident was when Tommy Boyle mistakenly charged the referee and both had to be attended to by the trainer. Cantrell got in a shot for Spurs that Dawson caught before Dick Lindley missed a good chance with a header from a centre by Bellamy. At the interval the score was 0-0.

Tottenham resumed the second half with only ten men, their centre-forward Cantrell injured. Burnley pressed home their advantage, forcing an early corner which was cleared. At the Burnley end, a Walden shot went just over Dawson's crossbar. Then a Burnley attack with Bellamy and Freeman broke down, but Bellamy later got in a good centre which just went over the Tottenham bar. A goal-bound Middlemiss effort was cleared off the line by Tommy Boyle's head. Burnley's best opportunity fell to Bert Freeman whose dribbling run and shot looked a certain goal, the ball hitting the inside of the Tottenham post which Joyce never saw, before re-bounding back into play. Following up, Freeman's header went just over the Spurs crossbar.

Twenty minutes into the second half, Cantrell returned to the field and was soon in the thick of the action. Ernie Edwards the Burnley trainer attended to Teddy Hodgson after he was hurt in collision with Clay which then put Burnley down to ten men. A Burnley move begun by Dave Taylor set Billy Nesbitt off down the left to centre for Freeman who shot just wide.

Tottenham now with the advantage in numbers pressed forward and Taylor fouled Cantrell in the penalty area. Mr Asson had no doubt and pointed to the spot from which Walden stepped up and made no mistake to give Spurs the lead. With ten minutes remaining, Burnley pushed forward and a Billy Nesbitt shot was just cleared by the Spurs 'keeper. With only minutes remaining, Spurs sealed their victory when a fast shot from Bliss from twenty yards out caught Dawson off-guard and couldn't stop the shot despite getting his fingertips to the ball. The game finished 2-0 to Spurs, Burnley suffering their first defeat since Christmas Day.

At Full Time: Tottenham Hotspur 2 (Walden pen, Bliss), Burnley 0
Attendance: 18,000

---xxx---

A Crazy Game Of Two Halves

Following their defeat at Tottenham, Burnley returned to Turf Moor for another Lancashire derby, this time against Preston

North End. Before the match, Preston were bottom of the League and had won only once on their travels. Burnley were fifth in the table and had not lost at home since Christmas Day. Burnley gave a home debut to George Milligan following Teddy Hodgson's injury at Spurs and Eddie Mosscrop returned to the Burnley side in place of Jimmy Bellamy.

Burnley v Preston North End, Turf Moor, Saturday 28 February 1914, Kick-Off 3:15 pm

The teams lined up:
Burnley: Dawson, Bamford, Taylor, Halley, Boyle, Watson, Nesbitt, Lindley, Freeman, Milligan, Mosscrop.
Preston North End: Taylor, Broadhurst, Rodway, Holdsworth, Broome, Dawson, Ford, Toward, Osborn, MaCauley, Barlow.
Referee: Mr L. N. Fletcher (Bury)

Around 2,000 Preston supporters made the journey to Turf Moor making it the best ever attended derby at Turf Moor between the two sides. Tommy Boyle won the toss and Burnley attacked the Bee Hole End. The Clarets had much the better of the preliminary phase, Eddie Mosscrop coming close on two occasions. Mosscrop and Billy Nesbitt were Burnley's' most prominent forwards in the first twenty minutes but it was North End that drew first blood shortly after. Ford got away from the Burnley defence and centred for MaCauley who met the ball and steered it into the net with his hand according to Jerry Dawson. Neither Mr Fletcher nor his linesmen saw the offence and awarded the goal to jeers and booing from the home crowd. Burnley immediately sprung into action. From the re-start Eddie Mosscrop won a corner. Mosscrop's centre was cleared, the ball coming out to Tommy Boyle whose fierce shot struck Rodway's arm. 'Penalty' cries went up around the ground and Mr Fletcher pointed to the spot. Boyle putting the Clarets on level terms from the penalty kick. From then on Burnley dominated. A forward-run from George Halley saw his shot fly just over the Preston crossbar. On forty minutes, Burnley won a direct free-kick on the edge of the North End penalty area after Bert Freeman was fouled. Tommy Boyle lined up the shot and struck the ball through the North End defenders to put Burnley ahead. With the interval approaching, George Milligan's pass found Billy Nesbitt who's long centre found Mosscrop who stole in between the defenders and scored Burnley's third to give the Clarets a deserved 3-1 lead at half time in the derby.

Home supporters were confident that the Clarets would improve on their score in the second half based on the dominance shown toward the end of the first half. Preston North End had other ideas. Burnley began the second half well but Preston adopted Boyle's tactics of swinging the ball to either wing and switching the attack. Sixteen minutes into the second half, Ford got in a centre from which Osborn netted to reduce the arrears, "letting the ball glide off the side of his foot" according to Sportsman. Now 3-2 to Burnley. Eddie Mosscrop had a glorious chance to put the Clarets further ahead but his chance was cleared by Rodway. With fifteen minutes to go and the light fading, some supporters were already setting off for the trams home. Bert Freeman was judged to have fouled his opponent close to the corner flag in the Burnley half. From Toward's free-kick, the ball dropped behind Boyle, rolled between Dave Taylors legs and in snuck Osborn to put Preston on level terms, 3-3! With the seconds ticking down it looked as if Burnley had thrown away another point. Preston redoubled their efforts. Only two minutes remained when North End were awarded a corner. The ball came across and Dawson saved it but a scuffle took place in the goalmouth. Dave Taylor found himself on the floor, "a player trod on or kicked his face above the eye inflicting a nasty cut and leaving another mark." Taylor staggered to his feet, Toward got to the loose ball and shot, the ball striking the crossbar and over the line and into the Burnley net. The referee was not listening to Boyle's complaints despite Taylor being kicked and covered in blood. He merely pointed to the centre-circle having awarded Preston the goal. Taylor then collapsed and had to be carried off, "in a dazed condition by the ambulance men." This was the last real incident of the game, with bottom side North End doing the double over Burnley and taking all the points.

At Full Time: Burnley 3 (Boyle 2, 1 pen, Mosscrop), Preston 4 (MaCauley, Osborn 2, Toward)
Attendance: 20,000 (Gate receipts of £460)

---xxx---

This wasn't the best preparation for next match, the FA Cup Fourth Round Cup tie against Sunderland at Roker Park in only seven days time. Burnley were mauled in the newspapers for turning a 3-1 half-time lead against the League's lowest side into a 4-3 defeat. The Clarets had not let four goals in at Turf Moor in over five years! Worse than that was the walking wounded count. Doc Hodges was busy most of the weekend patching up half the Burnley team; Dave Taylor, George Halley, Tommy Boyle, Billy Watson and Bert Freeman, all nursing cuts, sprains and bruises.

The following Monday, the Burnley players left for their training base at Lytham. Eddie Mosscrop was teaching and trained with Southport Central in the evening. Mosscrop was often seen doing his running along Southport promenade. By Wednesday, news on the injured players was much better and John Haworth named the same Cup team for Sunderland that had defeated Bolton. Levi Thorpe would travel with the team to Roker Park as reserve.

The Athletics News presented the portraits of the eight Quarter-final captains. Burnley's Tommy Boyle would again meet the formidable Charlie Thomson.

Figure 22: The Quarter-Final captains

Top Row L to R: Boyle (Burnley), Ferguson (Liverpool),
Hughes (Man City), Bache (Aston Villa)
Bottom Row: Thomson (Sunderland), Mitchell (QPR), Utley
(Sheff. United), Brittleton (Sheff Wednesday)

The FA CUP Fourth Round

Sunderland v Burnley

After Sunderland had knocked Burnley out at the Semi-final
stage in 1913, they went on to lose to Aston Villa in the infamous 1913 Final. Sunderland had never won the Cup. Their
local rivals Newcastle had and Sunderland were desperate to
take the trophy back to Roker Park. They had reached the
semi-finals four times and the Final once and were desperate to

win the trophy this time. Having lost in the Final in 1913, their supporters thought that surely it would be Sunderland's turn? The teams had met twice in the League already this season, during the festive period, Sunderland winning on Christmas Day, 1-0 at Turf Moor and Burnley managing a 1-1 draw at Roker Park on Boxing Day.

Reigning League Champions Sunderland were third in the First Division but recent results had damaged their hopes of retaining their title. In their last League game at Roker Park, they had lost 0-1 to Bradford City and over the last seven matches had won only three times. Tommy Boyle and his men knew they had to massively improve on recent performances to get any kind of result at Roker Park or their Cup journey would be over. Roker Park would be screaming cauldron of noise cheering the Wearsider's into the Semi-Final.

The day before the match, the Burnley players returned from Lytham to Burnley Manchester Road station on the 10:15 am train where they were joined by club officials before setting off for Sunderland. On Friday evening, the Burnley party were invited to the Sunderland Empire as guests of the Sunderland directors.

Burnley supporters could travel to the north-east in style in a first-class saloon car for six shillings return (30p) with match entry an extra shilling. The match itself was a sell out with all the tickets sold. Burnley took four thousand supporters to the north-east in four football specials that departed from Burnley's five railway stations from seven o'clock on Saturday morning.

Sunny weather greeted Burnley's travelling supporters on their arrival when they disembarked at Sunderland Central railway station at noon. Along the route to Roker Park, local cafes and pubs soon filled and the street vendors near the ground were selling all manner of items; badges, rosettes, photos of the players and teams, long coloured feathers and "squeakers" in the clubs colours. Injuries to the Burnley's players from the previous week had healed. Both teams would today be at full strength. Burnley would be unchanged for their fourth successive Cup tie, and a lucky omen.

Sunderland v Burnley, Roker Park, FA Cup Fourth Round, Saturday 7 March 1914 Kick-Off 3:15 pm

The teams lined up:
Sunderland: Butler, Hobson, Ness, Cuggy, Thomson, Low, Mordue, Buchan, Conner, Holley, Martin.
Burnley: Dawson, Bamford, Taylor, Halley, Boyle, Watson, Nesbitt, Lindley, Freeman, Hodgson, Mosscrop.

Referee: Mr J. Talks (Lincoln). Linesmen: Mr A.S.W. Conroy (Sheffield) and Mr A. Denton (Leeds).

At 3:15, the match referee, the diminutive Mr Talks, standing just four foot six inches tall, brought the two captains, Charlie Thomson and Tommy Boyle together to toss up. Boyle beat Thomson to the toss and elected to play with the sea breeze behind his team.

The game began at a frantic pace. Thomson conceding a corner in the first minute from a Dick Lindley effort. At the other end, Jerry Dawson pulled off a fine save from a Martin shot. Then Cuggy lost the ball to Eddie Mosscrop in who worked his way down the right wing only to be cleanly tackled and robbed on the edge of the Sunderland penalty area before he could shoot.

Bert Freeman won the ball in the centre and set Billy Nesbitt going on the left but the winger held onto the ball too long, his centre being cleared. On twelve minutes Burnley had a good opportunity from a Mosscrop centre and George Halley and Dick Lindley both tried to get the ball in the net through a crowded penalty area. The ball came out and Teddy Hodgson put the ball back in, but it was cleared. Then Billy Nesbitt had another good chance to score but his effort was cleared by the full-back, Hobson. Another Burnley attack saw Freeman and Nesbitt bang into each other in their eagerness to put the ball in the Sunderland net. Sunderland attacked through Martin but his effort was halted by Halley's right boot. The Burnley defender then had an excellent chance of his own, but Halley's fierce shot skimmed the crossbar. Mr Talks later admonishing Butler for "pulling the crossbar down." Two of Sunderland's forwards, Buchan and Mordue combined to create an opening but their effort was broken up by Taylor and Bamford, clearing Mordue's centre. At half time the score remained goal-less.

The second half began with a swift Burnley attack. Boyle set Nesbitt off but the little wingers centre had no one on the end of it and the ball went straight into the arms of Butler. Six minutes into the half, Dick Lindley going forward put the ball in the Sunderland net only for his effort to be ruled a yard offside. A Tommy Boyle foul on Conner led to a Holley free-kick but his shot sailed high over the Burnley crossbar. Then Teddy Hodgson and Dave Taylor were both injured in separate challenges but both resumed play after the trainer's aid. Bright afternoon sun shone in the Burnley players' faces and a Sunderland attack on the Burnley goal led to Jerry Dawson being unfairly charged after taking the ball with both hands. At the other end Freeman, Lindley and Nesbitt combined in a forward move but Nesbitt's shot went over the crossbar. The pace of the game picked up in the last quarter of the game as both sides sought the winning goal. With fifteen minutes remaining, Burnley's best effort of the second half came when a pass and move between Hodgson and Lindley broke down close to the Sunderland goal. A late Dick Lindley run saw him 'laid out' by Holley and there was a lengthy stoppage while the trainer brought him round. A Sunderland attack saw Bert

Freeman back defending, the ball striking his chest. Sunderland supporters behind the goal cried, "Penalty" but Mr Talks was having none of it and gave a corner instead, Charlie Buchan's header from the corner going over the bar. Burnley pressure was put on the Sunderland goal but Butler had already fisted away Mosscrop's centre when Lindley, 'knocked him into the net.' The last real effort from Sunderland saw Jerry Dawson run out of his area to head the ball into the crowd as Mr Talks brought proceedings to an end.

Burnley had played well and had not lost. They had a replay and another chance at Turf Moor the following Wednesday afternoon. The players on both sides had one or two knocks but all would hopefully be fit for Wednesday. The big question Burnley supporters were asking on their return to Lancashire was would winger Eddie Mosscrop be given permission by the Southport School Board to play mid-week?

At Full Time: Sunderland 0, Burnley 0
Attendance: 34,581 (Gate receipts £2,196)

---xxx---

FA CUP Fourth Round Results
Matches Played Saturday 7th March 1914

Match	Home Team	Away Team	Gate	Receipts (£)
1	Manchester City 0	Sheffield United 0	35,738	1,447
2	The Wednesday 0	Aston Villa 1	56,991	2,302
3	Liverpool 2	Queens Park Rangers 1	45,000	1,794
4	Sunderland 0	Burnley 0	34,581	2,196

Figures supplied by The Times

Fourth Round News

Only three goals were scored in all four matches played on Saturday. Cup holders Aston Villa progressed through to the semi-finals winning at Sheffield in front of the biggest crowd of the day, almost 57,000. Liverpool beat Southern League side, Queens Park Rangers at Anfield. The gates were closed at Manchester City an hour before kick-off in their tie with Sheffield United which ended goalless.

The draw for the semi-finals of the competition had paired the following teams.

Aston Villa v Liverpool, to be played at White Hart Lane

Manchester City or Sheffield United v Burnley or Sunderland.

Venue - This Semi-Final tie to be played at either at Old Trafford if Sheffield United were left in, or at Ewood Park, Blackburn if otherwise.

The FA Cup Fourth Round Replay

Burnley v Sunderland

Long queues of supporters seeking tickets for the replay began forming early on Monday morning outside Burnley secretary John Haworth's office. All the Brunshaw Road stand tickets had gone by Monday evening. The newly built Cricket-Field End terracing was ready to be used for the match, albeit without a roof. That end of the ground would accommodate 3,000 spectators. Efforts had been made to increase the cinder banking on the side opposite the Brunshaw Road stand with more material brought in over the weekend. The directors estimated that 50,000 people could be accommodated safely if needed and there should be no need to close the gates.

The Burnley players and officials returned from Sunderland late on Saturday evening. Dave Taylor, Billy Watson, Teddy Hodgson and Dick Lindley, who were all injured on Saturday, were all reported fit. Eddie Mosscrop had managed to secure his release from teaching duties at Southport and would occupy his usual berth on the right-wing.

The Sunderland players had also recovered from Saturday and had journeyed down to Lancashire on Tuesday. The team had stayed in Manchester overnight. The Wearsider's enjoyed lunch at Burnley's Bull Hotel before arriving at Turf Moor at 1:30 pm.

Local collieries, factories, foundries and many town centre shops closed on Wednesday from 1:00 pm until 5:30 pm, calling a 'half-day', which was normally on a Tuesday in the town. At some mills, the weaver's wives had offered to take their husband's places so they could attend the match.

The Turf Moor turnstiles opened at 1:00pm and from then on a steady stream of spectators paid over their shillings as kick-off time approached. Three thousand Sunderland supporters made the journey south, most of them wearing red and white and thousands of Burnley supporters wore their club colours. Brunbank in the Burnley Express, described the scene in and around Turf Moor before the match,

"Burnley for five hours was a pandemonium. Trams, trains, motors, motor charabanc's, motor-cycles, bicycles came like a fleet and all the streets flanking Brunshaw road were used as open-air garages. So great was the crush it was impossible to get through the Culvert, most people using Finsley Gate. The Sunderland contingent advertised themselves with penny buttonholes, decorated hats, umbrellas, tommy-talkers, speaking funnels, squeakers and painted rattles. One Sunderland man brought a black cat with red and white ribbons around its neck. On the ground the man dressed as a dog returned and Walter Place's son was again the Burnley mascot along with another Burnley youth dressed fully in claret and blue." The massive crowd took its toll on some people. One girl collapsed in the crush and there were other reports of people fainting. Brunbank reporting later that, "the crush was tremendous."

Figure 23: Burnley Supporters Sit On The New Cricket Field End Wall

Burnley v Sunderland, Turf Moor, FA Cup Quarter Final Replay, Wednesday 11th March 1914. Kick-Off 3:00 pm.

The teams lined up:
Burnley: Dawson, Bamford, Taylor, Halley, Boyle, Watson, Nesbitt, Lindley, Freeman, Hodgson, Mosscrop.
Sunderland: Butler, Hobson, Ness, Cuggy, Thomson, Low, Mordue, Buchan, Conner, Holley, Martin
Referee: Mr Forshaw (Birkenhead)

The weather was perfect for football by kick-off time as Mr Forshaw the changed match referee, brought the team captains together to decide ends, Tommy Boyle winning the spin. The noise inside Turf Moor was deafening with almost 50,000 filling the ground. Burnley kicked off, attacking the Bee Hole End with the sun and a light breeze at their backs.

It was another blistering start from Burnley with Eddie Mosscrop getting away down the wing, his first centre was too long, the ball going out of play. Sunderland cleared up field and attacked but the opening moments of the game were all Burnley. A more determined Burnley. Five minutes into the game Tommy Boyle had the ball in the centre of the field. His long sweeping pass out to the left found Billy Nesbitt in space. Nesbitt beat his marker and put in a good centre. Bert Freeman got on the end of it and his header rattled the Sunderland crossbar. The ball came out to Teddy Hodgson whose shot also hit the crossbar! Sunderland couldn't clear the ball and Hodgson's smart move found a gap in the crowd of players to weave the ball through a sea of legs to find the net for the opening goal. Sportsman in the Burnley Express, "whereat a mighty cheer rent the air."

The goal settled Burnley's nerves and had shocked the visitors. It put more fire into the Burnley attack and the Clarets had the greater part of the play in the first half. Bert Freeman and Billy Watson had good chances to increase Burnley's lead, both missing with good shots. Both Burnley wingers were enjoying the occasion. Nesbitt had an effort that hit the Sunderland post. Then Mosscrop came close to scoring with a fine run into the Sunderland penalty area, Butler clearing away the danger for the visitors. After that attack, the visitors slowly came into the game forcing consecutive corners. Throughout the first half, Jerry Dawson was the quieter of the two 'keepers with only two shots to stop, both from Martin and at half time Burnley led Sunderland 1-0.

Sunderland were expected to pick up their game in the second half and they did, showing a better quality of football than the first half. But it was Burnley who showed more steel and desire to win. The visitors found the Burnley defence on top form said Sportsman, "The intermediate trio (Halley, Boyle and Watson) especially Boyle, who was seen at his best, were ever on the alert in circumventing the in-roads of the visitors."

Fifteen minutes into the second half, clever work on the ball from Eddie Mosscrop, found Teddy Hodgson. Hodgson dribbled into the Sunderland penalty area where he was fouled by Ness. The crowd rose for a penalty but Mr Forshaw pointed to a free-kick just outside the Sunderland area. Boyle's free-kick was cleared but the ball quickly returned. Then Bert Freeman was fouled in a similar position as Hodgson was. Another free-kick was awarded. This time when Boyle took the kick, he sent the ball out to Mosscrop whose centre was cleared by Butler and the danger averted. Twenty-one minutes into the second half Burnley won another free-kick in a dangerous position after a foul on Lindley by Ness. The ball was sent out to the left and Mosscrop, who had switched wings with Nesbitt. Mosscrop twice beat Hobson and put a good centre into the Sunderland area. The Turf Moor crowd watched as Mosscrop's centre sailed to the far post where Dick Lindley was running in. Lindley timed his run perfectly, met the ball with his forehead and headed it into the far corner of the Sunderland net to make it 2-0 to the Clarets.

At this point Sunderland captain Charlie Thomson changed his team's tactics. Conner went to outside-right, Mordue went inside-right with Buchan in the centre. It was Burnley however who came close to scoring a third goal when a Teddy Hodgson strike went just wide of Butler's post. For the final fifteen minutes the Burnley defence was tested as Sunderland threw all their big men forward. It was at this point Sunderland lost Cuggy and down to ten men, Thomson had to re-arrange his side again. Then Billy Watson was badly fouled by Buchan in a challenge and needed attention. Jerry Dawson was the busier 'keeper in the closing minutes as Sunderland sought a break-through with only ten men. With only two minutes left on the referees watch, Conner pulled a goal back for the visitors. Burnley took their time but from the restart, Sunderland won the ball and raced forward in an effort to force extra-time. Boyle pulled all his men back to defend and the Clarets halted a barrage of attacks from the visitors. Finally, Mr Forshaw blew the whistle to the relief of the Burnley supporters who saw their team through the Semi-Finals for the second season in succession.

At Full Time: Burnley 2 (Hodgson, Lindley), Sunderland 1 (Conner)
Attendance: 49,737 (Gate receipts of £2,858, 9s (Burnley's biggest ever gate at the time.)

---xxx---

What the Papers Said.

Daily Mirror, "Sunderland are a bigger lot than Burnley, but they would have done better if they had saved their weight against the humouresly elusive Burnley."

Manchester Courier, "Burnley were on their toes from the start, the whole side was enthused and they practically ran Sunderland off their feet."

Manchester Guardian, "Burnley were excellent!"

Burnley's Semi-Final Opponents

The Manchester City v Sheffield United quarter-final replay was played at Bramall Lane on the afternoon of Thursday 12th March. The Burnley team without Freeman, Taylor and Mosscrop travelled over to Sheffield and the players watched the match from the stands, which went to extra-time and ended 0-0. A second replay was held at Villa Park, Birmingham on the afternoon of Monday 16th March. Sheffield United winning 1-0 to reach the Semi-Final.

Thunder, Fire and Storm

Three days after their victory over Sunderland, Burnley were back in League action at Turf Moor facing another side who had won through to the Semi-Finals, Liverpool. Injuries forced three changes for Burnley. The Scottish youngster Billy Pickering, who had been scoring well in the reserves, made his Burnley debut at centre-forward replacing an injured Bert Freeman. Levi Thorpe came in for Billy Watson and Bob Reid came in at full-back for Dave Taylor.

Burnley v Liverpool, Turf Moor, Saturday 14 March 1914 Kick-Off 3:00 pm

The teams lined up:
Burnley: Dawson, Bamford, Reid, Halley, Boyle, Thorpe, Nesbitt, Lindley, Pickering, Hodgson, Mosscrop.
Liverpool: Campbell, Longworth, Pursell, Fairfoul, Lowe, Ferguson, Sheldon, Banks, Miller, Dawson, Nicholl.
Referee: Mr G. W. Drewery (Hull)

The afternoon began with a strange incident prior to kick-off. The two teams emerged from the tunnel, but Burnley were not in their familiar claret and blue strip. Sportsman in the Burnley Express explains, "When the teams turned out Burnley were wearing blue and white striped jerseys, but owing to the similarity with those worn by the Liverpool team, whose jerseys instead of being red where black and white stripes, Burnley returned to the dressing room and donned their familiar colours!" When normality had resumed, Tommy Boyle won the toss and decided to play towards the Bee-Hole End. The high-tempo start that had been seen in recent games featuring Burnley, continued right from the first whistle.

The game was only three minutes old when an Eddie Mosscrop centre found Dick Lindley unmarked whose header found the back of the Liverpool net. Shortly after the re-start, Teddy Hodgson should have scored Burnley's second goal but his shot just missed the target. Burnley were constantly on the attack. Shots from Boyle and Levi Thorpe keeping Ken Campbell the Liverpool 'keeper busy. On twenty minutes Teddy Hodgson had the ball in the Liverpool penalty area when he was fouled. Mr Drewery never hesitated and pointed straight to the penalty spot. Tommy Boyle stepped up and placed the ball past Campbell to put Burnley 2-0 to the good. Following the Burnley goal, Liverpool came more into the game. On thirty minutes, Liverpool's Sheldon got away and centred for Banks to score to make it 2-1. It was a more even game toward half-time, Burnley holding on to their 2-1 lead.

For the first fifteen minutes of the second half, Burnley dominated the game. The Liverpool full-back, Longworth had to clear two certain goal-chances from off the Liverpool goal-line. Longworth then handled the ball in the area following a Lindley shot and Burnley claimed the penalty but Mr Drewery instead gave a corner. Eighteen minutes into the second half a lapse in concentration from the Burnley defenders let Miller in whose shot was parried by Jerry Dawson. The ball came straight back out to Nicholl who tapped in. 2-2. Liverpool pressed sensing the advantage and for ten minutes, they saw more of the ball. Around this point the light worsened and rumblings of distant thunder could be heard. The wind rose and the play which was fast and exciting according to Sportsman, was punctuated by flashes of lightning and more thunderclaps. There was a terrific downpour of rain during which Dawson made a fine save from Miller. It became difficult to see the ball in the cloudburst. The pitch started to hold water as huge pools of water appeared. On thirty minutes, Levi Thorpe splashing up field, let loose with a cannon of a shot from twenty yards out which Campbell never saw coming through the rain at speed to restore Burnley's lead. The playing conditions worsened and the Turf Moor pitch turned into a mud bath as the heavy downpour eased. Seven minutes after Thorpe's goal, Eddie Mosscrop won a corner. Running in, the debut-making Billy Pickering headed his first League goal and put the Clarets 4-2 up. Burnley were fully on top by the closing stages and four minutes from time George Halley began a move which was finished masterfully by Mosscrop. Mosscrop dribbling his way toward Campbell took aim and his shot struck the inside of the upright before crossing the line. On a stormy afternoon the soaking wet, mud-plastered Clarets ended worthy winners over Liverpool 5-2.

At Full Time: Burnley 5 (Lindley, Boyle pen, Thorpe, Pickering, Mosscrop), Liverpool 2 (Banks, Nicoll)
Attendance: 16,000 (Gate Receipts of £329)

---xxx---

Athletics News 16 March:
"The winners were well served by their reserves. Boyle was obviously suffering from the effects of the gruelling game with Sunderland."

The FA Cup Semi-Finals
The revised Semi-final draw had paired Burnley against Sheffield United following their 1-0 victory over Manchester City after two replays. Tickets were now on sale at Turf Moor for the match which would take place in two weeks time on the 28th March at Old Trafford, Manchester.

Aston Villa v Liverpool at White Hart Lane
Burnley v Sheffield United at Old Trafford

Mosscrop For England

Burnley's Eddie Mosscrop was selected for the full England side for the forthcoming International match against Wales in Cardiff on Monday 16th March. It was Mosscrop's first full cap.

"Mosscrop was magnificent against Sunderland. One excursionist from Wearside paid the little man a deserved compliment when he said, 'please teacher can we score a goal?'
His resource with the ball, his speed and his accuracy of centres combined with his unselfishness stamped him as an artist."
(Athletic News 16/3/1914)

---xxx---

CHAPTER SIX

The Semi-Final

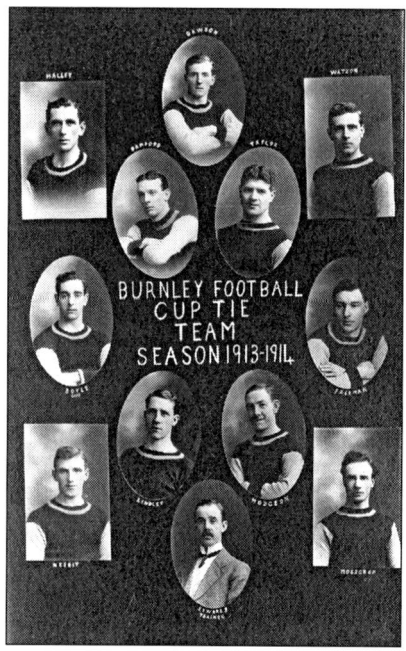

Figure 24

Clarets On International Duty

The demands on the Burnley players increased as the season continued with the International trial matches followed by the Home Championships. Eddie Mosscrop had played outside-left for England in the full international match against Wales at Cardiff on Monday 16 March, England winning 2-0 and Mosscrop having an excellent game. George Halley and Dave Taylor had played in the trial match between the 'Home' Scots and 'Anglo' Scots on the same day in front to 20,000 spectators in Glasgow, Taylor and Halley both in the Anglo-Scots side. Taylor was apparently the best full-back despite him playing with a swollen foot and picking up a knock to his knee. In 1914, there was no shutdown of the Football League programme for International games. If players were selected to play for their country, they turned out and the club suffered as a consequence. Due to their good form, a number of Burnley players came under the International selector's spotlight. No fewer than five Burnley players, Bert Freeman, Jerry Dawson, Tommy Boyle, Teddy Hodgson and Eddie Mosscrop were all 'possibles' for a call-up for the forthcoming English League v Scottish League match that was to take place at Turf Moor on Saturday the 21st Match.

Before that match, Burnley had to visit the North-East for the re-arranged League match against Newcastle United. Burnley were struggling with injuries to six players.

Tommy Boyle – lacerated toes against Liverpool.
Dick Lindley – groin injury and a cold.
Bert Freeman – knee tendon trouble, making progress.
Dave Taylor – swollen foot and knee injury from the Anglo-Scots game.
Jimmy Bellamy – suffering from pleurisy.

Dave Taylor was ruled out and Bob Reid filled in as full-back. Tommy Boyle was replaced by Levi Thorpe and Billy Watson was replaced by Ernest Bradshaw. George Milligan, Billy Pickering and Bill Husband, covered for the injured Dick Lindley, Bert Freeman and Eddie Mosscrop who couldn't play due to his teaching.

Newcastle United v Burnley, Wednesday 18th March 1914, St. James's Park Kick-Off 3:00 pm

The teams lined up:
Newcastle United: Mellor, Hampson, Hudspeth, Spink, Hewison, Hay, Douglas, Hibbert, Sheperd, Wilson, Goodwill.
Burnley: Dawson, Bamford, Reid, Halley, Thorpe, Bradshaw, Nesbitt, Milligan, Pickering, Hodgson, Husband.
Referee: Mr I. Baker (Nantwich)

Newcastle won the toss and had the advantage of the breeze in the first half. The home side battered the patched-up Clarets in the first ten minutes. United should have been at least two goals to the good but their finishing was poor and Dawson kept them out. On twenty-five minutes, United won a corner. The ball came out to Hibbert whose shot hit a defenders leg and deflected into the back of Dawson's net. Hibbert's goal must have been the only event worthy of mention of the first half. Sportsman expressed his frustration on how timid Burnley were in attack, "In the whole of the half, they only journeyed three times beyond the Newcastle 18-yard line."

John Haworth made changes at the start of the second period. The first change the travelling Burnley supporters noticed was Billy Nesbitt playing at centre-forward! Billy Pickering moved to inside-right and George Milligan to outside-right. Amazingly, Burnley's shape looked much better. After fifteen minutes, Burnley centre-forward Billy Nesbit scored with a fierce shot during a goalmouth melee to make it 1-1. Burnley then had their best period of the game up until the 75th minute. Douglas took Sheperd's pass and with Bob Reid slipping Dawson was left alone. Douglas made no mistake and put United 2-1 up. Jerry Dawson then saved a penalty following a Tom Bamford handball to keep the Clarets in the game. Eight minutes from time, Newcastle sewed up the points when Hibbert hooked the ball into the penalty area for Goodwill to score. Newcastle running out comfortable winners in the end, 3-1.

At Full Time: Newcastle United 3 (Hibbert, Douglas, Goodwill), Burnley 1 (Nesbitt)
Attendance: 15,000.

---xxx---

Burnley made a "gallant show" according to Sportsman but with so many injuries and several players playing out of their normal positions, the team performance couldn't be blamed. Burnley's only consolation was 'centre-forward' Billy Nesbitt's brilliant goal!

Women's Football in Burnley

Teams to play in Midweek Matches

An interesting article written in the Daily Express about women's football in Burnley said that, "A women's football club has been formed at Burnley and the first practice game will be played today - weather permitting. It is the intention to run two teams who will take part in matches in mid-week. The players will wear white jerseys and short navy-blue skirts over knickers. The ground of a Sunday school club has been rented and a ball with the initials "B.L.F.C." has been purchased. This will not be the first time that women have played football in the town for many years ago a team of professional women footballers opposed the town club." (Daily Express Tuesday 17/3/1914)

Figure 25: Burnley Ladies Play the Game

Burnley Invaded by Tartan Army

On Saturday the 21st March, Burnley Football Club played host for the first time to an FA International match, The English League playing the Scottish League. Each side were represented by players from their respective home countries. Selected for England duty were three Burnley players; Tommy Boyle, Teddy Hodgson and Eddie Mosscrop. As it was a Saturday, Burnley supporters had a difficult decision to make. Should they travel to Villa Park and watch Burnley in action in their League match or stay at home and cheer on the three Burnley players playing in the 'three lions' for England.

The game brought interest from across the country. The Football League management committees and their Scottish counterparts were present. New telegraphic equipment was installed at Turf Moor for the assembled pressmen to transmit their copy to the various press agencies in Scotland and London. Also making the journey to Turf Moor for the match came a tartan-wearing, kilted army of some six thousand Scots. Brunbank of the Burnley Express describes the scenes in Burnley that Saturday.

"One couldn't help but laugh heartily at the pranks the visitors played. They saw the comical side of everything and were like mischievous monkeys with their practical jokes and tricks.
One train arrived into Bank Top with scores of windows broken. A party stormed the station waiting room, re-arranged the furniture and proceeded to brew up with a kettle they had brought along. The Scots were intrigued with the dress of the local Burnley women wearing clogs and shawls. Scores of them following the women on their way to work in the mills.

One group stopped a horse and cart and took the horse from the shafts. Another group raided a fish cart playing 'catch' with the fish. One Scot pushed a bloater down his shirt. A window-cleaner was knocked from his ladder, the group catching him as he fell. A large body of Scots paraded St. James's Street seeking liquid refreshment. Many drank from flasks and bottles brought with them. One group hijacked a tram in St. James Street, the driver and conductor powerless. Another group commandeered a bread van, looted it of its contents - and then paid the baker the bill. The police however were very indulgent. Only one or two people were arrested. One Scot was badly cut in getting out of a public-house cellar after the trap door had fallen on him."

One of the things Brunbank described was the chant the Scots sang inside Turf Moor before the start of the game,

> Scotland will ne-ver fail
> Ne-ver fail, never-fail;
> Scotland will ne-ver fail,
> **No, no ne-ver!**

"it was sung to the old Sunday-school hymn, *Kind words will never die*. The verses varied between *Scotland will ne-ver die* and *Scotland will ne-ver lose*"

Like Aston Villa, Burnley had three players selected for the English side. Tommy Boyle had been suffering from bruised feet and a groin strain but had recovered and would play. Teddy Hodgson had recovered from his injury as had Eddie Mosscrop and lined up with the other English League players. Bob Crompton the Blackburn Rovers skipper was England captain.

Scottish League v English League Inter-League Trial Match, Turf Moor, Saturday 21 March 1914

Figure 26: English League and Scottish League Teams

Figure 27

The teams lined up:
Scottish League: Shaw (Celtic), McNair (Celtic), Dodds (Celtic), Gordon (Rangers), Wright (Greenock Morton), Nellies (Hearts), McAtee (Celtic), McMenemy (Celtic), Reid (Rangers) Croal (Falkirk), Smith (Hibernians).
English League: Hardy (Aston Villa), Crompton (Blackburn Rovers - captain), Boocock (Bradford City) Barber (Aston Villa), Boyle (Burnley), McNeal (West Bromwich Albion), Jephcott (West Bromwich Albion), Stephenson (Aston Villa) Peart (Notts County), Hodgson (Burnley) Mosscrop (Burnley).
Referee: Mr H. H. Taylor.

Abel Hudson had done a fine job in preparing the Turf Moor pitch for the occasion. A strong south-westerly breeze blew across the pitch as the teams appeared. The teams lined up for photographs and England captain Bob Crompton won the toss, electing to play with the wind towards the Bee Hole End.

The English side had the better of the opening exchanges and on seven minutes, Claude Jephcott got down the right wing and put in a good centre. Teddy Hodgson brought the ball down and hit it with force goal-ward. The ball hit Nellies on the goal-line but he could do little but deflect Hodgson's shot it into his own net and give England the lead. Three minutes later, Eddie Mosscrop worked his way down the left-flank toward goal. He cut inside, got into the Scots penalty area and was about to let loose when he was brought down by Wright. Mr Taylor had no option but to point to the penalty spot. Bob Crompton signalled to Tommy Boyle to take the kick. Boyle placed the ball and stepped back his usual ten yards. His shot flew past Shaw to put the English side two goals up with only ten minutes gone.

Directly after the goal, "a mishap occurred" according to Sportsman in the Burnley Express. Teddy Hodgson was kicked by the full-back Gordon and had to be attended to. "Though he resumed and pluckily stuck to his task he was handicapped by the injury."

England continued to have more of the play but the Scots came more into the game. Mosscrop and Jephcott plagued the Scots defence the whole of the first half. Mosscrop coming close on two occasions to scoring himself. On the first half's play, the English side should have been four goals to the good and they wished they had later.

Whatever was said to them in the dressing room, the Scots team were transformed in the second half. They pushed forward, sometimes with seven forwards to find a way back into the game. Two minutes into the second half, a centre from McAteer found Croal and the Scots pulled a goal back. The English were limited to attacks that came mainly through Mosscrop. Teddy Hodgson was clearly lame from the first half tackle but he limped on all regardless throughout the second half.

Eighteen minutes into the second half the Scots attacked and found Smith to centre for Croal who scored his second goal to put the Scots on level terms. Croal was hurt in scoring his goal and was taken off the field and he was absent a good ten minutes. The English were stunned by the Scots comeback. Sam Hardy in the England goal was now the busier goalkeeper and with eleven minutes to go the Scots took the lead. Good work on the right-wing by Reid, who cut inside his defender. unleashed a shot that went straight over Hardy's head and into the net. With Peart struggling to adapt and Hodgson injured, the English attack lacked bite and couldn't counter – attack. In the end the Scots won a memorable game 3-2.

At Full Time: Scottish League 3 (Croal 2, Reid), English League 2 (Boyle pen, Nellies o.g.)
Attendance: 34,607 (Gate Receipts £1,241 6s 6d - Admission Price 6d - a record at the time for an Inter-League match in England)

---XXX---

For one Burnley resident, the behaviour of the Scots visitors it was the final straw. Burnley supporters didn't escape his wrath either as the vicar of St. James's Church, Reverend Whitfield told the Editor of the Burnley Express,

BORDERLAND PLEASURES

"Some five thousand football excursionists came into Burnley early on the Saturday and for the rest of the day the town was turned into what is usually styled a pandemonium, a general assembly of evil spirits, whisky in this case appearing as Beelzebub, the chief of spirits. Disorder, drunkenness and extravagance prevailed, respectable people avoided the town and shopkeepers suffered and a sign of relief was raised when the railway companies again swallowed up the pleasure seekers whom they had disgorged in the early morning."

Then the Reverend brought his fire to bear on Burnley supporters...

"Take the English Cup competition at Sunderland. Thousands of our Burnley working men spent the whole time from 6:00 am on the Saturday to 6:00 am on the Sunday to see this match at Sunderland. We are told that the whole week's wages were selfishly and meanly taken up in many cases for the excursion that families were cruelly left un-provided for that tradesmen went unpaid for the weeks goods supplied to the homes which had to depend on further credit, that the pawnbrokers did a roaring trade the day before. The railway journey was largely taken up with gambling that many found themselves pounds in debt on their return and many unfit for work the day after."

(Burnley Express 4/4/1914)

Meanwhile at Villa Park

With three players playing in the International at Turf Moor and with four players injured, Burnley were down to just four regular first-teamers for the match at Villa Park. Dick Tranter, the youngster from the reserve team and former Padiham player made his Burnley first team debut. With Dawson out injured, reserve goalkeeper Ronnie Sewell came into the Burnley side for his first League match of the season and Bob Kelly came back into the first team.

Aston Villa v Burnley at Villa Park, Saturday 21st March 1914 Kick-Off 3:00 pm

The teams lined up:
Aston Villa: Anstey, Lyons, Weston, Morris, Harrop, Leach, Dyke, McLachlan, Boyne, Bache, Edgeley.
Burnley: Sewell, Bamford, Reid, Halley, Thorpe, Watson, Nesbitt, Kelly, Pickering, Tranter, Husband.
Referee: Mr H. Swift (Sheffield)

The makeshift Clarets "did exceedingly well" at Villa Park according to Sportsman. Ronnie Sewell in goal was reportedly, "a shining light."

Billy Watson captained the Clarets for the match and won the toss. Burnley wearing a changed strip of light blue and white stripes, kicked off. Villa had much more of the play but the Burnley defence held well. Ronnie Sewell made several good saves from distance. On thirty minutes a Villa attack opened the scoring when a centre from Dyke found Joe Bache. His shot hit Tommy Bamford's leg, the ball rebounding to Edgeley on the edge of the Burnley penalty area to score. At the end of the first half, Aston Villa led 1-0.

In the second half, Burnley again were on the defensive but Villa were poor at finishing in front of goal. The best Burnley chance fell to Billy Pickering. Bill Husband's shot from distance struck the Villa crossbar and from the rebound the ball found Pickering but he miscued and his scuffed shot was saved on the floor by Anstey. Burnley threatened to equalise late on but the Villa defence repelled the attack. At the end of a fairly uneventful match, Villa ran out winners, 1-0.

At Full Time: Aston Villa 1 (Edgeley), Burnley 0
Attendance: 25,000

---xxx---

The FA CUP Semi-Final

Preparations for the Match

Following Burnley's defeat at Villa Park, the players re-grouped in Lytham the following Monday. It was hard to tell who would show up at Lytham, there were so many players injured and carrying knocks.

The Semi-Final at Old Trafford was now only six days away. Teddy Hodgson had been for an x-ray on his ankle following the International match. The x-ray showed no bones were broken but Hodgson would probably miss the Semi-Final. Reserves Billy Pickering, Levi Thorpe and Bob Reid joined the Burnley party for Cup training as Ernie Edwards, Charlie Bates and Doc Hodges worked flat out getting the first-teamers fit for Burnley's biggest game of the season.

Figure 28: Burnley Players Enjoy the Sea at Lytham

L to R: Billy Nesbitt, Richard Lindley, Levi Thorpe, Jerry Dawson, Bob Reid, Billy Watson, Dave Taylor, Tommy Bamford. (Getty Images)

Figure 29: Football Training at Lytham

Sheffield United had already made a name for themselves in the competition for their 'robust style of play.' Sheffield's opponents in the First Round, Newcastle United, had limped off St. James's Park with only eight men, Sheffield winning 5-0. In the second round, United dispatched Bradford Park Avenue 3-1 at Bramall Lane and in round three, they had a convincing victory over Millwall, winning 4-0 at The Den. In their Quarter-Final, it took United three games to overcome Manchester City. For the second replay, City had lost the services of both of their first-choice wingers, Cummings and Cartwright due to injury.

Burnley captain Tommy Boyle knew all about United, particularly their captain, George Utley, his old defensive partner at Barnsley. Both men had begun their careers working in the South Yorkshire coalfield. They were brought up a pit village apart, Boyle in Platts Common and Utley in Elsecar. Both had joined Barnsley and had played in the team that met Newcastle United in the 1910 Cup Final. Both had experienced defeat in the replay a week later but Utley had gone one better than Boyle. When Boyle became a Burnley player in September 1911, Utley replaced him as captain and he lifted the Cup in April 1912 after Barnsley beat West Bromwich Albion in the Final. The two men may have been team mates once but today they would be slugging it out for a place in the Final.

What George Utley didn't know was the state of his opponent's health. Tommy Boyle had been suffering from pleurisy for several days before the game. Each time Boyle had drawn breath, he had winced from the pain in his ribs. Each time he moved he felt the pain. During the week at Lytham, Boyle had woken the Burnley Trainer Ernie Edwards at 4:00 am in agony. Jimmy Bellamy had been sidelined with the same complaint earlier in the month so it must have been 'something going around.' Under examination, Boyle masked the pain from

Doc Hodges who could tell he wasn't a hundred percent from the colour of his complexion. Boyle simply lived to play football. He had missed out on a Cup medal once and didn't intend to miss out a second time. He would not miss the greatest occasion of a footballer's career, in leading his team out at the Final, even if it killed him. Despite Boyle's illness, Doc Hodges shook his head and sighed and then passed him fit to play.

The Burnley directors met on the Thursday evening of the 26th March to select the team. The Burnley Express reporting the day before, that; "The composition of the side is doubtful at present owing to injuries." It didn't look good as the mid-week Express usually named *a* team even if it wasn't **the** team. The newspaper didn't even print the squad.

From 9:00 am onwards on the Saturday morning, thousands of Burnley supporters began arriving at railway stations all along the East Lancashire line from Colne to Accrington. From the station newsstand, supporters found out the latest team news for the match. As they boarded the twenty-four special trains bound for Manchester, it was a feeling of all-round relief. Captain Tommy Boyle would play and Burnley would field their strongest side. The same side for the sixth time in the Cup.

Old Trafford

Corporation buses and trams greeted the scores of trains arriving at Manchester Victoria and Piccadilly stations from all over the country as a 'human tide surged toward Old Trafford' from noon. One Sheffield supporter carried a giant scythe with a blade on the end decked in red and white. Numerous supporters had their faces painted in red and white. The flower sellers did a roaring trade selling coloured favours. There were

Burnley supporters carrying banners, wearing rosettes and "fool hats." Along the route to Old Trafford were stalls selling merchandise and souvenirs of the occasion; teddy bears clothed in the team colours, team photographs, match programmes, local newspaper vendors. On the ground, around 2:00pm, the players came out to look at the pitch, Sheffield first, wearing their suits. They were noisily greeted with cheers by the crowd. Unlike the previous rounds, there were no team mascots on the ground. However, according to 'Brunbank' in the Burnley Express, "The Burnley runner, George Brunton, did scramble over the rails and commenced to run around the enclosure in his bare feet, but he ran full tilt into the arms of some policemen and was removed. Although he only got thirty yards however, he got five shillings and ten pence collection. Evidently any popular demonstrating was tabooed."

Before the match and again at half-time, there were toffee sellers walking around the pitch 'feeding' the crowd's appetite for sweets. They would throw packets of toffee into the crowd and receive the pennies in return. The Football Association had only given licences to six news agencies to take photographs of the match. The Burnley Express were not among them and had to take their photographs from the terraces rather than sit at pitch side with the 'officials'.

It was a fine but breezy afternoon at Old Trafford and though the pitch was dry it had been heavily sanded. The Irwell Springs Band provided the pre-match entertainment right up to the moment the teams emerged from the player's tunnel. At just before three-o'clock, Tommy Boyle and George Utley led out their teams onto the pitch.

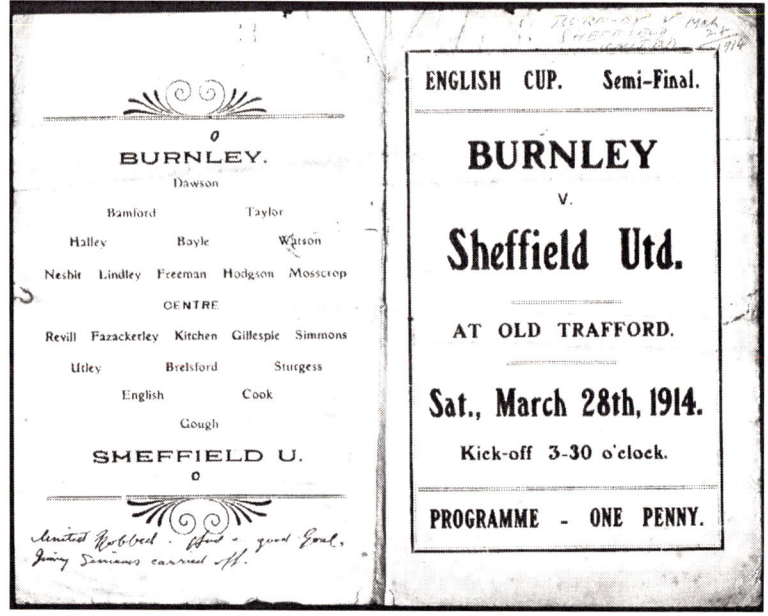

Figure 30: The FA Cup Semi-Final Programme

Sheffield United v Burnley, FA Cup Semi-Final, Old Trafford, Saturday 28 March 1914 Kick-Off 3:30 pm.

The teams lined up:
Sheffield United: Gough, Cook, English, Sturgess, Brelsford, Utley, Simmons, Gillespie, Kitchen, Fazackerley, Revill.
Burnley: Dawson, Bamford, Taylor, Halley, Boyle, Watson, Nesbitt, Lindley, Freeman, Hodgson, Mosscrop.
Referee: Mr H. H. Taylor (Altringham)

Mr Taylor called the captains together and George Utley beat Boyle in the coin-toss and United played with the breeze. As they had played in the earlier rounds, Burnley went on the attack right from the first whistle. Burnley hammered away for the first twenty minutes but the Sheffield defence broke down any attacks and neither Gough nor Dawson were severely tested. A Burnley corner that was met by Teddy Hodgson was

Burnley's first real chance, but Gough put the ball round the post. Burnley followed up with a header from Dick Lindley which Gough put out for a corner. Billy Nesbitt's next centre found Lindley again and his shot hit the crossbar before clearing for a goal-kick. It was close but not close enough. Then Bert Freeman had two chances, sending the ball just wide on both occasions, with Gough at full stretch as the ball whizzed past his post. After Hodgson had tested Gough on 22 minutes, Freeman put the ball in the net but Mr Taylor refused the goal, ruling him offside.

The Burnley goal wasn't in any jeopardy in the first half hour until United won their first corner. Simmons then hurt his ankle in a tussle with Dave Taylor and went off for the trainers' attention, returning ten minutes later. Following a free-kick against Tommy Bamford, Fazackerley put the ball in the Burnley net but his effort was ruled offside. A Tommy Boyle header looked to be going in, but the captain's effort was blocked on the line by George Utley's nose. Utley was felled, covered in blood that formed a round red patch on the front of the United captain's shirt. Following that incident, Eddie Mosscrop was marked out for some rough treatment by Sturgess who badly kicked the little winger from behind. Sportsman in the Express noted that Mosscrop wasn't the same for quite some time later. The last fifteen minutes of the first half was littered with niggling fouls from both sides, "The Sheffielder's were the greater sinners" said Sportsman. The worst feature of the half was the number of free-kicks and throw-ins which disrupted the flow of the game. Just before the interval the ball was crossed from United right and George Halley headed the wrong way, the ball striking the inside of Dawson's upright (the photograph, shown later in the newspapers showed how close United came to taking the lead, the ball leaving an imprint in mud on the inside of Dawson's post) and a quick move by Dawson saved the day. "It was a miraculous escape," said Sportsman.

Figure 31: Burnley Attack in the Semi-Final at Old Trafford

In the second period, Eddie Mosscrop was hurt again following another rash challenge by Sturgess in what appeared to be an attempt to kick Mosscrop out of the game. Gough was the first goalkeeper called into action, and then Fazackerley badly fouled Dawson in a United attack, kicking the Burnley 'keeper high up on his thigh while both players were in mid-air. A Bert Freeman run on goal looked promising. He got all the way to the penalty area before being brought down by Cook. From the free-kick, Boyle sent a flyer just over the United crossbar. United got more of the play as the match wore on and a limping Jerry Dawson just managed to fist out an effort from Kitchen. Burnley won a succession of free-kicks. Brelsford and Sturgess being the chief offenders, though Freeman was twice penalised for unfair shoulder charges. As the game progressed to its conclusion, Boyle and Watson who had both been hurt, "were in some distress", said Sportsman. The Burnley skipper holding his sides obviously in great pain. Eddie Mosscrop recovered and came back more into the game in the last tem minutes of the second half. Mosscrop looked to have a good chance to score all on his own but his progress was blocked on the edge of the box. As full-time drew closer, Jerry Dawson was troubled two or three times by Sheffield attacks and a dangerous United corner was cleared away well by Taylor. Shortly afterwards Mr Taylor brought the match to a close and both bruised and battered sides limped off the field.

At Full Time: Sheffield United 0, Burnley 0.
Attendance: 55,812 (Gate receipts of £3,777) inc. 14,000 travelling supporters from Burnley. This was then a record attendance for an FA Cup Semi-Final.

---xxx---

The Burnley dressing room at the end of the game looked like a war zone, all the players suffering damage to some degree. With Boyle struggling from the start and Mosscrop hurt and uncertain of release from teaching for the replay, it was difficult to see who would pull on a shirt for the replay at Goodison Park. Hamerold in the Burnley Express – "The injuries Burnley's men received were the outcome not of mischance but by design. Dawson was badly lamed by one of Fazackerley's insensate challenges, Taylor suffered to a less extent, Watson was elbowed out of the field and into unconsciousness, and all the forwards received some rude buffetings. Freeman and Lindley finding Brelsford so frequently guilty of shady tactics as to deserve censure. Utley thought nothing of putting his feet into Nesbitt's back. Mosscrop received one wild charge that completely spoiled him for the rest of the game."

After the final whistle at Old Trafford, thousands of spectators headed for the exits to catch their trams and trains home. The crush exiting Old Trafford was described by Brunbank in the Burnley Express.

"I am pretty comfortable in a crowd as a rule but on Saturday I came to appreciate the helplessness of a mere odd man.

To safeguard my money I had one hand in my pocket and never got it out again. My feet only touched the ground in little inch strides. For a hundred yards they never felt the ground at all and I never knew I was on the bridge till I was half over it for I could neither see nor walk. I am sore yet - in body as well as mind." Supporters made their way home slowly, feeling different to when they arrived. Brunbank again, "Going we were all agog with confidence, coming back we were depressed and dejected with not a shout or an excuse."

It had been a poor match from both sides who had tested and probed for each others weaknesses that had offered only few opportunities at either end. They had also tried to kick the other into submission. And it would all be repeated at Goodison Park on Wednesday.

In the other semi-final at White Hart Lane in front of 27,464, Liverpool clinched their place in the Cup Final by defeating the Cup holders Aston Villa 2-0 with both goals scored by inside-forward Jimmy Nicholl.

The Burnley players had just 72 hours to recover. The team attended the Russian Hydrotherapy and Turkish Baths at the Mitre in Burnley on Sunday afternoon and both Dawson and Boyle were reported to have benefitted. "Jerry was very despondent over his injury on Saturday after the match and thought he would not be able to play again this season." (Burnley News 1/4/1914)

Press Reports from Old Trafford:

"The officials at Old Trafford on Saturday were not satisfied that a legitimate goal had been scored. One was disallowed to each side but Sheffield claim that they did register a valid point in that Halley headed inside the goalpost and that when Dawson took the rebound the whole ball was within the net.

"The Athletic News printed two photographs, one showing the imprint the ball had left on the inside of Dawson's post with another photograph taken from a different angle. "They (the photographs) suggest that Sheffield won the match. Still we would be the last to declare that the evidence of the camera is irrefutable as much depends upon the position of the operator at the vital moment, and if we are to make the camera a new critic, the position of referees would become intolerable." (Athletics News 30/3/1914)

Manchester Guardian

The match between Burnley and Sheffield United was a miserable affair...Burnley were lucky that fears about Boyle's fitness to play were not realised. Boyle was one of the best men on the field." (Manchester Guardian, 30/3/1914)

Burnley's Cup Income so Far

Leaving the Semi-Final accounts out, Burnley have made the biggest profit to date. The receipts at their matches had been £8,810 compared with £8,445 for Liverpool, £7,476 for Sheffield United, and £6,580 for Aston Villa. The clubs take half the receipts less expenses directly connected with the matches and five percent which goes to the Football Association. (Manchester Guardian 30/3/1914)

Burnley Firm to Supply Cup Final Ball!

It was announced in the Burnley Express that, "Messrs Chas. A. Clegg Ltd of 10 Market Street Burnley, has been appointed as the official match ball provider for the 1914 Cup Final at the Crystal Palace, Sydenham."

Mossy for England

The Monday after the Semi-Finals, the FA announced the England squad for the forthcoming full International match against Scotland at Hampden Park. Among the eleven players, Eddie Mosscrop had won the selectors nomination and would play for England.

The FA CUP Semi-Final Replay

Injuries Force Changes to Burnley Cup Team.

April Fools Day and it was near pandemonium at Burnley Bank Top station on Wednesday morning. Only three trains had been prepared to take six thousand Burnley supporters to Merseyside for the replay. There were simply not enough train carriages and hundreds of fans were left on the station platform with no means of getting to Goodison Park.

As it was a 'half-holiday' in Liverpool, there was a good crowd for a midweek match. The match attracted a number of Liverpool supporters (their team playing away at Newcastle in a re-arranged game) to witness who their team would play in the Final. From Kirkdale Station, along Westminster Road and all the way to Goodison Park, large numbers of spectators wearing their respective team favours were seen carrying their lucky mascots, loud-hailers, banners and decked out in either red and white or claret and blue.

Sheffield United v Burnley, FA Cup Semi-Final Replay, Goodison Park, Wednesday 1 April 1914, Kick-Off 3:00 pm

The Burnley team came out onto the pitch early and received a great welcome, but the big surprise among the Burnley supporters that had managed to make it to Goodison Park was the appearance of Ronnie Sewell on the pitch and not Jerry Dawson. Sportsman noted, "The Burnley section of the crowd were very quiet before the match but the Sheffielder's were very confident to all appearances." It was the first time Burnley's line-up had changed in seven Cup matches. Since joining the

Clarets from Gainsborough Trinity in February 1913, Ronnie Sewell had spent most of his time keeping goal in the reserves, playing in the Central League in front of crowds of a few thousand. He had only one Burnley first team appearance to his credit this season against Aston Villa at Villa Park in March where he had performed well, but Burnley had lost by a single goal. Burnley supporters were asking themselves how Sewell would cope with the big occasion, with a place in the Final at stake. Sheffield United also had one team change from the first game. Hall replacing the injured Simmons.

All the other ten Burnley outfield players were declared fit to play. Eddie Mosscrop took up his usual place, and after bed rest, Clarets captain Tommy Boyle had recovered from his bout of pleurisy over the weekend. The captain had got his colour back and was looking more like his old self as he met George Utley in the centre-circle to shake hands and toss the coin for a second time. It was a fine afternoon on Merseyside as Mr Taylor once again got proceedings underway.

**Figure 32: Tommy Boyle Leads Out Burnley
For the Semi-Final Replay.**

Figure 33: Semi-Final Replay Programme

The teams lined up:
Burnley: Sewell, Bamford, Taylor, Halley, Boyle, Watson, Nesbitt, Lindley, Freeman, Hodgson, Mosscrop
Sheffield United: Gough, Cook, English, Sturgess, Brelsford, Utley, Kitchen, Gillespie, Hall, Fazackerley, Revill.
Referee: Mr H. H. Taylor (Altringham)

Sheffield United kicked off, with Burnley playing towards the Stanley Park End. Mr Taylor was, "down on rough play" right from the outset and the game was a much "cleaner" affair reported Sportsman, "Sheffield's proneness to hacking the man was checked at the outset."

Burnley won a series of early throw-ins on the left and an early shot from George Halley was headed away by Cook. On the wings, Utley and Sturgess had the better of Eddie Mosscrop and Billy Nesbitt in the early exchanges. United's full-back, English, was injured in an early Burnley attack, from which Mosscrop's first centre was cleared before Teddy Hodgson could intercept. United, with the wind at their backs, punted the ball up-field at every opportunity, trusting their forwards to get hold of it. The Burnley back line of Bamford, Sewell and Taylor stood firm, Sewell seeing a lot of the ball early on which allowed him to settle into his role. Mid-way through the first half, the ball came to Bert Freeman for his first real chance. Freeman spotted a gap in the United defence, set off on one of his runs but his progress was finally blocked. Freeman's second chance came when Cook in the United defence was floored, but this second effort went behind the goal.

Two Eddie Mosscrop attempts, the first cleared by Brelsford and then a second, saw the United keeper' pull off a fine save. "Burnley meant business" reported Sportsman and in the next minute a shot from Hodgson straight at Utley, burst his nose, as in the first game. Sheffield then had their best opportunity to take the lead. United centre-forward Billy Gillespie was running on goal. He drove the ball obliquely toward the right-hand side of Sewell's goal, the ball going away from the goalkeepers reach. But Sewell calculated the strength and direction of the ball perfectly, "and flung himself, cat-like," and palmed the ball round for a corner. "It was mastery and artistic in its brilliance" said Sportsman, "it was little wonder he had a special ovation all to himself before and after the interval." The strong wind tended to carry the ball long, so that any long balls pumped forward were not reaching the Sheffield forwards and going out for Burnley throw-ins. The wind was a big factor in the first half as the sides went in for the interval with the score goal-less.

As the second half began, the wind had dropped slightly, Burnley playing with a lighter breeze at their backs. "Only once did Sheffield ever look like scoring," said Sportsman. Ronnie

Sewell, after catching a dropping shot which was about a foot inside the top left hand corner, had, "a few pointed words to Fazackerley who went for him." A determined Bert Freeman set off on a run on goal. He was edged to the left away from goal but managed to reach the touchline and cleverly back-heeled the ball to a waiting Mosscrop who's rising shot Gough did well to palm away. From the goal-kick a Sheffield attack through Kitchen saw him hit a low shot that Sewell saved at the expense of a corner. United hadn't heard the referees whistle and Billy Gillespie played on and put the ball in the net. Bert Freeman had several more solo attempts on goal and almost scored with, "one of his glorious screw-shots - which seem to curl like a boomerang." All Gough could do was tip it under the bar and Mosscrop running in could only see the ball strike the crossbar and roll on top of the Sheffield net. Another Freeman effort looked like a clear penalty when he was bundled over in the area, his penalty claim ignored by Mr Taylor.

Almost half an hour of the second half had gone, "and we were all looking like watching extra time", said Sportsman, "when Boyle completely changed the picture." Nesbitt playing now on the left, the captain having switched his wingers over, had been fouled and Billy Watson put the ball down for the free-kick, just in front of the goal to the right. Watson's kick led to both Mosscrop and Freeman having shots blocked by Gough and Cook respectively. From Cook's clearance Sportsman describes. "Then the ball went to Boyle who was waiting. It was as if he knew where the ball would come." Boyle ran in and met the ball with force, it flew towards Gough but he had no chance of stopping it."

Brunbank in the Express, "it was 28½ minutes into the second half. Those who saw it will for ever when they hear of good goals say, 'Did you see that goal of Tommy Boyle's?'

It crashed into the net like a projectile from a machine-gun and I believe that if the goalkeeper had been in the way it would have knocked him down, or if it had caught his outstretched arm it would have broken it."

After two hours of football, the deadlock was finally broken and there was only one team in it. Burnley wanted another goal and Boyle's men attacked United vigorously. After Burnley's goal, any weary legs in the team were strengthened with renewed purpose. Burnley didn't sit back. Burnley wanted another goal. Teddy Hodgson hit the ball square across the Sheffield box but no Burnley player could get on the end of it. Dick Lindley was then ruled offside for no reason with three Sheffield defenders in front of him!

Five minutes remained when a Freeman attack ended with "a nasty kick in the face." Another free-kick netbuster from Boyle was only just saved by Gough. In the final seconds a bloodied Freeman was about to bang the ball into the net when it hit Gough's body and deflected over the crossbar. "Thus ended a semi-final replay which, if not adorned with brilliance, was a mighty struggle," concluded Brunbank.

At Full Time: Burnley 1 (Boyle), Sheffield United 0
Attendance: 27, 266 (The Times gave the figure as 35,000)
Gate Receipts of £1,731

---xxx---

What the Papers Said,

BURNLEY FOR CUP FINAL. Sheffield United beaten on their merits in hard game at Liverpool. "Burnley deserved to win on the run of play" (Daily Mirror 2/4/1914)

BURNLEY FOR THE FINAL!
Twenty-eight minutes after the interval, Boyle, the Burnley captain and centre-half put a fine finish upon an excellent personal display with a shot no goal-keeper could have stopped.

Watson had taken the free-kick for a foul by Cook on Nesbitt and he swung the ball across the goal mouth. Hodgson tried to find the net, but Gough, the United keeper' pushed the ball out. Mosscrop returned it and Utley headed it out to Boyle who took the ball on the half-volley and crashed it into the net.
(Daily Mail 2/4/1914)

BURNLEY FOR THE PALACE.
BOYLE SCORES ONLY GOAL IN CUP REPLAY.
The only goal of the match scored eighteen minutes from time by Boyle, their captain. The goal came in unexpected manner. English mis-kicking, let in Lindley who shot. Gough saved but the ball was met and returned by Boyle who was about eight yards out.
(Daily Express 2/4/1914)

A PRICELESS GOAL!
BOYLE'S WONDERFUL SHOT.
BURNLEY IN THE CUP FINAL AT LAST.

"What then was it which wrought the wondrous change from Saturday?
It was Boyle – the subtle difference between Boyle ill as on Saturday, and Boyle, bubbling with life, energy and directness as on Wednesday. Boyle's magnetic influence electrified the nerves of every defender till they became perfectly tuned to the situation; and from beginning to end there was never a slip. It was Boyle, here, there and everywhere tackling, heading as far as some men can kick, swinging the ball to the wings…a great leader he was on Wednesday." (Burnley Express 4/4/1914)

LIVERPOOL POST AND MERCURY
Burnley did not play nearly so well…They have gone stale and have suffered severely through leading men being injured. Sewell was excellent in all he did.
(Liverpool Post and Mercury 2/2/1914)

SHEFFIELD DAILY POST

The better team won. In the second half Burnley always seemed to have the whip hand. Freeman was a splendid leader even though he did appear to be walking in his sleep now and again. But that is Freemans little way. Boyle and Watson were great half-backs and Sewell saved the game in stopping Gillespie's shot. (Sheffield Daily Post 2/4/1914)

Real Rejoicing

Leaving Goodison Park at the end of the match, Burnley supporters were in good spirits, cheering and singing at the top of their voices, noted Brunbank. "There were scores of cars but not enough trams which were all filled before they left the depot. On the way home as the trains passed through Blackburn, Accrington and Padiham, there were crowds to re-echo the expressions of pleasure which were voiced by crowds of trippers who flocked to the windows of the compartments."

In Burnley itself there was an atmosphere of unrest. "After three-thirty that afternoon until quarter past five, almost everyone's thoughts were fixed on something else than the matter immediately at hand. Even the sedate city fathers in the Burnley Council Chamber found municipal matters somewhat dull in comparison."

The news that Burnley had beaten Sheffield United reached the town shortly after five o'clock. "The crowds outside the newspaper offices in Manchester Road and on St. James Street went frantic over the joyful intimation that Burnley had scored and the shout of triumph could be heard streets away." The news seemed to spread from street to street, from mill to mill and workshop to workshop like wildfire. There were some lively moments in the mills and workshops when the news reached them." In the Burnley Council Chamber, there were shouts of excitement and from the moment the result was known, "the streets in town thronged with people discussing the result, details of the play and the arrangements for getting to The [Crystal] Palace. Many holiday club funds will now be drawn upon and between now and then there is likely to be rigid economy to raise the 'necessary'."

The Burnley team with the exception of Freeman who stayed with friends in Liverpool and Mosscrop and Watson who had travelled home to Southport, returned from Liverpool by the 8:55 pm train. Waiting for the team at Bank Top station were upwards of three thousand Burnley supporters. At just past 11:00 pm, the train steamed into the station to great cheers. Teddy Hodgson was first out of the carriage to loud cheers. Hodgson managed to escape the gathering. George Halley and Ronnie Sewell came next but didn't. Sewell was raised shoulder high, the crowd carrying him along Standish Street all the way to Market Place with hundreds of people following behind. Sewell later managed to escape and set off at a run towards the centre of town. Tommy Boyle was submitted to the same 'chairing' treatment as Sewell for a minute or two before he managed to escape and several of the other players were followed home by their ardent supporters.

The football club received many messages of congratulations on the team's success. Philip Morrell, the Liberal Member of Parliament, soon after 8:00 pm despatched the following telegram to Harry Windle, the Burnley chairman.

"Warmest congratulations from Lady Ottoline and myself on Burnley's great victory. Hope directors and players will honour us by dining with us here after final on April 25th.
Letter Following – Philip Morrell."

From that afternoon, Burnley's success in reaching the Cup Final at the Crystal Palace was the main subject of conversation in the pubs, clubs, workplaces and among families. Cup fever struck Burnley and the whole population was under its influence.

By the following Saturday, the 4th of April, local travel company's in Burnley were advertising trips to the Cup Final,

ADVERTISEMENTS

CUP FINAL, APRIL 25th
Book Early At Althams'!
Return Fare 12 shillings.
If you require Saloon Travel, Meals, Drives, Hotels or any other special arrangements call without delay at any of
ALTHAMS' BRANCHES.

---xxx---

WHITTAKER'S Ltd. (Est. 20 Years)
Cup Final Party Outing - only 21 shillings.
Includes Railway Fare, Drives, Three Good meals,
Admission to Palace and Ground, Conductor etc.
Extra Drives for those not going to match.
No Extra Charges.
Book at once to avoid disappointment. 2s 6d deposit.
J. B. Whittaker 19 Brooklands Terrace, Burnley or his agents.

---xxx---

For any Burnley supporters who couldn't make the Semi-Final, they could see all the action from the first game at Old Trafford any time during the week at the 'newly opened' Tivoli Picture Palace in Burnley.

TIVOLI PICTURE PALACE

The Management have secured a number of
exclusive features this week:
Big Game Hunting in Central Africa –
following a seven month expedition.
**Burnley v Sheffield United. Cup Semi-Final at
Old Trafford (matinees and evenings)**
The Club of Black Masks
And another exciting episode of **Count Zarka**
and finally,
'In the Bishop's Carriage.'

---xxx---

Not Sheffield Again?

The Burnley players had a rest day on Thursday before meeting
up again at Turf Moor on Friday morning ahead of the
following days League match. It was with none-other than
Sheffield United, this time At Bramall Lane and the third
meeting between the sides in a week who must have been sick
of the sight of each other by now. After missing out on a trip to
The Crystal Palace, George Utley's men took swift retribution
for their Cup exit. For Burnley, Ronnie Sewell kept his place as
Jerry Dawson still wasn't fit and Dick Tranter replaced Bert
Freeman (suffering a bruised face). Bill Husband provided
cover for Eddie Mosscrop who was on England International
duty at Hamden Park. Mr Taylor from Altringham again took
charge as referee for his third encounter between the two sides
in a week.

Sheffield United v Burnley, Bramall Lane, Saturday 4 April 1914 Kick-Off 3:00 pm

The teams lined up:
Sheffield United: Gough, Cook, Richardson, Brelsford, Hawley, Utley, Revill, Gillespie, Kitchen, Fazackerley, Evans.
Burnley: Sewell, Bamford, Taylor, Halley, Boyle, Watson, Nesbitt, Lindley, Tranter, Hodgson, Husband.
Referee: Mr H. H. Taylor (Altringham)

Sheffield United stood in sixteenth position in Division One, only four points above the relegation places with Burnley in ninth and with games in hand. With the season drawing to a conclusion, the Blades desperately needed the points to move away from the bottom two.

Sportsman noted in the Burnley Express how different the performances of both sides were from only three days before. "Sheffield played a game which was streets ahead of anything they did during the Cup-ties, and by contrast Burnley were the reverse."

Ronnie Sewell was the busiest man on the field and in the first fifteen minutes he stopped two good goal opportunities from Utley. With twenty minutes gone, United won a corner. From Revill's cross, the ball hit a Burnley defender and landed at Gillespie's feet who put the ball in the net before Sewell could move. Eight minutes later, United doubled their lead when Fazackerley scored with a swift hook shot from a pass by Gillespie. Tommy Boyle moved Teddy Hodgson to centre-forward and he had a good chance to pull a goal back but his shot went over the crossbar. Other than that one Burnley chance, Gough in the United goal had little to do. At half-time United led 2-0.

With the second half eight minutes old, Billy Gillespie put the game beyond Burnley's reach with a headed goal from a United corner. Then Kitchen made it four-nil, fifteen minutes from time as he raced in on goal with only Sewell to beat, Burnley having pushed too far up field. And to cap off a miserable afternoon for the Clarets, Fazackerley scored a fifth goal for the Blades after a good effort from Evans. "Burnley were rather fortunate that one or two more goals were not scored against them," wrote a despondent Sportsman.

At Full Time: Sheffield United 5 (Gillespie 2, Fazackerley 2, Kitchen), Burnley 0
Attendance: 18,000

---xxx---

In the international match at Hampden Park on the same day, Eddie Mosscrop had won his second full international cap for England. Mosscrop had, along with most of the England side and according to the (English) newspapers account, a poor game as England went down 3-1.

Easter 1914

The Middlesbrough League game at Turf Moor was another match that had been rearranged after Burnley's Cup run. It was played on a Monday afternoon before Burnley's smallest home crowd of the season. After three League defeats on the trot, Burnley were sliding down the League table and were only five points above the relegation places. Several players were suffering from their exhaustive Cup run. The Middlesbrough game came only two days after Burnley had received a good kicking from the boots of George Utley and company. That match had sidelined both Tommy Boyle and Teddy Hodgson. Jerry Dawson was still recovering from the injury he picked up in the first Semi-Final and Eddie Mosscrop was teaching so Bob Kelly came into the side.

Bert Freeman returned after his facial injury and Dave Taylor took over as Burnley captain. Middlesbrough had to make three changes of their own from the weekend, Heyworth, Stirling and Stage all coming into the side.

Burnley v Middlesbrough Turf Moor, Monday 6 April 1914, Kick-Off 3.00 pm

Burnley: Sewell, Bamford, Taylor (c), Halley, Thorpe, Watson, Nesbitt, Lindley, Freeman, Tranter, Kelly.
Middlesbrough: Williamson, Heyworth, Walker, Davidson, Jackson, Malcolm, Stirling, Carr, Elliott, Tinsley, Stage.
Referee: Mr Garner (Barnsley)

A stiff breeze blew across Turf Moor as Williamson beat Dave Taylor for the choice of ends, Middlesbrough playing with the wind and Burnley defending the Bee Hole End. Despite the wind in their faces, Burnley started the game well. Bert Freeman seemed back to his old self and after receiving the ball from Thorpe, he set off with Kelly in support. Kelly took the ball forward before he floated the ball across to Freeman only for 'Boro's centre-half, Jackson to head clear. George Halley pushing forward and had a good effort saved and Billy Nesbitt's centres were becoming more dangerous as the game progressed. With fifteen minutes gone, Halley found Freeman unmarked. Working inside the 'Boro half backs, Freeman found an opening and his shot found the back of the Boro' net. Good combinational play between Kelly and Freeman led to two more Burnley opportunities before Middlesbrough equalised on 25 minutes. A breakaway from midfield by Elliott, who was possibly a yard offside, shot with force, the ball rattling Sewell's crossbar, "causing a shower of whiting" according to Sportsman. From the re-bound, Carr, running in, side-footed the ball into the Burnley goal and the teams went in at the interval at 1-1.

In the second half Sportsman noted that, "Burnley had the better of the play and were the rather more dangerous team, controlling the ball very well when the teams changed ends." With the wind in their favour now, the Clarets should have capitalised as they looked more confident. For the first twenty minutes of the second half, Middlesbrough were kept on the defensive. A Burnley shot struck Davidson's arm in the penalty area but the appeal from the Burnley players was turned down by Mr Garner. Billy Nesbitt was then shoved in the back but the resulting free kick by Burnley was wasted. A succession of shots, the first by Billy Watson and then from Thorpe, followed by Halley were all saved by Williamson. Middlesbrough had rarely travelled over the half-way line when on 26 minutes a quick attack saw Elliott race forward from his own half to score and give Middlesbrough the lead. Middlesbrough suddenly came to life with more attacks. One effort hitting Sewell's crossbar. During the closing phase of the game, Dave Taylor pushed his troops forward and sent in a splendid long shot from a free-kick which Williamson saved on the goal-line. The Burnley forwards pressed forward to find the equaliser but the Middlesbrough half-back line held fast. Middlesbrough saw the game out, the final score being 2-1 in their favour.

At Full Time: Burnley 1 (Freeman), Middlesbrough 2 (Carr, Elliott)
Attendance: 7,000 (Burnley's lowest gate of the season.)

---xxx---

It was Burnley's fourth League defeat in a row and with only four League games left, the Clarets were only five points above the relegation places. Their form had to improve soon or they could find themselves sucked into a relegation fight that could affect their performance in the Cup Final, now less than three-weeks away.

It was Easter week with two games in two days, but the League fixtures had been kind, giving Burnley two home games against Everton and Derby County. The Clarets urgently needed a return to their post Christmas unbeaten form. They needed all their key players fit again and a little bit of luck that had eluded them of late.

Herbert Bamlett to be Cup Final referee

Figure 34

Before Easter, The Football Association announced that the referee for the Cup Final would be none other than Herbert Sydney Bamlett. Bamlett's appointment must have brought cries of despair from several quarters in Burnley. The Athletics News in profiling Bamlett as part of their lead-up to the Cup Final said,

"The Football Association announced in their last meeting the appointment of Mr H. S. Bamlett of Gateshead-on-Tyne to act as the Cup Final referee. Mr Bamlett is a native of Sunderland where he was born some 32 years ago. He joined the Durham Association in 1901 and joined the Football League and Southern League list of referees in 1907-08. He has had his 'little troubles' [not stated what these were] and has been subjected to criticism over his interpretation of the offside rule. Last Saturday he officiated at Glasgow at the Scotland v. England International." (Athletic News 6/4/1914)

For the visit of Everton, Burnley were once again without the services of first-choice goalkeeper Jerry Dawson but apart from his omission, the Clarets lined up as they had done in the replayed Cup Semi-Final with the same outfield players that had beaten Sheffield United.

Burnley v Everton, Turf Moor, Good Friday 10 April 1914, Kick-Off 3:00 pm

The teams lined up:
Burnley: Sewell, Bamford, Taylor, Halley, Boyle, Watson, Nesbitt, Lindley, Freeman, Hodgson, Mosscrop.
Everton: Fern, Thompson, Maconnachie, Weller, Wareing, Grenyer, Chedgzoy, Jefferies, Parker, Bradshaw, Harrison.
Referee: Mr T. P. Campbell (Blackburn).

It was a sunny afternoon and there was a good attendance at Turf Moor for the Good Friday afternoon encounter with Everton. Tommy Boyle was fit again and won the toss and Burnley played toward the Bee Hole End with the wind. An Eddie Mosscrop attack from the kick-off was flagged offside as Burnley gained the upper hand in the early minutes of the match. A Tommy Boyle long shot was caught by Fern before Bert Freeman had his first chance of the game with a low shot that just went wide of Fern's right-hand post. Dick Lindley was next in line with a goal-scoring chance but his attempt was cleared by Thompson. From the clearance, Everton broke and won the first corner of the match. From the corner-kick, Parker the Everton centre-forward, had a good header saved by Sewell. Then a cross from Harrison came to Chedgzoy, but he made poor use of his chance and Billy Watson cleared. Eddie

Mosscrop combined well with Dick Lindley and Fern had to come off his line to foil another good Burnley goal attempt.

Bert Freeman got in a good shot which Fern managed to save on his knees, turning the ball round the right-hand post. It was all-out attacking from Burnley as Billy Nesbitt centred, and then Eddie Mosscrop struck the Everton post. The break-through came mid-way through the first-half. Tommy Boyle found Teddy Hodgson with a good pass and he worked inside to find Dick Lindley whose hard, low shot beat Fern to put the Clarets in front. Burnley should have gone further ahead from a Nesbitt corner, the ball twice coming out the Burnley half backs to knock the ball back into the area only for Everton to eventually clear. Everton had the occasional attack but Burnley were looking the much stronger and more organised side with Tommy Boyle commanding his forces well. Just before the break, Halley, Boyle and Watson had again pushed forward, right to the edge of the Everton area and each of them had shots saved by Fern. A rocket shot from Boyle bounced off an Everton defender to end the half, before the teams went in for tea with Burnley leading 1-0.

Burnley pressed straight from the start of the second half seeking a second goal. Four minutes in, a move started by Dave Taylor led to Burnley's led to it. Taylor found Nesbitt, whose jinking run down the left put in a good centre which dropped just in front of Freeman. It was a typical Freeman dribble and run ended in Burnley's second goal. "It was Freeman's finest goal this year and richly deserved the enthusiastic cheers it elicited," said Sportsman in the Burnley Express. Burnley looked hungry for more and forced a corner straight from the re-start. Boyle found Hodgson whose header was saved by Fern. Then a claim for a Burnley penalty was turned down by Mr Campbell. Everton attacked and in the process put the ball in the net but the effort was flagged offside by the linesman. Another dangerous Everton attack followed but that was safely cleared away by Tommy Bamford. "Burnley's passing was up to their best standard," noted Sportsman and as Everton looked to score, their forwards couldn't make any impression. After his goal Bert Freeman looked to have got his old confidence back. Dave Taylor was hurt in an incident that put Burnley down to ten men temporarily. Meanwhile a run on goal by Freeman led to Fern coming out to meet him. Bert was about to let loose when Fern took the ball from his toes and was hurt in the process. Fern looked dazed and was helped off the field for attention but like Taylor, he later returned after treatment from the Everton trainer.

An Everton attack through Bradshaw saw Everton come close, the ball striking Sewell's crossbar and Watson steering the ball away to safety. Another Everton attack saw Bamford clear the ball far over the grandstand roof and into Brunshaw Road. Fern in the Everton goal, was clearly unwell and had to leave the field again (he was later hospitalised in Burnley Victoria Hospital, suffering concussion) and Macconachie went in goal with Weller as full-back. With the Blues down to ten men, Burnley pressed home their advantage in the final minutes before Mr Campbell blew his whistle to end the game, the Clarets winning 2-0.

At Full Time: Burnley 2 (Lindley, Freeman), Everton 0
Attendance: 20,000 (Gate receipts of £538 11s 6d) Gate pooling with Everton had been agreed back in August agreed, the two clubs would pool the gate monies at Goodison Park and Turf Moor and the clubs would split the income. With this arrangement, Burnley benefitted to the tune of just over £200.)

---xxx---

This had been a much better performance by Burnley, their first League win in nearly a month. With Boyle back in the middle directing the play, his tactic of attacking at speed and in numbers combined with the regular change in the direction of his attack, had paid dividends. Bert Freeman had looked much sharper and had enjoyed the match against his old club. Burnley's four match losing streak had come to an end. The two points were welcome in Burnley's quest for League safety. Burnley were in ninth place after the Everton result but were only six points above the relegation zone. A good result in Saturday's game against Derby County who were battling against relegation, would secure the Clarets First Division status. Burnley did not want to be going into Cup Final week with their future uncertain.

Tom Charlton Badly Injured

Former Burnley inside-left Tom Charlton, who had moved to Blackpool in December 1913 after scoring three goals in seven appearances for the Clarets, was badly injured in a Good Friday game between Blackpool and Leicester Fosse at Blackpool. Charlton slipped over a player's foot, and in trying to recover himself fell and his head came into violent contact with another players knee. Charlton was unconscious and the ambulance men and two doctors ferried him to hospital. Suffering a severe depressed fracture of the right-side of the skull, Charlton was operated on by Dr Richardson, who removed several pieces of bone. Charlton was only given a slight chance of recovery at first but since he has made good progress, "his vitality surprising the doctors." (Burnley Express 15/4/1914)

---xxx---

CHAPTER SEVEN

Cup Fever

The great fallacy is that the game is first and last about winning. It is nothing of the kind. The game is about glory.
                                                    - Danny Blanchflower

Brilliant Burnley

Burnley fielded the same eleven for their second Easter game against Derby County. With three League games to go and Burnley six points above County in the relegation zone, the Clarets needed to secure the points today, or possibly face a relegation scrap in their final two League games. It was the last home game before the Cup Final and the home supporters wanted to see a good Clarets performance, before everyone set off to London for the Cup in just two weeks time. The Burnley faithful were not disappointed.

Burnley v Derby County, Turf Moor, Easter Saturday 11 April 1914, Kick-Off 3:00 pm

The Second Round Cup encounter with Derby had been a tight affair, Burnley winning 3-2, Teddy Hodgson scoring a hat-trick. Derby had come back at Burnley throughout that game. In the corresponding League match at the Baseball Ground in December, Burnley had lost 3-1.

Derby's centre-forward, Henry Leonard who had missed the Cup-tie, was back in the side replacing Steve Bloomer. Derby's leading scorer, the winger Horace Barnes was Burnley's biggest threat. He had scored 25 League goals from the left wing but despite that Derby were bottom of the League, their defence having leaked goals all season. Jerry Dawson was still on the injured list but the news was good, he was undergoing light training on his injured leg and should be fit for the Cup Final. Ronnie Sewell kept goal for the Clarets for his fifth game in succession.

The one person all Burnley supporters were surprised to see was the match referee. Cup Final referee Herbert Bamlett marched onto the pitch in place of the scheduled referee, Bamlett stepping in at the last minute to replace the unwell Mr Hargreaves. According to Sportsman, "Bamlett was given a 'cordial' reception by the home crowd."

The Teams lined up
Burnley: Sewell, Bamford, Taylor, Halley, Boyle, Watson, Nesbitt, Lindley, Freeman, Hodgson, Mosscrop.
Derby: Scattergood, Atkin, Waugh, Barbour, Buckley, Bagshaw, Reader, Moore, Leonard, Barnes, R.H. Callender.
Referee: Mr H. S. Bamlett (Gateshead)

Burnley captain Tommy Boyle lost the toss and the Clarets began playing toward the Cricket-Field End. It was bright, sunny and a slight wind blew toward the Bee Hole End as Derby began well and won a few of the early skirmishes. "The play was fast and of an excellent quality, with Burnley the more aggressive side," said Sportsman. Derby attacked first through Barbour and then Leonard, Sewell pulling off two fine saves, Leonard putting the ball past Sewell only for his attempt to be ruled offside. On ten minutes Dick Lindley won the ball and passed inside to Freeman. The pair moved forward into the Derby half. They combined well passing the ball to each other as both cut through the half-back line. Lindley's final pass to Freeman left him to dribble to the edge of the penalty area and fire a low shot past Scattergood, to great cheers around the ground. "It was one of the finest pieces of play seen for a long time," enthused Sportsman. Derby came straight back at Burnley. After the re-start, Ronnie Sewell flying to his left, pulled off the save of the match, turning a certain goal around the post. "The pace was fast and of the highest order," described Sportsman, the play moving from end to end.

Sewell was later injured when clearing the ball after coming into contact with Billy Watson's elbow, but he was alright again shortly after. On 35 minutes, Watson began the move that led to Burnley's second goal. Watson's pass found Freeman in the centre-circle. He fed Mosscrop out on the right, Freeman running forwards as Mosscrop fought his way down the flank riding several flying tackles. Mosscrop saw the Burnley centre-forward signalling for the ball and placed the ball just in front of him, and Freeman from considerable range got in a fast screwing shot which entered the far corner of the net far beyond the reach of Scattergood. Two nil to Burnley! Four minutes before the interval, Derby pulled a goal back when Horace Barnes got in a fast shot which Sewell fisted against the crossbar but couldn't prevent the ball going over the line and an exciting first half came to an end with Burnley leading 2-1.

The second half began quietly. Derby came out and their forwards looked for an equaliser but Scattergood had more work to do than Sewell. With twenty minutes gone, Dick Lindley had the ball and was tackled by one of the full-backs. Freeman running in, picked up the loose ball, slipped round a defender and had the ball in the net for his hat-trick! 3-1 to the Clarets! The home supporters were enjoying seeing the centre-forward on such great form. Derby pushed forward knowing they had to get something from the match or their season would end in relegation. A determined Tommy Boyle won the ball. Boyle fed Lindley and with his back to goal scored Burnley's fourth with a sublime overhead kick. Derby's defence were all over the place. Two minutes later it was Lindley again with a hard shot from ten yards out who found the back of the Derby net for his second goal after fine work by Freeman to make the score 5-1 in favour of the Clarets. Burnley had looked like they could score when they wanted and the second half had been an excellent team performance.

At Full Time: Burnley 5 (Freeman 3, Lindley 2), Derby 1 (Barnes). **Attendance:** 19,000 (Gate Receipts of £423)

---xxx---

Burnley had found the right kind of form, and according to the Burnley Express's Sportsman, "Burnley were superb. Football the likes of which has not been seen at Turf Moor since the Bolton and Sunderland Cup-ties. Burnley were on the top of their form." The team had not picked up any injuries and more importantly, the result meant Burnley had secured their place in the First Division for next season. The team could now focus all their efforts on preparing for the Cup Final in a fortnight's time. In other news from Turf Moor, Ronnie Sewell who had been sought after by a number of First Division clubs had signed a new contract for the Clarets for next season.

Liverpool Investigation

The joint FA and Football League Commission investigating the Liverpool v Chelsea match, [of the previous season] concluded that no case was to answer regarding inducements not to play to their ability. The case had been brought by Mr H.G. Norris. (The Times 12/4/1914)

H.G. Norris was a sports journalist and director of Woolwich Arsenal when this game took place at Anfield in March 1913. Liverpool lost the match 2-1. Chelsea and Norris's club, Arsenal were both battling against relegation. Norris claimed that Liverpool had not shown enough desire to win the match. The claim was brought before the Football Association and Football League and an investigation followed which dragged on through the 1913-14 season with the conclusion that there was no case to answer. The accusation Norris had made had incensed the Liverpool players. Liverpool's, Ephraim Longworth writing in the Liverpool Evening Express of 5th April 1914 said, "…that Liverpool players deliberately lay down and allowed other sides to win…there is not an atom of truth in the suggestion." At the end of the 1912-13 season, Arsenal had been relegated on 17 points, Chelsea staved off the drop and Burnley later took Arsenals place in the First Division.

Cup Final Week

After their encouraging victory over Derby County, the Clarets spent the following week at Lytham at their training base.

One game stood between Burnley and the Cup Final, a League fixture against Manchester City at Hyde Road. The Sky Blues were in fifteenth position and had secured their place for next season so there was nothing riding on the result. Jerry Dawson was fit again and returned in goal after a five-match layoff with a leg injury, as his understudy Ronnie Sewell returned to the Reserves. John Haworth's latest injury concern was Bert Freeman who had wrenched a knee against Derby the previous week after scoring four goals in the last two games. Freeman's place was filled by Levi Thorpe.

The Burnley players arrived by train at Manchester Victoria station at 11:00 am on the Saturday morning. They enjoyed a light lunch in the city centre at the Mosley Hotel before setting off for Hyde Road in a fleet of taxis. One taxicab with Hodgson, Bamford, Halley and Thorpe in it had turned into Manchester's Downing Street, close to the football ground, when the driver attempted to pass between a tramcar and a lorry. The taxi became jammed between the two vehicles. "Matters were quickly remedied, however the players being none the worse for their somewhat startling experience," according to Sportsman. The players soon laughed it off but it could have been more serious. Summer-like weather greeted the players and Burnley's travelling supporters on arrival at Hyde Road.

Manchester City v Burnley, Hyde Road, Saturday 18 April 1914, Kick-Off 3.00 pm

The teams lined up:
Manchester City: Smith, Henry, Fletcher, Hughes, Hanney, Hindmarsh, Cumming, Wynn, Howard, Browell, Dorsett.
Burnley: Dawson, Bamford, Taylor, Halley, Boyle, Watson, Nesbitt, Lindley, Thorpe, Hodgson, Mosscrop.
Referee: Mr J. T. Howcroft (Bolton)

Tommy Boyle lost the toss and Burnley faced the breeze and the bright sun as City kicked off. City had the better of the play in the opening phase and the Clarets had little in goal attempts in the first quarter of an hour. It was shortly after that disaster struck for the Clarets. City's centre-forward, Fred Howard was running in on the Burnley goal to meet a centre from the right. Jerry Dawson went up to claim the cross but he collided with Howard's knee which hit him in the side, in the ribcage. Dawson fell to his knees in agony. He went off the field clutching his ribs for attention for a long period. Boyle put Dave Taylor in goal, but later Dawson returned to the fray, not wanting to let his team mates down.

On eighteen minutes, City had a throw-in and the ball was crossed into the Burnley penalty area by Dorsett. The ball looked to be going out of play but Wynn reached it and hooked the ball back and over an outstretched Dawson and into the net. It was clear that the injury to Dawson was more serious and he was in pain. On 25 minutes Dawson could stand it no longer and left the field. Tommy Boyle put Dave Taylor back in the goal and the Clarets resumed with ten men for the rest of the game. Burnley attacked down both flanks, seeking the equaliser. Mosscrop being cheered when he weaved his way past three City defenders in succession before finally losing the ball. Eleven minutes before the interval, Howard popped up again scored past Taylor for City's second and at half-time the home side led Burnley, 2-0.

During the interval it was reported that Dawson was suffering no more than a bruised rib, "and that the injury was not so serious as first feared," according to Sportsman. John Haworth took no chances however and Dawson remained in the dressing room and Dave Taylor wore the green jersey for the second half.

City's numeric advantage gave them more of the play though the Clarets did often threaten. In one Burnley attack through

Billy Watson the Burnley half-back was fouled by Henry. The normally quiet Watson was incensed, "and assumed a threatening attitude toward the culprit, but Mr Howcroft intervened and the players shook hands," noted Sportsman. Twenty minutes into the second half, Billy Nesbitt centred accurately for Teddy Hodgson to head in and pull a goal back for the Clarets to make it 2-1 to City. After the goal, Burnley looked more composed with ten men, but a City attack thirty minutes into the half saw them restore their two goal lead when Browell scored. City wrapped up all the points three minutes later when Browell headed his second goal and City's fourth goal past a befuddled Taylor.

At Full Time: Manchester City 4 (Browell 2, Wynn, Howard), Burnley 1 (Hodgson)
Attendance: 25,000

---xxx---

Kestrel in the Burnley News was outraged at the rough tactics of the hosts. "One can only compare City with Sheffield United for rough play except that the Hyde Road men were even the more deliberate in their actions. I have rarely seen three more deliberate fouls than those on Dawson, Lindley and Watson but also the easy way in which the referee [from Bolton] took the City tactics was very surprising." The City full-back, Henry, was identified as the main perpetrator. "...first charging Lindley in the back and then kicking him on the ankle... on one occasion Henry had his legs around Hodgson's neck," according to Kestrel.

On the confrontation between Henry and Billy Watson...
"One knows Watson is not easily aroused to retaliation but there was little wonder that he should raise his fists when Henry deliberately kicked his legs from under him as he [Watson] had beaten two players in a dribble. The two players stood up threateningly; there was a scuffle between them and

a half-dozen other players. No blows were actually struck but it was pretty close. On the edge of the disputing band stood the referee, arms folded making no effort to bring the matter to an end. Then when tempers had simmered down and the players had separated, he called Watson and Henry together and persuaded them to shake hands." (Burnley News 22/4/1914)

Burnley reserves v Manchester City reserves at Turf Moor.
In the reserve match at Turf Moor against Manchester City, Burnley gave debuts to four newcomers. Thompson of Bedlington, Green of Congleton, John Heaton of Padiham and John Mitton the former Portsmouth player. Burnley beat City 2-1, Green scoring on his Clarets debut, and the other goal scored by Burnley full-back Bob Reid.

Back to Lytham

Figure 36: Burnley Players Train on the
Green on Lytham Seafront.

Figure 37: Burnley Players Outside Gaskell's Hotel in Lytham.

After the defeat at Hyde Road, the Burnley players travelled straight back to Gaskell's Temperance Hotel on Clifton Street in Lytham for a weekend of rest followed by five days of Cup Training. The Final now had even greater prominence following the announcement made in The Times and other national papers on Saturday the 18th of April;

KING TO ATTEND CUP FINAL

"The King has indicated his intention to be present at the Cup Final. His Majesty will have to leave at half-time and the Cup and medals will be presented to the winning team by Lord Derby." It was also stated that the normal Royal day-wear of dress coats was toned down to fit the occasion, "silk hats won't be worn but bowler hats and short coats." (The Times 18/4/1914)

As Prince of Wales, and like his father, The King had a keen interest in horses. He played tennis and golf but his real passions were sailing and shooting. He was an excellent shot, once bagging 1,000 birds in six hours. In later life he had taken up stamp-collecting and built one of the finest collections in England. He had visited several rugby internationals at Twickenham but had seen little association rules football.

The King's attendance would be the first time a reigning monarch had attended a Cup Final. It raised the stakes of the game massively. The King's presence would mark the Final as a history-making event. The King coming to watch the people's game. The winning team captain would receive the trophy from Royal hands for the first time. Cup history would be made, headlines written and photographs taken that would be wired around the Empire. That news must have played hard on the mind of the Burnley players as they prepared by the seaside for the Final. Goalkeeper Jerry Dawson had his own concerns, nursing his aching ribs, courtesy of Fred Howard's knee. Dawson had only just returned to the Burnley first team after recovering from a leg injury in the Semi-Final and had less than a week to prove his fitness or could miss out on a place in the Final.

Burnley's Cup Final opponents Liverpool had played their final away game of the season at Middlesbrough where they had been thumped 4-0. The club had rested several of their key players; Campbell, Lacey, Sheldon and Longworth in their preparation for the final. But not their influential captain. On the long train journey home to Merseyside, the Liverpool captain Harry Lowe had injury problems of his own. Lowe had retired for the second half of the Middlesbrough match nursing a damaged knee.

Cup Final Tickets

Burnley had sold out their allocation of seated tickets, the club announcing that no tickets for the reserved positions were now left. The club reported it had sold all its seating allocation at The Palace including 2,500 covered stand seats at five shillings and 5,000 uncovered seats at five shillings. 8,000 ground tickets had also been sold. These figures didn't include those turning up to pay on the day at the park entrance (6d to enter the park) and a further shilling to stand on the terracing. Burnley could have as many as 18 – 20,000 supporters inside the Crystal Palace watching the match. 120 saloon parties had been pre-booked with the train companies in Burnley for local businesses, firms, clubs, pubs and factory social clubs going to the Final. Burnley's four main Cup tour organisers, Abraham Altham's, Thomas Cook's, Whittakers' and The Co-operative Society, all reported strong demand.

Monday 20th April 1914

On Monday evening the King and Queen attended the opening concert of the opera season at Covent Garden. Nelly Melba, the Australian soprano made her entrance to rapturous applause for the opera, La Boheme, conducted by Mr Albert Coates. The following day, Tuesday, The King and Queen made a three-day visit to Paris where they were greeted by the French President, Raymond Poincare. The Royal Family stayed at the Elysee Palace until Friday morning, their visit helping build a new spirit of 'entente cordiale' between Britain and France. The Royal couple would return to England early on Friday evening for Royal engagements and for the King's visit to the Cup Final on the Saturday afternoon.

Liverpool Set Off For London

The Liverpool team set off for London on Monday morning and set up their training headquarters in Chingford at the Royal Forest Hotel. The team had stayed at the same hotel for the Semi-Final match against Aston Villa at White Hart Lane.

On the teams departure from Liverpool, a supporter had scribbled Liverpool 2, Burnley 1 on the side of their carriage. Harry Lowe, the Liverpool captain said, "We mean to win, but so too do Burnley. However all things being equal, I fancy we shall just pull it off." The Reds Irish forward, Bill Lacey said, "I think we ought to bring it off, but you never can tell."

There would be no 'hard' training at Chingford, the players merely resting there in view of Saturday's strenuous game.

It was too hot for training according to 'Centaur' in Wednesdays Daily Express,
"The orders for them were to take it easy…their 'work' yesterday afternoon consisted of strolling about the golf course." Centaur described the current warm spell and, "If the weather continues as at present, a society for the prevention of cruelty to professional footballers may be formed at once and an appeal made to the Football Association to allow Burnley and Liverpool to play the Cup Final at six o'clock in the morning."

Figure 38: The Liverpool Squad

Back Row L to R, Speakman, McKinley, Lacey, Nicholl
Middle Row T. Watson (manager) Fairfoul, Pursell, Campbell, Lowe, McConnel (Trainer), E.A. Bainbridge
Front Row L to R, Metcalf, Sheldon, Miller, Ferguson, Longworth

Dawson's Injury News

On Wednesday April 22nd it was stated in the Burnley Express that Dawson's injury was, "…to his cartilage and not actually to the ribs There is considerable soreness but his breathing was much better yesterday morning (Tuesday) in fact he was allowed to indulge in a little ball practice. Trainer Edwards expects him to play on Saturday but Sewell will be held in readiness. The team are enjoying golf, badminton and boating and indulging in gentle football kicking and taking brine baths."

The April Heat-Wave.

The newspapers reported that there had been no cloud over Britain for three days. At Lytham, the Burnley players enjoyed 12 hours of sunshine and it was 70 degrees in the shade, remarkable temperatures for April. In London, temperatures reached 74 degrees and it had not rained for a week.

In Other News

Mad Women Destroy £250,000

At the meeting of the State Assurance Company in Liverpool yesterday, the chairman stated that the total insurance losses attributed to the militant suffragettes during 1913 were estimated at £250,000. (Daily Express 22/4/1914) By April 1914, the suffragettes had been responsible for over a hundred acts of 'outrage' including; bombings, arson, window-breaking and the disruption of sporting events.

American Marines Land at Vera Cruz

American Marines from two US battleships, Utah and Florida, landed at the port of Vera Cruz and had seized the Custom

House. They sustained 24 casualties in the fire-fight and four marines were killed in fierce fighting. A German steamship heading for Mexico, the Ypiranga has arms and ammunition aboard that the Mexicans purchased some time ago. After a unanimous vote in the House of Representatives, the members give President Wilson the mandate he needed. He has instructed Rear-Admiral Fletcher to, "use his discretion, but prevent the guns reaching General Huerta."

The Final Tie – Mr Morrell's Invitation
(Letter to the Editor of The Burnley News)

"Sir. A great many of your readers will be coming to London on Saturday to see the match; and if any of them would like to spend a part of their morning in seeing over the Houses of Parliament I shall be very glad to have the privilege of meeting them and showing them over. I propose to be at the big gates leading into the Palace yard at 9:00 am on that day when I shall be pleased to see any of my friends and constituents who are able to be there and take them over the buildings. If you could send me a post-card to 44 Bedford Square so I know what numbers to expect."

Former Burnley Captain Drops into Poetry
In Wednesday's Burnley Express, former Burnley captain and goalkeeper James McConnell writing from Massachusetts in the USA said, "Though many miles away from Turf Moor, we have many anxious moments on Saturday afternoons awaiting the results of the football matches in England." McConnell penned the following poem;

Then up, lads and at it,
Though cold be the weather;
And if by perchance
You should happen to fall,
There are worse things in life
Than a tumble on heather,
For what is life
But a game of football.

Now up in London town, my lads
So you know what waits for you
You've been very near it once before,
Though it slipped you very true
But now your chance has come my boys
Set about it like good men
And do the work you never shirk
We have faith in you now as then.

Thursday 23rd April

Thursday was St George's Day and it had been a duller day in London and rained slightly but not much. The Daily Express forecaster predicted that Liverpool would beat Burnley in the Final, despite the Clarets beating the Reds more convincingly over the course of the season. The Liverpool team had attended the Hackney Empire in the evening. There was further news on the King's attendance at the Final. The King would attend the match and stay until the end but was scheduled to leave before the presentations, but if His Majesty's other engagements permitted, he would stay and present the trophy and medals but any speeches would be dispensed with.

Winston Churchill's driver fined for speeding

At Bow Street Police Court, Winston Churchill's chauffer was in the dock accused of speeding. The offence had taken place in St. James's Park where three park-keepers timed Churchill's car travelling over a one-furlong distance at 17 miles per hour. This contravened the speed limit of 12 mph in the park. Churchill's witness was a detective-sergeant who told the court that he was sat next to the driver of the vehicle and at no time did he go over the limit. Churchill was not present in court and the driver who had a similar motoring speeding offence from the previous month was fined 40 shillings plus costs.

Burnley Team Return From Lytham

Burnley's training regime at Lytham had included several activities, "The most stimulating day at Lytham when a sea breeze tempered the heat of a powerful sun. For the greater part of the week there has been a dead calm and much of the Burnley players time has been spent sailing. Rowing has formed a new and decidedly beneficial feature and the arms have been brought into play by liberal exercise at golf. There has been much walking and practically no ball practice." (Daily Express 24/4/1914)

The players travelled back to Burnley from Lytham on Thursday afternoon and stayed overnight at Cronkshaw's Hotel, their home training headquarters. "Tommy Boyle is quite himself again," said Sportsman, "but the Burnley team will not be named until Saturday morning"

Friday 24th April 1914

The Burnley Team Depart
Huge Scenes at Station

From early on Friday morning, crowds began gathering at Burnley Bank Top railway station to wish the team good luck and see them off to London. The scene resembled that which greeted the team after their win at Goodison Park in the Semi-Final. The streets leading up to the station were packed with hundreds of well-wishers. The Burnley party of about 40 people; players, trainers, directors, and wives, arrived at 10:00 am. When they appeared on the platform they were given a hearty reception and Jerry Dawson whom it thought would not be fit to travel, was given the warmest cheer. All the players looked fit and well including Ronnie Sewell, Bob Reid and Levi Thorpe, the three reserves. The players wives travelled in the clubs saloon carriage together and were all joyous and happy. Before the Clarets set off on the 10:16 am train, Burnley captain Tommy Boyle told the press at Bank Top Station that, "all the men were well and in the pink of condition," he said, "every man will try hard and I believe Burnley will win."

The Burnley players all very looked smart in their suits, wearing matching claret and blue ties. But only nine of the eleven first team players were present. It was known Eddie Mosscrop was being picked up at Wigan station, but where was Bert Freeman? A phone call was made to the station master at Burnley Barracks station and Freeman was found on the platform there.

The train bearing the name plate, "East Lancashire's Hope" pulled in and the Burnley party climbed onboard, the first four carriages reserved by the football club. When all were onboard, the carriage doors were slammed shut and the stationmaster raised his flag for the train driver to pull out. The Burnley players waved to the crowd from the carriage windows and the train slowly left the packed platform, to a sea of raised hats, waved handkerchiefs, cheers and hurrahs. As the train picked up speed over the viaduct, five fog detonators that had been placed on the rails, went off in a succession of loud booms that echoed across the town.

Dawson's Injury Concern

The only Burnley player over which there was any concern was goalkeeper Jerry Dawson. Dawson was still suffering from badly bruised ribs. He had some ball practice at Lytham but the Burnley Express reported on the 25th April that, "he is not sure of himself and Sewell is being prepared for an emergency."

Friday's Manchester Guardian also picked up on Dawson's injury, "It is stated that Sewell may play in place of Dawson who was injured the previous Saturday. [That information may show that the decision to replace Dawson with Sewell was not the shock news it was thought to be in some sources. Dawson had been suffering for the past month, first with a leg injury from the first Semi-Final game and then the rib injury he sustained at Manchester City. It would only have been common sense to have Sewell on standby for the Final.]

Burnley Reserves also were playing Bradford City in the Central League at Valley Parade on Saturday afternoon and Burnley's third choice goalkeeper would have been told he was needed for the match to play in Sewell's place.

Burnley Blind Enthusiast

The Manchester Guardian told the story of a Burnley supporter, a blind paper boy who had not missed a League match or Cup tie all season, "He has expressed his intention of going to London last night to 'see' the Final. So interested was he a few years ago when the 'snowstorm' match was played, he was then living at Blackburn, that he walked all the way and went on the ground as soon as the gates opened. He got wet to the skin but walked it back to Blackburn. That's enthusiasm. He's a merry chap and can always be heard behind the Bee Hole goal. (Manchester Guardian 24/4/1914)

Up West On A Friday Night

Figure 39: Charterhouse Square and Hotel, Smithfield (2014)

Figure 40: The London Palladium Programme 1914

After a lunch served on the train, the Burnley party arrived at London's Euston railway station at 4:00 pm. A fleet of taxis decorated in the club colours was waiting and drove the party to Smithfield and The Charterhouse Hotel where they stayed for three nights. The hotel was Burnley's regular base for matches in the capital. An early evening dinner was arranged at 5:00 pm where the team were joined by the former Burnley captain, Alec Leake, who was now the head coach at Crystal Palace F.C. Leake passed on his knowledge of The Palace facilities, the ground and of his experiences in the Cup. Before he left, Leake bade the Burnley team and party goodbye and said, "May I wish you from the bottom of my heart the very best of luck." (Daily Express 24/4/1914)

As usual on a Friday evening, London was bustling. As the weekend began, the streets were thronged with commuters making their way home, theatre-goers arriving and tourists taking in the sights including the newly arrived contingent from Burnley. At 6:30 pm, The King and Queen returned from their visit to Paris at Victoria Station. Before that, the Burnley party departed Charterhouse Square for the first house show at the London Palladium to see the variety performance, 'Town Topics.' The comedy show starred George Robey - 'The Prime Minister of Mirth' along with Ella Retford, whose big hit was, 'She's a Lassie from Lancashire' and Billy Williams - 'When Father Papered the Parlour.' Other classic musical-hits; 'Boiled Beef and Carrots', 'Daisy, Daisy,' Keep Right On to The End of the Road, and 'Who's your Lady Friend' were performed during the show.

Across town at the Holborn Empire, Londoners were amazed as the worlds first colour film, 'The World, The Flesh and the Devil,' was screened in Kinemacolour, while at His Majesty's Theatre in Haymarket, George Bernard Shaw's play, Pygmalion was staged for the first time. In Covent Garden at the Royal Opera House, the Australian soprano, Nelly Melba, was on her fifth performance in a week. Front row seats at the opera costing one guinea. *'Hello Ragtime'* was playing at the London Hippodrome, while all through the West End; noisy café's belted out ragtime hits like Irving Berlin's, *'Alexander's Ragtime Band.'*

Burnley Supporters Depart

The majority of the cotton mills in Burnley closed on Friday night at 6:00 pm and wouldnt re-open until Monday morning, some had even closed until Tuesday. A large proportion of the towns population would make the journey to see the Final, predominantly male supporters but there were a number of females,

"Most of the excursionists carried the Burnley colours in their headgear or button-holes whilst the women enthusiasts in many cases wore costumes in which the Burnley colours were the dominant note. Fourteen special trains left Friday night with approximately a thousand on board each train." There was no worry about the future and the crowds that departed during the night were boisterously happy. The local Co-operative Society in Burnley ran a special train with about a thousand people on board. Every seat at the Palace was sold a month ago and you couldn't get one even if you offered two guineas." (Manchester Guardian 25/4/1914)

The cost of the going to the Cup Final would have been expensive, with the cheapest train ticket costing 12 shillings for a day return, (Altham's price - GNR and other train company prices may have been slightly cheaper.) A day out would have been the equivalent to almost a weeks pay for a manual worker, but this was the Cup Final, and money was found, somehow. "To go to London was the only thing thought of, even if sideboards and pianos were sold to pay the expenses." (Manchester Guardian)

"Despite the depression in the cotton trade in consequence of which the mills are running short time, the bookings have been unusually heavy and scenes unprecedented in the history of Burnley excursions were seen at Bank Top and Manchester Road stations last night," said the Burnley News.

By the time the pubs and clubs had called last orders in Burnley, thousands of supporters started making their way to Burnley's five railway stations to catch the overnight trains. Up to 12,000 people, more than a tenth of the population left on the overnight trains and they were joined by another 4,000 who departed early the following morning. "There was lusty cheering at the stations as the trains departed and much playing of the various instruments which made excruciating music," said the Manchester Guardian. The main overnight route taken was via the GNR East-Coast line via Wakefield a journey time of six hours that would see the claret and blue army arrive at London King's Cross, St Pancras and Marylebone stations around dawn.

Advertisement

CUP FINAL REFRESHMENTS
Saloon Parties for London can be supplied with;
HAM, BEEF, TONGUE, or
PORK SANDWICHES, PORK PIES etc.
On most reasonable terms.
George Haffner and Son, Pork Butchers
16 Yorkshire Street Burnley.

---xxx---

Liverpool Supporters Depart

There were similar scenes in Liverpool. At Liverpool Lime Street and Central stations, thousands queued at midnight for the special trains. People joined at Birkenhead, Woodside,

Bootle, Huyton, Earlestown and St. Helens. More trains departed at midnight for London from Warrington, Wigan and Manchester. One of the liveliest departures was a party of Liverpool dock workers and their wives. While waiting for their 11:00 pm train at Alexander Dock station, they danced on the platform to the strains of concertinas. Thomas Cook and Son, told the press that 25 hotels had been booked for the weekend and over 30 restaurants reserved. Cook's were expecting a large number of visitors that would decide to stay in London until Monday or Tuesday.

The Burnley Cup Team

The Burnley team, a set of lads
Who always play the game
And season after season they
Keep adding to their fame.
For stamina no one can beat,
They never do give up;
That's the reason why, I think,
They'll win the English Cup.
In goal there's Jerry Dawson
Who's very hard to beat;
He does his work in splendid style,
And does it very neat.

Then there's Bamford and there's Taylor,
Two backs of great renown
Who in the tightest pressure
They can always hold their own.
In Halley, Boyle and Watson,
Three half-backs really fine;
No matter who they play against,
They're always sure to shine.
In the centre there is Freeman,
Who leads the forwards well;
About his speed and shooting
Many goalkeepers can tell.

On the left there's Hodgson and Mosscrop
Two of the very best
Who never give the opposing backs
A single minute's rest.
At inside-right there's Lindley who's very clever too;
He plays with head as well as feet
And passes very true.
The last to praise is Nesbitt
A youngster who is fast
And though he is not quite a star
He's a trier to the last.
Now the Burnley boys are going strong
I think you will agree
And why they should not win the Cup
I really cannot see.

(By G.W. Burnley Express, April 1914)

---xxx---

Final Preparations At The Crystal Palace

The Times described the final preparations that had been made at the Crystal Palace on the Friday. "The Royal Box, gay with crimson covered rails and the Royal Arms is in the Pavilion Stand between stands A and B in the middle of the west side of the ground so that the sun is behind it in the afternoon. The Royal Party is expected to number fourteen. The King will not pass through the Palace on his way to the ground. He comes as a guest of the Football Association and not the Crystal Palace Company."

The Times went on to describe the grounds, "The Crystal Palace grounds are just now beautiful with all the spring flowering shrubs and trees in flower. Just inside the Sydenham gate by which the royal party will enter is a magnolia tree in full and very abundant blossom. Thence the drive winds past the lily tank, the surface of which is covered by lily beds just now. The wide park like stretches if undulating turf are brilliantly emerald at this time of the season with an abundance of blossoms of berberry, magnolia, lilac and flowering cherries. Above the cycle track past the Eddystone Lighthouse and across the Grand Avenue with its lines of Plane trees to the Pavilion stand, The King will have an opportunity to see it at its best." (The Times 24/4/1914)

Precautions Against Suffragists

The Times also gave details of the security arrangements at The Palace. "Unusual precautions have of course, been taken to protect the Palace and the football stands against danger from suffragists. Ever since the attack on the Rokeby Venus* all the

---

(*The Rokeby Venus is a 17th century painting of a nude by Velazquez that hangs in the National Gallery. On the 10th March 1914 the painting was slashed by suffragette Mary Richardson in protest over the recent arrest of fellow suffragist Emmeline Pankhurst.)

entrances into the Palace grounds as well as the doors from the grounds into the Palace itself, have been closed at 7 o'clock each evening. It was thought best not to allow any persons in the grounds after it grew dusk. Since it was intended that the King intended to be present at the Cup Final, precautions have been increased and the structures about the football ground in particular have been under close watch by night and day."

"The Crystal Palace grounds offer an obviously tempting mark to a suffragist with a taste for outrage, filled as they are with a number of buildings of all sorts and sizes which must be necessarily be difficult to keep under surveillance. The temptation to incendiarism may be diminished by a suspicion that not a few of the buildings could be destroyed without exciting any great public grief." (The Times 25/4/1914)

The Football Association and the Crystal Palace company faced with the Royal party's security would be taking no chances. A large security presence was in evidence at the Palace on the day of the match. "A small army of men had been engaged at the Palace to prevent any suffragette disturbances," said the Burnley News. There were a large number of police surrounding the Pavilion and also stationed around the pitch.

There was another visitor to Sydenham, a regular at this time of the year. "Those who go to the Palace today may have a chance to hear the cuckoo, for the birds were calling yesterday for the first time this year on the wooded slopes of Sydenham Hill almost as if they had come on purpose to see the match. This is four days earlier than their arrival last year." (The Times 25/4/1914)

Liverpool Are Cup Favourites

The Daily Express, the Daily Mirror and now the Times all favoured Liverpool to win the Final. "In the preliminary ties,

Liverpool certainly distinguished themselves more than their opponents." That was an interesting analysis bearing in mind Liverpool's drawn game at Anfield with Barnsley, then a win over the Gillingham, a draw and a replay against West Ham and 2-1 victory over QPR. Three clubs who were not in the Football League at the time. The first time Liverpool had met a First Division side was in the Semi-Final against Cup holders Aston Villa. "Their [Liverpools] victory was a magnificent achievement," lauded The Times.

Burnley meanwhile had beaten four First Division sides along the way - then a record which The Times had clearly overlooked...

"Burnley have no such triumph to their credit in the Cup competition. They beat Sunderland, last years finalists in the replay on their own ground after a drawn game at Roker Park, but this and other victories were won by a process of 'plugging away,' helped by all the good luck that was going. In view of these circumstances, Liverpool are the favourites..." (The Times 24/4/1914)

That article would have made welcome reading for any of the Burnley party travelling to London on Friday afternoon. It would have incensed any Burnley supporters reading it and would have certainly brought a reaction from the Burnley players had they seen it. It would have given the unfancied Burnley, all the motivation to win the match they needed.

As the Burnley players returned to Charterhouse Square after their visit to The Palladium and an early night, they knew tomorrow might be their only chance. Two Burnley players knew what tomorrow would bring. Full-back Dave Taylor had tasted victory in the Cup Final three years before with Bradford City. He already had a winner's medal. In 1910, Tommy Boyle had played at The Palace in the Final, his Second

Division Barnsley team drawing 1-1 with Newcastle United. After Barnsley had led for much of the game, Boyle had seen victory snatched away from him in the final minutes following a disputed offside goal. The following week, Barnsley lost the replay 2-0 at Goodison Park. Boyle knew he might not get a third chance. It had to be tomorrow or nothing.

In Burnley, working late in the Burnley Express newspaper offices, before he caught one of the overnight trains, Sportsman had finished his copy and was searching for the right headline for Saturday's Cup Final special edition. After some deliberation, the words finally came. He used a form of Lord Nelson's rallying call to his forces on the eve of the Battle of Trafalgar in 1805. Four words that said everything;

BURNLEY EXPECTS – THE CUP

---xxx---

CHAPTER EIGHT

Send Them Victorious

And in the year 1198, the English king met his great enemy at Gisors,
where he was victorious. And at the height of battle, The Lionheart
roared his mighty battle cry, "God and My Right," and cast
the French king into the river. And from thenceforth
the words became his Royal Arms.

– Anon.

The Royalites

Turf Moor, Burnley, 13th October 1886

On Wednesday the 13th of October 1886, Burnley received a Royal visitor when Prince Albert Victor arrived to officially open the newly constructed hospital. After naming the hospital in honour of his grandmother, Her Majesty The Queen Victoria, the Prince travelled to Turf Moor where he sat and watched a fund-raising football match in the afternoon between Burnley and Bolton Wanderers. Burnley played in pale blue and white vertical stripes and white knickers, while Wanderers played in red, white and blue vertical stripes. There was a good attendance for a midweek afternoon match as most of the town were normally working. The funds raised by the charity football match were all for the local hospital and some local dignitaries had paid up to a guinea to sit close to the Prince.

"After opening the Victoria Hospital, the Prince re-entered the carriage and was driven through the streets, his passage through which was marked with the most gratifying demonstrations of loyalty. From the hospital to Turf Moor the cheering was enthusiastic and continuous, culminating in a deafening outburst as he stepped on to the grandstand in sight of ten thousand persons assembled to witness the match between Burnley and Bolton Wanderers first teams. As may be assumed, great preparations had been made for the comfort of the Royal party. The front of the grand stand had been painted and permission had been given to use the Royal Arms. The whole scene was strikingly effective and, when play was in full swing, it was so exceedingly animating that His Royal Highness and party, who were evidently much interested in the game, frequently cheered the players whenever any particularly clever feat was performed. It had originally been intended that the prince should leave after witnessing the play for about

20 minutes but so interested were the party that they remained until half-time, being on the field exactly 50 minutes.

Both teams appeared in new jerseys and the home team had new caps to match their blue and white jerseys. As they entered the enclosure the players who were loudly cheered, gave His Royal Highness a pleasing salute. Half-time arrived with the score at 3-1 in favour of the Wanderers and the Royal party left amid a gratifying outburst of enthusiasm. In the second half, Sugg and McFetridge exchanged positions with the best effect. Burnley again showed their superiority in passing but they were ineffectual in front of goal and they retired with the declared result 4-3 against them. Over 9,000 paid for admission and there are 700 members. The net receipts were £209 and after all expenses (which are expected to be £100) have been paid, the balance will be handed over to the Hospital fund." (Burnley Express 16 October 1886)

Shortly after that charity match, Burnley were nick-named, 'The Royalites,' and for a number of seasons after The Prince's visit, the Burnley players shirts bore the Royal Arms. But for some reason later, the Arms disappeared from Burnley's shirts shortly after the 1894-95 season.

But they were about to re-appear again…

Cup Final Day

Early Morning, Saturday 25th April 1914

As the Burnley players slept on in Charterhouse Square and their opponents in Chingford, a new day was breaking over London. From just before 6:00 am, the first of the chartered trains carrying thousands of football supporters from Burnley, Liverpool and towns across the north began arriving at Kings Cross, St. Pancras, Marylebone and Euston railway stations. As the trains pulled in to the platforms one after another, their bleary-eyed passengers, sporting their team's favours, formed a human mass of noise and colour that spilled out of the stations and into Euston Road.

Too excited to sleep, most of them had stayed awake during the long overnight journey south. For most of the travellers, it would be their first visit to the capital and the furthest they had ever travelled from home. Hungry, they emerged from the railway stations into a different world. A world without chimneys, canals, mills and factories. The giant metropolis. Wide tree-lined roads, noisy traffic, huge seven storey buildings, hotels, churches, monuments and statues, department stores, tree-lined squares. People speaking in different accents. People of different colours, from all over the Empire. Strange eating establishments pouring out even stranger smells.

At 6:00 am it was light and London was already awake. Red-liveried London omnibuses drove up and down Euston Road. In their wake, black taxicabs, lorries, trucks and cars, their horns warning the newly arrived visitors not to step into the busy road. Visitors on the pre-booked saloon parties, were met outside the railway stations by a fleet of omnibus's that would take them on early-morning guided tours of the City, taking in the major landmarks, the Tower Of London, St. Paul's Cathedral and Westminster Abbey. Around the same time as the overnight travellers arrived in London, the second wave of day-trippers were preparing to set off that would see them arrive in the capital for lunch-time, in ample time to reach Sydenham for the match kicking-off at 3:30 pm.

Most of the cafes in and around the railway stations quickly filled (from as early as 2:00 am café's were selling bacon and eggs according to the Burnley Express) so the masses fanned out and, "took possession of The Strand, Piccadilly, Holborn and Regent Street." Some visitors headed for London's main tourist spots. Trafalgar Square, Downing Street and the Houses of Parliament. A number of visitors headed for the station escalators to experience the underground railway. Some hailed taxis or jumped on passing omnibuses, but most of the visitors set off on foot. The early morning sunshine warmed the travellers. With bright blue cloudless skies, it would be another glorious day in the capital. In Southampton Row, Tavistock and Russell Squares had daffodils and tulips out in full bloom, their huge oak and yew trees in full leaf. It was going to be a warm day and most travellers had come unprepared for the heat, dressed in heavy overcoats over their Sunday best suits.

There was a rush on the newspaper stands to pick up the latest London morning editions. The Times informing the visitors, "Those arriving by train could have free entrance (if they presented their tickets) to Madame Tussauds with "new attractions and tableaux plus cinematograph performances." Regent's Park Zoological Gardens were advertising, "The World's Greatest Collection of Exotic Animals from across the Empire," which opened its gates at 9:00 am. Entrance was one shilling for adults and sixpence for children. Westminster Abbey opened at 7:00 am and provision was made for visitors to be conducted around the Royal Chapel. (The Times 25/4/1914)

**Figure 42: London Underground Poster Promoting
Football (London Transport Museum)**

**Figure 43: Piccadilly Circus in 1914 (London
Transport Museum)**

On the roads, London's public transport had changed in recent years. Gone were the horse-drawn vehicles of a few years ago, replaced by the faster, cleaner, petrol-driven motorised omnibus that could carry up to 35 passengers.

Saturday the 25th of April was Princess Mary's 17th birthday. The event was celebrated at Buckingham Palace by a 'young people's party.' The King and Queen would be with their daughter in the morning before their separate engagements in the afternoon.

From 9:00 am, Burnley's Member of Parliament, Phillip Morrell and his wife Lady Ottoline took up to 400 Burnley constituents around the Houses of Parliament. They were assisted by Mr F.E. Harvey the MP for Leeds and Sir Frederick Cawley the MP for Prestwich. One Burnley resident, Mr. J. Beaumont had written a reply to Philip Morrell stating,

"Dear Mr Morrell, I shall be very pleased to accept your invitation for a visit through the Houses of Parliament. I have reached the age of 72 years and I am coming to London for the first time bringing my five sons with me. Hoping we shall have a good time and win the Cup."

It would be a long day for the Morrell's, who would be hosting a post match dinner for the Burnley team and invited guests at the Connaught Rooms on Queen Charlotte Street later that evening.

**Figure 44: Lady Ottoline Morrell Outside
the Houses of Parliament.**

In Charterhouse Square at 9:30 am shortly after breakfast, the Burnley team did some light exercise in the square across from the hotel. At 11:00 am. John Haworth gathered them all together to discuss the day's programme and the team. Ronnie Sewell would play, Jerry Dawson had told Haworth he was not fit and would not want to let the team down. It was a noble move by Dawson as he wouldn't receive a medal, regardless of Burnley winning. Across London in Chingford, Tom Watson, the Liverpool manager, spent the morning giving a final fitness test to his captain, Harry Lowe. Lowe didn't make it. He too would miss out on a Cup medal. Ephraim Longworth would take Lowe's place in defence and Bob Ferguson would captain Liverpool for the match. Losing their influential captain at such a late stage was a bitter blow for Liverpool probably more so than Dawson's loss, as Sewell had played in the Semi-Final Replay and also in the League.

Their team briefings and selection matters over, John Haworth and Tom Watson left their team hotels and travelled to Mansion House, where they met up for a lunch engagement with Sir Thomas Bowater, the Lord Mayor of London. The Burnley players had an early lunch themselves before departing from Charterhouse Square at 1:30 pm in a fleet of taxis, closely followed by the Burnley directors, players' wives and fiancées.

At Football Association Headquarters in Russell Square, Cup final referee, Herbert Bamlett and his linesmen Mr Talks and Mr Rogers, were receiving their last-minute briefing from officials and checking their equipment. Bamlett had a new silver whistle for the final, presented to him by the boys from his old school in Gateshead. At 32, Bamlett would be the youngest ever Cup final referee. The three men would travel down to Sydenham together at 12:30 to check the pitch and facilities. There would be no chance of bad weather calling the game off today. The hot sun would have a more draining effect on the players and officials than four inches of snow.

Getting To The Crystal Palace

Burnley and Liverpool supporters had two possible rail routes to get to The Palace which was served by three railway stations, two of which were attached to the 'great glass house.' There was another station at Penge, a five minute walk away from the Park.

The Brighton Line electric train service from London Bridge and Victoria ferried passengers to the low-level station which was straight outside the football stadium. The return fare to Sydenham was one shilling. The South Eastern Railway catered for passengers from the City stations, Holborn, Ludgate Hill, Elephant and Castle and Brixton and also from Victoria. These trains ran to the Palace high-level station where passengers could get off the train and walk through The Palace hall, past the centre-transept, down the grand staircase and out to the grounds by bearing to the right.

The late arriving supporters from Burnley, landing in London at noon had two possible Underground routes to choose from. The City and South London Underground Line (Northern Line) to London Bridge, for the direct train or they could take a London omnibus service.

Two regular bus services ran to The Palace. The Number 49A service travelled to The Palace from Shepherds Bush. The Number 3 bus ran from Camden Town went via Oxford Circus, Regent Street, Charing Cross, Westminster, Kennington, Brixton and Dulwich. The journey time was 72 minutes, the cost 5d. An additional 250 motor buses had been provided by the London General Omnibus Company for the Final and special arrangements for parking for charabancs and buses had been made at the Park.

The King's Route to Sydenham

The King was scheduled to leave Buckingham palace at 2:55 pm in an eight car motorcade that would take in an eight-mile route via; Buckingham Palace Road, Eccleston Bridge, Belgrave Road, Bessborough Street, Vauxhall Bridge South, Lambeth Road, Stockwell Road, Brixton Road, Effra Road, Water Lane, Dulwich Road, Norwood Road, Croxted Road, Dulwich Wood Park, Palace Parade and Crystal Palace Park Road arriving at 3:20pm. The Royal route was decorated with flags and bunting with thousands of people standing on the pavement and waving as the King passed by.

The King had visited the Crystal Palace to see a football match before. As patron of the Football Association, he attended the International match between England and Scotland April 1909 when he was Prince of Wales. He had attended rugby internationals at Twickenham and most recently he had attended the Army Cup final at Aldershot with Queen Mary present.

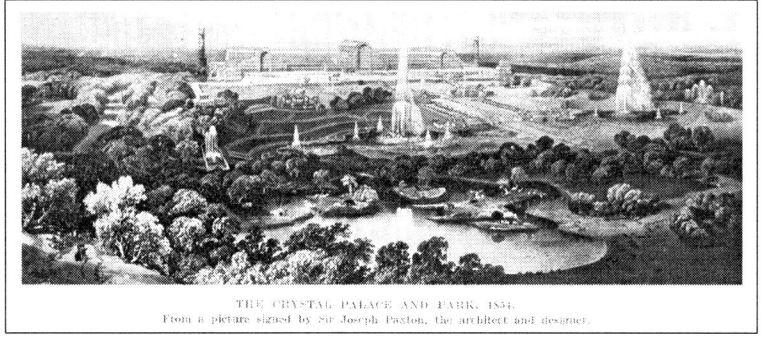

THE CRYSTAL PALACE AND PARK, 1854.
From a picture signed by Sir Joseph Paxton, the architect and designer.

Figure 45: The Crystal Palace

The Crystal Palace

The Crystal Palace was originally built in Hyde Park for housing the Great Exhibition of 1851. The huge cast iron, wood and glass structure was built in pre-fabricated sections that were bolted together like a giant construction kit. When the Great Exhibition ended, the structure was simply dismantled and moved to Penge Common in Sydenham where the building was extended with extra sections and re-erected. The re-built Palace was opened by Queen Victoria in 1854. The Palace was a vast building. At over a third of a mile long and 128 feet high, inside the Palace were a number of themed areas or 'courts.' In addition to the various touring exhibitions that took place took place there, the permanent exhibits included, Egyptian, Greek, Roman, Byzantine, Medieval, French, German courts that each contained cultural exhibits and artefacts from the Empire and around the world. There was an industrial court showing off Britain's industrial and military prowess, where steam locomotives, petrol engines, cotton-looms, printing presses, pumps and even washing machines were on display. There was an additional space for a full-size orchestra for concerts, operas and music festivals that could seat 4,000 people. In the evening of the Cup Final, for an extra sixpence, spectators could watch an exhibition boxing match featuring the heavy-weight champion, Bombardier Billy Wells.

The original Palace grounds were enclosed inside a high perimeter wall occupying 200 acres of land. The park grounds were designed and landscaped by Joseph Paxton into several areas. There were Italian gardens with huge water features. To provide enough water pressure for the fountains, Isambard Kingdom Brunel was brought in to design the giant water towers seen at each end of the Palace building. Other areas in the park contained a giant maze and an English garden. The Crystal Palace and the park were designed as an attraction for the whole family. In the lower lake area, Benjamin Hawkins produced 33 life-sized concrete models of then discovered dinosaurs, several of which are still in the park.

Following The Palace's re-opening in 1854, the following decades saw the popularity of the Crystal Palace's fall and with newer attractions in central London drawing the crowds, something fresh was needed to bring the people back.

Figure 46: Crystal Palace Entrance.

**Figure 47: The Crystal Palace Dinosaurs
in the Lower Lake**

Football Comes To The Palace

In the twenty years prior to 1893, the Cup Final had been held at London's main sporting venue, the Kennington Oval, the home of Surrey County Cricket club. In addition to test and county cricket, The Oval had also played host to football and rugby internationals. In 1892, at the suggestion of J. J. Bentley the Football League President, the FA agreed to trial the next Cup Final outside of London for the first time and chose the Manchester Athletic Ground in Fallowfield as the venue. In the 1893 Cup Final in Manchester, Everton met Wolverhampton Wanderers. Wolves ran out winners 1-0, but there was controversy over the conditions for spectators inside the Fallowfield stadium. The official attendance was given as 45,000 but it was later estimated to have been closer to 60,000. A number of pitch incursions took place before and during the match after which Everton complained to the FA. The Final was never held there again and a new location for the Cup Final was sought, preferably back in London. The 1894 Final was held at Goodison Park which drew a crowd of only 37,000, reducing the FA's income further, leaving the governing body with some tough decisions to make.

40 years after the Crystal Palace had opened, in 1894 the Crystal Palace Company received a proposal to use the park for important sporting events. Cricket and football matches had already been played in the open spaces of the Palace Park, so why not redevelop the park for sport and bid to host major sporting events like the Cup Final?

The Crystal Palace Company identified an area in the centre of the park that currently occupied the two huge water fountains that could be adapted for football and other sports. The north fountain area was re-developed with a running track for athletics and a velodrome for cycling, while the southern fountain area was turned into a football and polo pitch. The fountains were removed and the land drained, levelled and turfed over. Grass banked terracing was landscaped around the pitch, forming a shallow oval-shaped bowl. Two stands and a central pavilion were erected to the Crystal Palace side of the football arena. After a thorough assessment of the stadium and the amenities at The Palace, the FA were satisfied and awarded the Crystal Palace Company a contract to host the 1895 Cup Final. After a successful first year at Sydenham where attendances had risen on the previous years Final, The Crystal Palace became the new home of the FA Cup Final.

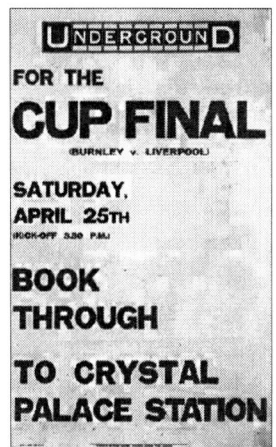

Figure 48: The London Underground
Poster for the 1914 Cup Final

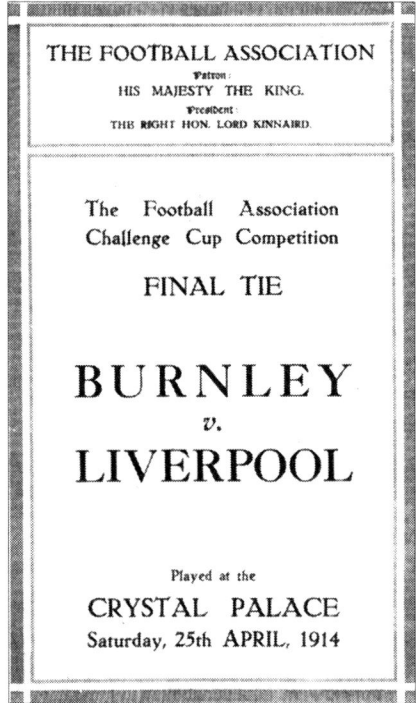

Figure 49: The Official Cup Final Programme.

Cup Final Food

Inside the Crystal Palace building were a number of eating facilities, restaurants and tea rooms; "Dinners from one shilling to five shillings per head, cold collations, and luncheons are provided in great variety and the *bon vivant* may enjoy his entremets and pates, while the third-class excursionist is content with 'bread and cheese and a pint of porter." (Crutchley's London Guide 1865)

The park grounds opened from 11:00 am, and from then on a steady stream of people began to arrive bringing with them their picnics and packed lunches that they could enjoy on the grassy slopes of the park. Several huge catering marquees had been erected for the thousands that would come. The contract awarded to feed the thousands of visitors went to Messrs. J. Lyons and Co. Ltd, The tea-house chain. The Times listed their food order as; 75 rumps of beef, 25 sirloins of beef, 35 ribs of beef, 60 loins of mutton, 100 shins of mutton, 250 fowls, 150 hams, 1 ton and a half of pressed beef, 400 heads of lettuce, 1 ton of potatoes, 12,000 sandwiches, 2,500 veal and ham pies, 25,000 pats of butter, 30,000 rolls and butter, 75,000 slices of bread and butter, 25,000 buns and scones, 48,000 slices of cake, 6,000 pastries, 1500 gallons of milk, 1500 dozen bottles of minerals, 1000 dozen bottles of beer, 2000 gallons of beer. (The Times 24/4/1914)

The Lucky Dressing Room

The Burnley players arrived at The Palace at around 2:00 pm. According to the Burnley Express, Alec Leake had told the team at dinner on the Friday evening to 'try and get there early to pick the visitors dressing room.' They did just that, arriving at the ground before the Liverpool team. Leake had said that the winning team at The Palace had always had the visitors' dressing room. Beneath the pavilion as the dressing room clock ticked toward 3:30, the players went through their mental preparations for the game. Ernie Edwards and Charlie Bates, the Burnley backroom staff, had already set out the players' kit. Claret stockings with a single light-blue band. Long white knickers with a draw-string pull. Claret and light-blue shirts with long sleeves hanging on the wall hooks. Claret and blue shirts that now bore the Royal Arms. Embroidered in silver thread and sewn onto a patch of claret fabric on the left side of the chest, positioned over the heart. The symbolic lion facing the unicorn. The motto beneath, Dieu Et Mon Droit - *God and My Right.* Four words handed down nine centuries. The war cry of the Lionheart. Four words carried into battle by English monarchs ever since. Four words now worn by eleven men.

Figure 50: Eddie Mosscrop's shirt with the Royal Arms

Meanwhile At Turf Moor

Back at Turf Moor that 3:00 that same afternoon, the annual Burnley and District Sunday School Charity Shield Final was taking place between two local sides, Walk Mill and Burnley Lads Club. Admission 3d. There was a good attendance of around 2,500. Many who had come down for the match that afternoon were those who couldn't afford the cost of going to London and just wanted to be at the ground to pick up the news on progress in the Final. The secretary's office had a telephone, and the line would be red-hot all afternoon as calls were made to find out the latest score from Sydenham.

In Bradford at Valley Parade

Over in Bradford, Burnley Reserves were in action playing their final Central League fixture of the season at Valley Parade. The Burnley team of Walker, Jones, Gunton, Shaw, Hampson, Brown, Lorrimer, Mitton, Earnshaw, Tranter and Husband must also have had their minds elsewhere. At half time the Reserves were 5-1 down and by the final whistle they had lost 8-1, Burnley's consolation goal scored by the youngster, Alf Lorrimer.

The Times printed a list of the Royal party and guests sitting in the Pavilion.

The FA Cup Final Official Guest List - Peers and Patrons

Figure 51: His Royal Highness King George V.

The official guest list was given in The Times as;

His Majesty, The King, George V, Royal Duchy of Lancaster,
Lord Kinnaird
Lady Carnarvon
Lord Derby
The Earl of Portsmouth
Earl Howe
Lord Desborough
Lord Faber
Lord Porchester
The Lord Mayor of London
The Honourable Arthur Stanley
The Honourable F G Curzon
Sir Charles and Lady Wakefield
Sir Claude MacDonald GCMG
Sir David Burnett

Others

(The Times included a separate list of 'Others' in addition to the Royal Party.)

Sir Harry Hornby MP (Conservative member for Blackburn)
Sir George Pragnell
Lieutenant Colonel Humphrey, Sheriff of London
The Mayor and Sheriff of Chester
The Mayor of Burnley James Sellars-Kay
Mr W Hayes Fisher MP (Conservative member for Fulham)
Mr F E Smith KC MP (Conservative member for Liverpool Walton)
Colonel R G Chaloner MP (Conservative member for Liverpool Abercromby)
Mr Samuel Roberts MP (Conservative member for Sheffield Eccleshall)
Mr G Cave KC MP (Conservative member for Kingston)

Mr Henry Pike Pease MP (Liberal Unionist member for Darlington)
Mr F W Goldstone MP (Labour member for Sunderland)
Sir J H Yoxhall MP (Liberal member for Nottingham)
Mr Philip Morrell MP (Liberal member for Burnley)
Sir J H Roberts MP (Liberal member of Denbeighshire West)
Mr Samuel Hill-Wood MP (Conservative member for High Peak and then chairman of Glossop North End FC)
Mr F. W. Wall Secretary of the Football Association

Outside the Crystal Palace in Anerley Hill, Church Road and Westwood Hill, scores of street vendors were selling all manner of souvenirs of the Cup Final. There were football-related mementos, miniature FA Cups, squeaking dolls, paper trumpets, rattles, claret and blue and red and white rosettes, coloured headgear and official match programmes. Supporters arriving at the Palace by the various routes found they had to pay first to get into the park despite many of them already holding a ticket.

"On arriving at the Palace, many spectators were astonished to find they had to pay a shilling to enter the Palace Building in addition to the cost of watching the match!" (Burnley Express 29/4/1914)

Pre-Match Entertainment

From 1.30 pm the pre-match entertainment had been provided by three military bands, The Band of the Irish Guards, The Liverpool Regiment and the Drum and Fife Band.

By 3:00 pm, most of the stand seats had filled and the stadium was filling up. In the crowd was Thomas Holt Freeman, Bert Freeman's father, who had travelled 13,000 miles from Australia by fast steamship to see his son play in the final. As kick-off approached, it was a warm, sunny, summer-like afternoon. The players would soon feel the heat in their long-sleeved cotton jerseys. The sunshine of the previous week had baked the pitch hard. It was as dry as a bone, the dust kicking up as the military bands marched across the pitch. "The pitch was as hard as concrete. It was baked and cracked. There were cracks in it so wide you could get your fingers in...," said Brunbank in the Burnley Express.

Sportsman in the Burnley Express gave his summary of the stadium, "I don't think the ground is the best in the country on which to play a Final, except perhaps for its holding capacity, for the going at any rate at this time of year, was anything but conducive to the best football. The weather was summer-like and the surroundings of the Palace were in their richest garb. I never saw the foliage of the forest trees and the blossoms of the fruit trees to such perfection as on Saturday. The weather was summer-like and quite unsuitable for such a struggle as that in which Burnley and Liverpool were engaged. And the ground was too hard, which was combined with the wind and the lively ball to spoil the game from a football point of view.... two or three day's rain would have made it better!"

High in the trees that lined the south side of the arena, opposite the pavilion, several supporters had climbed up in the branches to get a better view. But it wasn't the safest of places to watch the game according to Ivan Heald of the Daily Express, "I went to the Cup Final but I'm sorry I cannot tell you much about the game other than Nicoll's shot in the first half. It was at that point that the Burnley spectator who sat on the bough above me kicked me off the tree in his excitement. He was no end of a sportsman though and offered to exchange boughs with me at half-time." (Daily Express 27/4/1914)

His Majesty Arrives

At 3:15 pm, five minutes before the King's arrival, the Royal Standard was unfurled and run up the flagpole on top of the Pavilion to great cheers around the stadium. Five minutes later and right on time, the Royal motorcade arrived. The King emerged from his car wearing a grey suit and in his buttonhole he wore a red rose to signify the all Lancashire Final. The King was met at the Pavilion entrance by the two leading Football Association executives, Lord Kinnaird and Lord Derby, followed by the FA Secretary F. W. Wall and other football and civil dignitaries and the three match officials.

The King was ushered up to the front of the Pavilion where he stood to the admiration of the crowd as the combined bands struck up the national anthem. Lord Derby sat on his right and Lord Kinnaird on his left. According to Sportsman, "The National Anthem was never more heartily sung by an assemblage of Britishers."

Figure 52: The King in the Pavilion

Prior to the kick-off both teams with the referee and officials in the middle, lined up in front of the pavilion and cheered His Majesty. The team captains, Tommy Boyle and Bob Ferguson were called back from the line to be presented to the King by Mr F. W. Wall, the Secretary of the Football Association. After the national anthem was sung, Tommy Boyle and Bob Ferguson then sportingly raised 'Three Cheers for the King.' British Pathe film footage of the Final shows the players and officials lined up in front of the pavilion. As the two teams turn to take to the field, all but one player lifts the perimeter rope and ran onto the field. Burnley's Billy Nesbitt wanted to be different. Nesbitt attempted to jump straight over the rope, but the rope caught in his boot studs and he fell over.

THE TEAMS

BURNLEY

Ronald Walter Sewell: Goalkeeper. Born Middlesbrough. Age 24. 5 feet 10 inches, 12st 6 lb. Previous clubs, Wingate Albion, Gainsborough Trinity. Joined Burnley in a three-player deal in February 1913.

Thomas Bamford: Right-Back. Born Horwich. Age 26. 5 feet 9 inches, 12st 2lb.
Previous clubs, Darwen. Joined Burnley during the 1909-10 season.

David Taylor: Left-Back. Born Bannockburn, Scotland. Age 27. 5 feet 10 inches, 12st 10 lb. Previous clubs, Glasgow Rangers, Motherwell, Bradford City. Joined Burnley in a £1000 transfer from Bradford City in 1911.

George Halley: Right Half-Back. Born Cronberry, Scotland. Age 26. 5 feet 9 inches 10st 10lb. Previous clubs, Kilmarnock, Bradford Park Avenue. Joined Burnley in £1,200 transfer from Bradford Park Avenue in 1913.

Thomas William Boyle: Team Captain and Centre-Half. Born Hoyland. Age 27. 5 feet 7 inches, 11st 3 lb. Previous clubs, Barnsley. Joined Burnley in a £1,250 transfer from Barnsley in September 1911.

William Watson: Left Half-Back. Born Southport. Age 25. 5 feet 8 inches, 11st 13 lb

Previous clubs, Southport Central. Joined Burnley from Southport Central in 1909.

William Nesbitt: Outside-Right. Born Portsmouth, Lancs. Age 22. 5 feet 7 inches, 10st 12 lb. Previous clubs, Portsmouth Rovers. Joined Burnley as an amateur, in 1911.

Richard Lindley: Inside-Right. Born Bolton, Age 28. 5 feet 7 inches 10st 8 lb
Previous clubs, Oswaldtwistle Rovers. Joined Burnley in 1908-09.

Bertram Clewley Freeman: Centre-Forward. Born Handsworth, Age 28. 5 feet 9 inches, 13stone. Previous clubs, Aston Villa, Arsenal, Everton. Joined Burnley in 1911.

Edward Hodgson: Inside-Left. Born Chorley, Age 28. 5 feet 5 inches, 10st 7 lb.
Previous clubs, Chorley. Joined Burnley in 1911.

Edwin Mosscrop: Outside-Left. Born Sheffield, Age 22. 5 feet 7 inches, 9st 8 lb.
Former club Southport Central. A full-time schoolteacher. Joined Burnley in 1912.

Burnley Reserve Players:
(Travelled but did not play.)
Bob Reid (Full-Back), Levi Thorpe (Half-Back)
Jerry Dawson (Goalkeeper) travelled with the team but was injured.

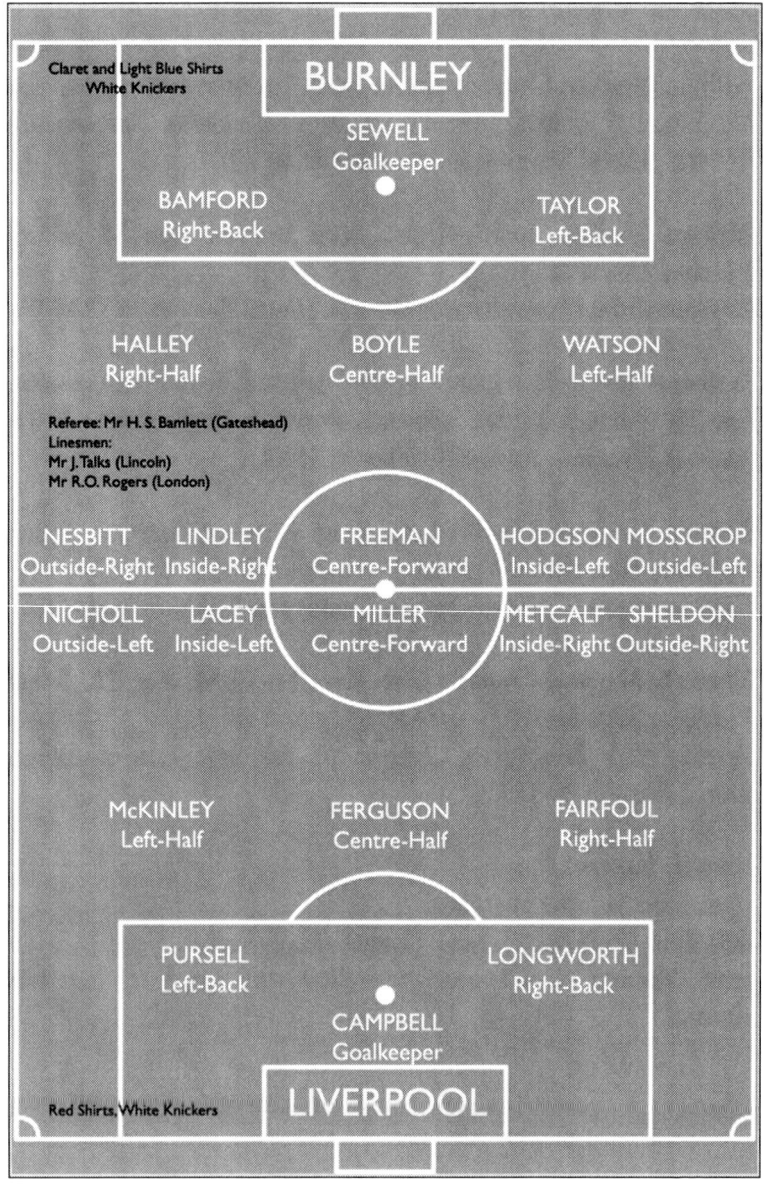

Figure 53: The Teams

LIVERPOOL

Kenneth Campbell: Goalkeeper. Born Glasgow. Age 22. 5 feet 11 inches, 11 st. 9lb. Previous clubs, Clyde Vale, Rutherglen Glencairn, Cambuslang Rangers. Joined Liverpool in May 1911.

Ephraim Longworth: Right-Back. Born Halliwell near Bolton. Age 26. 5 feet 8 inches, 11 st. Previous clubs, Halliwell Rovers, Hyde Street St. Georges and Bolton Wanderers. Joined Liverpool in 1910.

Robert Purcell: Left-Back Born Campbelltown, Ayrshire. 5 feet 11 inches, 11 st. 12lb. Joined Liverpool in 1911.

Thomas Fairfoul: Right Half-Back Born West Calder, Scotland. Age 32. 5 feet 9 inches, 11st. 10lb. Previous clubs, Doon Athletic, Kilmarnock, Third Lanark. Joined Liverpool in 1913.

Robert Ferguson: Captain. Centre Half Born Cleland, Lanarkshire. Age 27. 5 feet 11 inches, 11st. 6lb. Previous clubs, Third Lanark. Joined Liverpool in 1912.
Stand in captain for the Cup Final in place of Harry Lowe.

Donald McKinley: Left Half-Back Born Glasgow. Age 23. Previous clubs, Newton Swifts. Joined Liverpool in 1910.

John Sheldon: Outside Right Born Clay Cross, Derbyshire. Age 24. 5 feet 7 inches, 10st 11lb. Previous clubs, Nuneaton Borough, Manchester United. Joined Liverpool in November 1912.

Arthur Metcalf: Inside Right Born Sunderland. 5 feet 7 inches, 10st 11lb. Previous clubs, Durham Schoolboys, North Shields Athletic, Newcastle United. Joined Liverpool in 1912.

Thomas Miller: Centre-Forward Born Motherwell 5 feet 9 inches 11st 5lb. Previous clubs, Larkhill Hearts, Glenview, Lanark United, Hamilton Academicals.
Joined Liverpool in February 1912.

William Lacey: Inside Left Born Enniscorthy, Wexford, Ireland. Age 25. Previous clubs, Shelbourne, Everton. Joined Liverpool in 1912.

James Nicholl: Outside Left Born Port Glasgow. 5 feet 8 inches, 11st 2 lb. Previous clubs Cambuslang Rangers, Airdrie, Middlesbrough. Joined Liverpool in January 1914.

Liverpool Reserve Players
(Travelled but did not play)
S. Speakman (Right-Back), E. Peake (Centre-Half) T. Gracie (Inside-Left), J. Dawson (Outside-Left) Henry C. Lowe (Captain injured and did not play. Travelled with party)

The Form Guide

Going into the Cup Final, Liverpool had lost four consecutive League matches. They were 17th in the League with 33 points from 37 games. Preston on 29 points had already been relegated along with Derby County on 26 points. Liverpool had a goal difference of minus 17.

Burnley's form over the season was better. Over their last four games they had won two and lost two. Burnley were 12th in the table on 35 points from 37 games and had a goal difference of plus 8.

Goals Scored in the 1913-14 FA Cup
Liverpool (14), Lacey 5, Miller 4, Nicholl 2, Sheldon 1, Metcalf 1, Ferguson 1.
Burnley (12), Hodgson 5, Lindley 3, Freeman 2, Halley 1, Boyle 1.

Once the formalities and preliminaries had been dispensed with it was down to business. The biggest game of the 1913-14 football calendar.

Burnley v Liverpool, The FA Cup Final, The Crystal Palace, Saturday 25 April 1914. Kick-Off 3:30 pm.

The teams lined up:
Burnley: Ronnie Sewell, Tom Bamford, Dave Taylor, George Halley, Tommy Boyle, (c) Billy Watson, Billy Nesbitt, Dick Lindley, Bert Freeman, Teddy Hodgson, Eddie Mosscrop.
Liverpool: Ken Campbell, Ephraim Longworth, Bob Purcell, Thomas Fairfoul, Donald McKinlay, Bob Ferguson, John Sheldon, Arthur Metcalf, Tom Miller, William Lacey, James Nicholl.
Referee: H.S. Bamlett (Gateshead) Linesmen: Mr J. Talks (Lincoln), Mr R.O. Rogers (London)

Match referee Bamlett brought the two captains together in the middle. Boyle won the toss and decided to play with the breeze at Burnley's backs. The bright afternoon sun cast long shadows across the ground as Herbert Bamlett blew his new silver whistle and Burnley's Bert Freeman kicked off in the 1914 Cup Final. The Clarets started well, Sportsman saying that they had the better of the approach play, but "the play lacked the fire one would expect to see in a game of such vital importance and the prevailing feeling was that the players at the start were troubled with nerves." Though Burnley showed the neater football, Liverpool were quite as dangerous. The players found it difficult to get hold of the ball with the rock-hard pitch. With ten minutes gone, Dave Taylor slipped on the hard ground, his studs making no impression and Jimmy Nicholl struck the ball hitting Taylor full in the face. "It appeared to stun Taylor but the probability is it saved the Burnley goal."

Ronnie Sewell settled into his role and foiled an attack by Tom Miller by coming off his line. Had he stayed there, "he might well have been beaten and he disconcerted the on-coming forward who shot just outside the post," said Sportsman.

Figure 54: The Final Gets Underway

Figure 55: Action During the Match

While Ronnie Sewell was tested a few occasions, Ken Campbell in the Liverpool goal, had more work to do and a shot from Dick Lindley was saved at the expense of a corner. Burnley did the greater part of the pressing but the best chance fell to Liverpool's Arthur Metcalf that the Burnley half-backs cleared. Every now and then Burnley got their two wingers moving. Eddie Mosscrop's first centre came across but when it landed it bounced too high on the hard ground for the forwards to get a hold of. Bamlett's whistle was heard to often as the ball went into touch for numerous throw-ins and several off-sides. "The result was that the exhibition was comparatively poor during the initial stage, but even allowing for the heat, play did not descend to the level of the semi-final at Old Trafford. On the whole, the play of the first stage was even," said Sportsman as Herbert Bamlett blew his whistle to bring the goalless first half to a conclusion.

With the bright sun, the players were glad to leave the field for a well-earned ten minute rest and refreshment. During the interval, the crowd were entertained once more with the regimental bands marching up and down the pitch to the strains of, *"Here's to the maiden of the bashful fifteen."* His Majesty had enjoyed the atmosphere and though his schedule had planned for him to leave early, he stayed for the whole of the second half to see the match to its conclusion.

The players came out for the second half and for the first ten minutes the play continued much like the last ten minutes of the first half. Both sides had attacks only for the defences to block the forward play. But after the players had settled down, the game improved. Sewell was the first keeper' to be tested and then Dick Lindley won Burnley's first corner of the second half at the Liverpool end. Sewell then made two good saves, with both Taylor and Bamford busy. Fourteen minutes into the second half, Burnley got a break. Sportsman picks up the story, "there was no doubt in the minds of Burnleyites as to the outcome of the fray, though in fairness it should be said that Liverpool played up well after the fatal blow as the sequel showed it to be, inflicted by Freeman. From a throw-in on the right, Nesbitt sent across to Hodgson who cleverly headed the ball to Freeman, who in a twinkling, first time shot without any pulse-beating preliminaries shot the ball into the far corner of the net. Campbell had not the ghost of a chance. For a spell nobody knew exactly what had happened, but there were a few Burnleyites behind the goal and they first gave the welcome news to the onlookers at a distance for they, like the Liverpool defenders were completely bewildered by the rapidity with which the feat was performed. It was a fine goal."

Figure 56: Freeman Scores!

The Express's other reporter Brunbank reported the goal slightly different, "The goal which settled it was a masterpiece. So far as shooting went, up to that point nobody felt that a goal would ever be scored if the teams played all afternoon and night. But it was Freeman's unexpected that happened. He has a knack of doing just what nobody thinks possible. Hodgson who all through the game had trapped the ball better than any man on the field leaped high in the air and had headed the ball over the half-back and before anybody realised what had happened, Freeman darted in like a flash of lightning and taking the ball before it touched the ground hooked it with his instep into the left-hand corner of the net half-way up the net upright with Campbell and his two backs helplessly looking on." (Brunbank, Burnley Express 29/4/1914)

From the restart Liverpool came at Burnley and had two good opportunities to equalise, only to be thwarted by Sewell's further acrobatics. A Mosscrop centre found Lindley who was given the best opportunity to put Burnley two-up, but his shot struck the corner of Liverpool's post and crossbar. A second

Mosscrop run saw him cut inside and shoot but his effort went over the crossbar. Liverpool then caused a great deal of anxiety in Burnley's defence as three successive attacks directed towards the Burnley goal which Sewell and the defence just managed to clear. One Liverpool effort was a long dropping shot from Nicholl just inside the Burnley half, "which he [Sewell] secured after the fashion of an out-fielder at cricket after watching the flight of the ball and patiently waiting for it," said Sportsman. Another Sewell save on his knees, was quickly followed up by another save just under the crossbar. In the last quarter of the game, both Taylor and Boyle needed attention from the trainer. First Taylor was hurt and then Boyle was injured in a collision with Fairfoul. The Burnley captain looked in agony at one point and had to be taken from the field. He returned shortly after but not before Hodgson was accidentally kicked in the face and at one point Burnley only had only nine fit players on the field. Hodgson returned to the game with a sticking plaster over a cut, his shirt bloodied. As the Burnley players kept Liverpool at bay for one final time, Herbert Bamlett blew his whistle to end the game and give Burnley victory.

At Full Time: Burnley 1 (Freeman), Liverpool 0
Attendance: 72,778 (Gate Receipts £6,687)

---xxx---

At the final whistle there were scenes of joy and jubilation around the stadium from the thousands of travelling Burnley supporters and sporting congratulations and applause from Liverpool's supporters. Burnley captain Tommy Boyle, stood in the centre-circle, hands on hips. It had been an eight year struggle in trying to win the Cup first at Barnsley and now Burnley. His dream had come true. For thousands of Burnley supporters around the ground, they could go all the way back to Alec Leake's team and the disappointment they'd all felt when Burnley had lost to Manchester United in the replayed 'snowing' game. Then there was the bitter disappointment of the 1913 Cup run which had ended in the mud at St. Andrews. After years of struggle with nothing to show, all their dreams, hopes and prayers had finally come true. Burnley had won The Cup and it was hard for them all to believe it.

In front of the pavilion, the stewards were busy arranging the press and photographers into line in order to take pictures. Pictures that would be syndicated and wired across the country and beyond. A large contingent of uniformed policemen, their primary presence to avoid any suffragette demonstrations, (which never materialised) formed a cordon for the two teams and officials as they left the pitch. The Liverpool team led by Bob Fergusson climbed the Pavilion steps first to receive their runners-up medals from His Majesty. The Burnley players nervously waited on the pitch, trying to remember all the things they had been told before the game, to bow to the King, only speak if you are spoken to. Tommy Boyle lined up his team. When the last Liverpool player had passed by the Cup and had started down the steps, the FA stewards called the Burnley captain and his team forward.

Boyle climbed the steps first. As British Pathe film footage shows, the Burnley captain paused halfway up the steps and pulled up his shirt sleeves to the elbows. At the top of the stairs the Burnley captain bowed to His Majesty and shook the King's outstretched hand. The King gave a few words of congratulations before handing Boyle the Cup decorated in claret and blue ribbons.

Boyle moved down the balcony toward where Lord Kinnaird was standing and the FA Secretary, F. W. Wall who handed him his gold Cup-winners medal. Boyle took the medal and thanked him and nodded. Smiling, *beaming*. Boyle paused on the balcony and then the steps for more photographs with the Cup in his arms, as scores of camera flashbulbs went off. Boyle descended the steps carrying the trophy, 'like a babe in arms', onto the pitch for more photographs. Each Burnley player followed the captain and went through the same ritual, bow, give thanks to His Majesty and receive the medal before returning back to earth. After the long journey starting in the First Round against South Shields back in frosty January, the ceremony was all over in a matter of seconds.

Figure 57: Tommy Boyle Is Presented With The Cup

Tommy Boyle and Bob Fergusson were interviewed by the press straight after receiving their medals. Boyle said, "It has been a great struggle, a great game. Liverpool have striven magnificently. I think we were just the better team and deserved to win."

Bob Ferguson, said it to have been "a grand struggle". "Whilst I would have liked to have won the Cup," he said, "Burnley had played hard, every player was a sportsman and they each deserved their success."

The News Reaches Burnley

At Turf Moor, at the Charity Shield Final which had kicked off at the same time as the Cup Final, an increasingly anxious crowd were eager to know what was going on. From when the match kicked off at 3:30 pm, the telephone in the secretary's office rang every ten minutes with updates from Sydenham.

The crowd were given the news from a youngster who carried a board around the pitch with the time and the score, "Ten minutes, no score"; "Twenty minutes, no score"; "Half-hour, no score" and "Half-Time, no score." When another message came through with "No score yet" in the second half, people began to resign themselves to a draw and a replay. The mood completely changed once news of Freeman's goal came through.

"All at once two or three people came running out of the players' entrance and their shout was taken up by the crowd with hearty good will. 'Burnley must have scored' they said but it was some moments before the youth with his score board began his triumphal procession around the field. His board read, 'Burnley 1, Liverpool 0; Freeman scored.' There was much cheering and hat waving among the small crowd. When the final whistle came there was another burst of frantic cheering. It was a few minutes given over to ecstasy and the joyful culmination of a period extended over about four months, which had played havoc with the emotions of staunch supporters of the winners of the English Cup." (Burnley Express 29/4/1914)

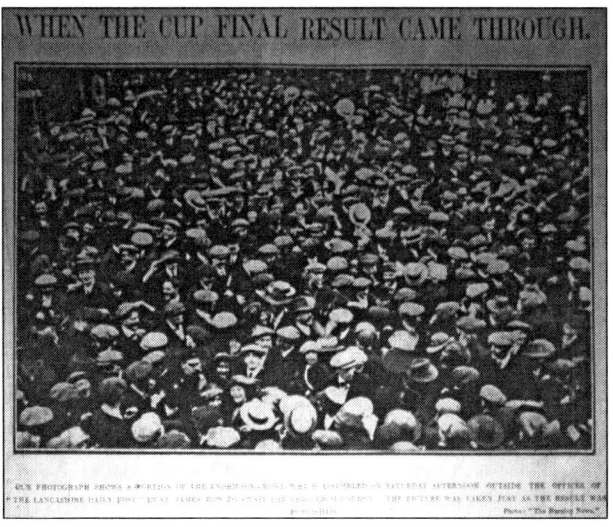

Figure 58: Crowd Outside Newspaper Offices in Burnley.

In Burnley centre, a large crowd of people had gathered in St. James's Row outside the offices of the Lancashire Daily Post. "In the centre of town there was a large concourse of people which extended from Yorkshire Street to the bottom of Westgate," reported the Burnley Express. Once victory had been confirmed the celebrations started. It was like no other Saturday night in town with drinking and dancing in the streets. Town-centre pubs ran out of beer before closing time and there were scenes like nothing before as the whole population joined in the celebrations. By early Saturday evening, 'Funeral cards of Liverpool' were being sold in St. James's Street with the verse:

> Ah! If they only had not fancied
> That football they could play,
> We should never had a reason
> For a Funeral today.

Following his presentation of the Cup and medals to the players, The King left the Pavilion shortly after 5:30 pm. The Royal party made their way back along the same route, returning to Buckingham Palace for Princess Mary's birthday party.

The Burnley team didn't have much time at The Palace themselves. It was gone 5:30 pm and the team needed to get back to Charterhouse Square to change for dinner. Tommy Boyle carried the Cup, (news photographs mostly show Boyle hold of the Cup and not any of his team mates) and the team made their way slowly back in their taxis along the crowded roads to Smithfield. Along the way, making their way back to central London, were the thousands of jubilant Burnley supporters who had cheered the team on through all the Rounds of the Cup, now heading for home. Tired but happy. It had been a long but truly wonderful day. The stories they would tell when they got home. Stories they would tell their children. Stories they would tell their grandchildren. Memories that would live forever. They had been there on the day and seen their team win the Cup in front of the King. As Burnley supporters, at that moment, after experiencing season after season of Cup defeats and watching 'bigger' clubs take the big prize, they must have felt an overwhelming feeling of emotion to have been there and been part of it all. Part of history.

The Celebration Dinner

The celebration dinner was hosted by Philip and Ottoline Morrell at The Connaught Rooms, Great Queen Street, Kingsway. The building located in-between the Freemason's United Grand Lodge of England and next door (in 1914) to the Freemason's Tavern where in 1863 the Football Association was formed. (A wall plaque erected in 2013 now depicts the location.)

Figure 59: The Connaught Rooms. Inset Lord Kinnaird.

Figure 60: The Connaught Rooms Banqueting Hall.

Figure 61: Philip and Lady Ottoline Morrell

Guest of Honour was Lord Kinnaird, the former amateur footballer and now President of the Football Association who sat at the top table with 'The Cup' alongside the Morrell's. Also present at the top table were; Burnley's Mayor, James Sellars Kay, Lord Weardale, Albert Smith MP (Clitheroe) Alderman Whitehead JP President of Burnley Football Club, Harry Windle, Chairman and Burnley directors and their wives. (Strangely John Haworth's name was not listed in the Express). All the Burnley players along with Jerry Dawson, Bob Reid and Levi Thorpe the Burnley trainers, their wives and fiancées were there along with other guests and members of the press.

As the guests had arrived, they were greeted by Philip and Lady Ottoline, and once everyone had gathered they sat down to dinner which consisted of;

> **The Cup Final**
>
> **Connaught Rooms, Holborn, London.**
>
> **Consommé Burnley,**
>
> **Sole Florentine,**
>
> **Chicken Casserole or Saddle of Lamb,**
>
> **Mushrooms on Toast or Peaches in Ice,**
>
> **Followed by Coffee**

The dinner was accompanied by music. During dinner, the Cup was filled (reports say not what with – presumably champagne) and was passed around to all the guests in turn to drink from and it was cheered along its route around the room.

The After Dinner Toasts

After dinner had ended, the first toast was offered to 'The Burnley Football Club,' by Philip Morrell. Morrell began,

To the Winners of the Cup! (applause) Those four words were he thought more eloquent than any number of speeches. The winning of it would be remembered in Burnley for many a long day (applause).

He thought he might fairly say that no such day had Burnley known in its long hundreds of years of history, during which it had grown from a little town of 5,000 inhabitants to the great town they knew now, as there would be that day (hear, hear). Everywhere the people would be saying, "We've won the Cup" and that was enough. He was glad to know that of the 15,000 spectators who he was told came from Burnley – a great many of whom came to the House of Commons that morning (laughter) there would not be one who would not go back happier thinking that his town and team had won the greatest trophy in the football world. (Applause) And as to Boyle and the men who had played that day, he could say on behalf of every one of his constituents that they were proud of them. They have made the name of the town famous throughout the country. Burnley was known for its cotton and for its education but he was bound to say it was still more famous on account of its prowess in the football world. They were not only proud of the fact that they had won a great victory, but they were proud of the way they had won it. (Loud applause.) It had been a great day for them all and in asking them to drink to the Burnley Football Club he coupled with the toast the names of Alderman Whitehead, Mr Windle and Mr Boyle. (Applause)

In seconding the toast, Lord Weardale expressed his pleasure at the opportunity of seeing so many friendly faces from a town which would always hold a place in his heart. That was, continued Lord Weardale, an auspicious occasion and one in which he was pleased to take part because his acquaintance with the Burnley F. C. went back many years when Alderman Whitehead and his friends were struggling with all sorts of difficulties. Burnley had had its ups and downs in football; in the days he remembered it was chiefly 'downs' (laughter).

Now, however they were on the 'up-gradient' and they could readily forget the old days and only remember the triumphs of today. He ended on, "Bravo for Burnley."

The Cup was passed round, one of those who drank from it was Bert Freeman's father (Tom Freeman) who, wearing Burnley's colours had come into the room. When his identity was known there was much cheering.

Alderman Whitehead, Burnley F.C.'s President responded to Lord Weardale's words. He began, "I have been twenty years waiting for this day, and am exceedingly happy." He said they all owed a great debt to the players (hear, hear). When Burnley had been drawn against Bolton Wanderers he was told by many that they had met their fate, but the players rose to the occasion and gave an exhibition of football at Turf Moor such had not been seen for a long time. Whitehead's main thanks went to Jerry Dawson who had ruled himself out of the Final.

"When he was injured the previous week they felt it would almost be a calamity if he could not be fit for the Final and they felt so much that he should play that they left it to him to decide. Like the grand and great sportsman he is (loud applause). Jerry had said, "I might as well tell you, gentlemen that I don't feel quite fit, and if I were injured in the first minutes of the match it would probably mean that they would have to play with ten men."

That said Alderman Whitehead showed Dawson's made of good stuff and his love for the game and for his club (loud applause) here he had the opportunity of getting if not a winning medal at least a runners-up medal, but for the good of his club he gave his chance up (loud applause). In thanking Mr and Lady Ottoline Morrell for their hospitality Whitehead said he felt sure the winning of the Cup had given as much pleasure to them all.

Harry Windle was loudly cheered as he rose to speak and remarked he was not less proud than the others because they had the opportunity of celebrating such an occasion. At one time and within his time of football management, too, it would have seemed scarcely dignified for many of the gentlemen present that evening to sit down to dinner in the company of professional footballers. Now however, throughout the length and breadth of the land professional footballers were looked up to as members of the community as much as men of other professions. Windle said he was proud to see the President of the Football Association present and proud to be chairman of the club during the time Burnley had won the Cup. In winning the Cup he thought, throughout England no one would begrudge Burnley their victory (loud applause).

As to the players, on behalf of the directors he congratulated them on the splendid manner in which they had behaved and he added his sympathies to the others with Dawson and also to the reserve men (Reid and Thorpe) who had trained with them but who had not been able to play in the games. He particularly congratulated one player on the many honours he had won in his first season of first-class football that was Mr Mosscrop (Applause)

As Windle concluded he too added that Burnley had had difficulties in their time, but now they had won everything they had taken part in except the First Division Championship (When someone in the audience said, 'NEXT YEAR') and applause as he sat, Tommy Boyle rose to speak.

"I am very pleased, seeing I am captain of the Burnley club at having won the English Cup (loud applause). I had hard lines at not winning it when I was with Barnsley and they won it after I left. But since I came to Burnley we only just got beaten for promotion the first year, last year we won promotion and this year we have won the Cup. (Loud Applause) I wish to thank Lady Ottoline and Mr Morrell for the kind way they have entertained us tonight and I hope and think we shall win the English League Championship next year (Applause). I sympathise with Liverpool but from the bottom of my heart I hope they may win the Cup next year." (Loud applause and cheers.)

Mr C.E. Sutcliffe, member of the Football League and formerly Burnley Football Club, who had been invited, wired the following congratulations, "Regret cannot join you, rejoice with you that Burnley's first Royal soccer team. Have deservedly won first Royal Final. A glorious climax to a wonderful season of remarkable progress. Hearty congratulations to all. Hurrah and again Hurrah over and over again."

Another wire came from Turf Moor, "From Burnley Sunday School League at Turf Moor. Heartiest congratulations on splendid victory. Great reception at Turf Moor. Gate £36."

Albert Smith MP gave a short speech as to how the day had gone. He reflected on the day when Prince Albert Victor, the King's late elder brother had visited Turf Moor for the opening of the Victoria Hospital. Then he introduced the next speaker, Lord Kinnaird, The Football Association President.

Lord Kinnaird began by thanking his guests for the dinner and praised the players and the club for the way they had conducted themselves in all the rounds to the Final. He said, he believed the Football Association was a great educational establishment, they were teaching the great principle that the greatest thing for a young man to do was to play for his country and his club without caring a pin what happened to him (hear, hear).

When he heard what Dawson, their goalkeeper had done he felt that men realised that they must take those disappointments for granted. They knew it was a great sacrifice it must have been and yet Dawson never hesitated (loud applause).

It reminded him of the time when the Old Etonian team first won the Cup. The captain Sir Francis Marindin was not well, and in spite of the temptation he decided not to risk his team's chances and had stayed in bed and allowed a present member of Parliament who still took a great interest in the game, Sir John Rawlinson the opportunity of playing in the Final and getting a Cup medal. Kinnaird praised Burnley's determination in rising from the Second Division to the First and after missing out on the Final last year, winning in it this season and that it showed other clubs what they could do with the same determination.

Speeches followed from The Mayor of Burnley, James Sellars Kay, and more words from host Philip Morrell that followed Lord Kinnaird, but the final words went to the hostess of the evening, Lady Ottoline Morrell who rose to great cheers.

"I am very pleased to be able to say what an enormous privilege and pleasure it has been to me to welcome you here tonight because I have known you all at a distance for many a long day, and I take a tremendous interest in football. I think you all merit every bit of praise showered on you when you return on Monday. Perhaps I am prejudiced in your favour and am not acquainted with football its wide sense but I take a tremendous pride in your football team, because I think there is no team playing such an honourable, splendid and true game as you play (Applause). One thing I always notice is it is always our men who get hurt! (Laughter) I feel it is a real privilege to know under more intimate circumstances the heroes I have looked upon for many a long day," (loud applause).

Lady Ottoline drank from the Cup and was later flattered when Bert Freeman and several other members of the Burnley team begged her to go back to Burnley with them to join in the victory parade on Monday afternoon.

After the speeches, the celebrations continued with music and dancing before the party eventually broke up in the early hours and the Burnley team returned to Charterhouse Square. Later, at Bedford Square, Lady Ottoline wrote to [her lover] Bertrand Russell, describing the evening's celebrations and her affection for the team: "They look upon me as their mascot, but I had to decline their requests to travel back to Burnley with them."

Earlier in the evening just after the Final had finished, there had been a train accident that had involved a number of football supporters from Manchester making their way home from London.

TRAIN COLLISION IN TUNNEL
Cup Final Excursionists Injured near Finchley Road

Hundreds of Cup-Final excursionists had an alarming experience in an accident which occurred while they were travelling homewards on the Great Central Railway yesterday afternoon. The accident occurred in Canfield place near the Finchley Road Metropolitan Station and the train was the 5:30 pm from Marylebone to the midlands and north of England.

A number of extra coaches had been attached to the train in order to accommodate holders of two-day tickets. So great was the load was the train was unable to pull the load up the gradient past Finchley Road and the train came to a standstill with several rear coaches in the tunnel. An auxiliary engine was sent for but when the driver arrived he failed to see the stationary train and the engine crushed into the back. Passengers were thrown onto the floor and one was hurled out of the carriage into the tunnel. Local doctors and members of St. John Ambulance rendered first aid at the scene and sixteen persons were taken to Marylebone at St. Mary's Hospital suffering cuts, bruises and shock. The most serious case was a Mr Pomphret from Openshaw Manchester who suffered a fractured rib and other injuries along with a number of other football enthusiasts from the Manchester district."
(Daily Express 27/4/1914)

The majority of the thousands of football supporters who were at the Cup Final had a safer journey home. They left Euston, St. Pancras, Kings Cross and Marylebone railway stations on the 'midnight specials' on Saturday night and began arriving home bleary eyed at 6:00 am on Sunday morning.

Sunday 26th April 1914

After breakfast on Sunday, some of the players went to church and at 10:00 am the Burnley party took in a motorbus tour that visited Shepherd's Bush. Kew Gardens, Old Richmond Park, Hampton Court, Virginia Water and Windsor. On their return the players had free time on Sunday evening where some took in an evening stroll along the Thames Embankment and a short boat trip along the river.

Figure 62: The Burnley Team Relaxing

The Newspaper Headlines

THE KING SEES BURNLEY WIN THE CUP. (Daily Mirror 27/4/1914)

Figure 63: Daily Mirror Front Page 27/4/1914

BURNLEY BRING HOME THE ENGLISH CUP
Boyle's Men Win The First Royal Final.
Unprecedented Scenes of Enthusiasm and Rejoicing

The first Cup Final ever honoured by the presence of the King, was won at Crystal Palace on Saturday by Burnley by the only goal. It was a Royal Lancashire day. The two finalists hailed from the County Palatine, from Burnley and from Liverpool. The Duke of Lancaster, as the King is now toasted in our County, witnessed the entire game, shook hands with the respective captains and presented the Cup and medals, and the majority of the crowd had gone up from the northern area. The game was – well, "nowt to shout about." We won and that's all that need be said here. (Burnley Express 29/4/1914)

**THE CUP FINAL – BURNLEY'S NARROW VICTORY.
LIVERPOOL BEATEN BY A GOAL TO NIL.** (The Observer 26/4/14)

**THE KING HANDS THE FOOTBALL CUP.
A DULL FINAL BUT FOR HIS MAJESTY.** (The Manchester Guardian 27/4/14)

THE KING AT THE CUP FINAL – VICTORY OF BURNLEY.
(The Times 27/4/1914)

**BURNLEY RECEIVE THE CUP FROM KING GEORGE.
THE KING WITNESSES THE ENGLISH CUP FINAL.** (The Athletics News 27/4/1914)

**ENGLISH CUP FOR BURNLEY.
KING PRESENTS CUP – UNIQUE HONOUR FOR BURNLEY.** (Hull Daily Mail)

**BURNLEY WIN ROYAL FINAL.
FREEMAN'S GOAL BRINGS VICTORY.** (Manchester Courier)

**BURNLEY WIN THE CUP!
BRILLIANT VICTORY AT THE CRYSTAL PALACE.**
(Burnley Gazette)

The Daily Express was less emphatic over Burnley's victory…

THE KING SEES A FUNEREAL FINAL Worse Game on Record, Redeemed by His Majesty's Presence (Daily Express 27/4/1914)

In gothic type during their match report; The Daily Express
wrote (rather unkindly),
Here Lie the Remains of the Worst Cup Final on Record." (P8,
27/4/1914)

BLIND CRITIC OF THE CUP TIE

One of the most interesting figures at the Cup Final was
Mr W. Meredith a blind man from birth, who was brought from
Manchester in connection with the National Institute for the
Blind. Mr Meredith has been a familiar figure on football grounds
in the north and had mastered his details of the game thoroughly.
At the Crystal Palace, relying chiefly on sounds, he followed the
play with amazing confidence and was frequently able to name
the player in possession of the ball and describe what he was
going to do with it. "I liked Sheldon very much, he is a great
forward but holds the ball too long," said Mr Meredith, and
"the Burnley side struck me as a very robust one, they played
vigorous football and swung the ball about in fine fashion."
Mr Meredith's accuracy in following the game is explained by
his keen sense of sound. He could tell by the interval of time
between the sound of a kick and the sound of it bouncing how
far and in what direction it has gone." (Daily Express 27/4/1914)

A Heroes Welcome

The Burnley party checked out of the Charterhouse Hotel at 10:00 am on Monday morning and a fleet of taxis ferried them to London's Euston station. A large group of supporters and well-wishers was already there to meet them in the station. Also at Euston, were Philip and Lady Ottoline Morrell which was quite a surprise to the Burnley players. Lady Ottoline had three bouquets of flowers made up of claret carnations with blue iris. She presented these to Mrs Whitehead, Mrs Windle and the last one to a blushing Annie Varley, Tommy Boyle's fiancée.

Also at Euston waiting on the adjacent platform were the Liverpool team and officials waiting for their 10:57 train to Lime Street. Like Burnley, they had to return home to play their final League game of the season, against Sheffield United at Anfield. Once the Burnley players had all climbed aboard, the carriage doors were slammed shut and the train bearing the plate, 'CORONATION' pulled out. The Liverpool players sportingly cheering as the Burnley train left. In the first saloon carriage, Tommy Boyle placed the Cup, the handles adorned with claret and blue ribbons, on the table by the window. The Cup was filled with lemonade on the way back as it was a match day, Burnley hosting the final League game against Bradford City at Turf Moor that kicked off at 6:30 pm.

The train made good time and stopped first at Wilmslow at 1:40 pm where a portion of the train was detached. There were people gathered on the platform and Tommy Boyle held the Cup at the train carriage door for the small crowd to see. The train continued via Stockport and Droylsden and reached Manchester Victoria station at 2:30 pm. As the train pulled in it was met by a group of Manchester railway workers, porters and gangers, all offering their congratulations. Manchester Victoria was where the Burnley players said goodbye to team-mate Eddie Mosscrop, who waved as he set off across the station concourse for the Southport train. He wouldn't play against Bradford as he was due back at school teaching the following morning.

While the train had stopped at Wilmslow, a wire had been sent to Affleck and Brown's store in Manchester, to have twenty yards of wide claret ribbon and the same amount of blue to be waiting for them at Victoria station. While the train was halted, the engine was decorated with the material by the engine driver, John Haworth and the two Burnley trainers.

From 2:00 pm in Burnley centre, crowds had begun gathering outside the Town Hall. The local schools began closing early so the children could get a good view of the procession passing along Accrington Road from Rosegrove to Turf Moor.

"From Manchester, the train had a triumphal run" said Sportsman, "East Lancashire people were as proud of Burnley's success as if it had been any other team from the area. As the train steamed past mills and workshops, workers could be seen at the windows waving flags and cheering. Particularly was this the case in the vicinity of Bolton, Darwen, Blackburn and Accrington. At these stations there were more demonstrations of delight. People came from all over. From Ramsbottom, Bacup and Blackburn in one direction and Nelson, Colne and Trawden in the other. Never has the district been so stirred and the beautiful weather which prevailed, made the affair quite a brilliant success. The streets at Accrington were packed with people and as the train passed over the arches the people cheered vociferously." (Burnley News 29/4/1914)

The train steamed on its last leg through Huncoat and Hapton, past factories, mills and farms. People waved from foot-bridges and the trackside on the final part of its 220 mile journey home. Just five hours and twenty minutes since departing Euston, 'Coronation' reached its final destination, Burnley's Rosegrove station at 3:50 pm. As the train steamed in to the platform, twelve fog signals placed on the track went off in quick succession signalling the train's arrival to the waiting crowds.

As the decorated train came to a standstill, the shouting of those on the platform was increased by the cheering of the occupants of the train, the people going frantic as Boyle appeared proudly bearing the Cup which was adorned with claret and blue ribbons. Two bands – The Briercliffe Band and the National Reserve Band struck up 'See The Conquering Hero Comes' as the players stopped for photographs before climbing the steps to the station exit.

Figure 64: Tommy Boyle on Rosegrove Station
Platform (Getty Images)

Sportsman in the Burnley Express estimated there were around 10,000 people waiting around Rosegrove station and the junction of Accrington and Rossendale Road. Willie Holt's on the corner of Rosegrove Lane and Accrington Road had a banner saying, "We Watched You Win And We Congratulate You." Many of the crowd were wearing Burnley colours and some were wearing 'specially made round caps of claret and blue material.'

"Boyle came out of the station with the Cup to great cheers, followed by Freeman and Sewell, to climb aboard their transport. The procession comprised of six horse-drawn vehicles, and seven or eight motors. In front was a motor car with the Chief Constable then came the bands with the mounted police and after this a charabanc with the directors, officials and players. Boyle being on the front seat holding the Cup. In the next vehicle were the player's wives and sweethearts and lastly the pressmen and behind this were the motors and carriages." (Burnley Express 29/4/14) [Photos actually show the Burnley Team with the Cup on board a wagonette not a charabanc]

"Never before have scenes been witnessed in Burnley as were seen when the Cup-winning team came home on Monday bringing the much-coveted trophy with them. Thousands came from as far away as Bolton to see The Clarets take part in a victory parade journey by a wagonette from Rosegrove Station to Turf Moor by way of Burnley's town hall on Manchester Road. Some workers had been granted the afternoon off, some lost a whole days pay to catch sight of their heroes." (Burnley News 29/4/14)

Figure 65: The Procession at Rosegrove

Crowds up to six deep in places on both sides of the road, lined the length of Accrington Road. People stood on steps and in their gardens. Some waved from shop doorways, balconies, upstairs windows, even rooftops. Some were perched on advertising boards as the Burnley team made their way slowly toward the town centre. So thick were the crowds in places, the police had a difficult job keeping the route clear and in Accrington Road, "there had been one or two unpleasant incidents." At the end of Accrington Road, bunting was strung across the road and miniature silver cups were seen here and there, the crowd getting ever denser as the procession moved slowly forward. All the trams were temporarily stopped at the Mitre as the procession passed into Trafalgar Street.

Figure 66: The Procession Reaches The Mitre.

After the carriages had entered Trafalgar Street, a shower of confetti fell on the procession from one of the mill windows. It was so hot holding the Cup aloft, Boyle had to remove his jacket, completing the journey in his waistcoat and shirt sleeves. Bunting adorned the length of Trafalgar Street, where workers waved from fire escapes and shouted from open windows.

When the procession had reached the end of Trafalgar Street, the spectacle that met their eyes was the most wonderful of all. The trams were stopped at the junction with Manchester Road with their drivers, conductors and passengers standing and waving as the procession went past, turning left toward the town hall. From the Canal Toll House all the way down the hill to St. James Street, all you could see was a sea of people. A solid mass of people, waving, cheering and singing. The band played and led the procession toward the Town Hall as the players were greeted with congratulatory banners hung from windows, welcoming home the team. Flags of all sizes were flying, coloured bunting flapped in the breeze hung from lamp-posts decorated the way. The noise was deafening.

The Burnley Express described the scene in Manchester Road.

"Manchester Road has never been so thronged as it was on Monday afternoon. From two o' clock a steady stream of people poured into it and by 3:00 pm, the sight was a memorable one. In front of the Town Hall was a dense mass of humanity and the thoroughfare seemed black with folk downwards as far as the 'Centre' and upwards as far as the eye could see. It was a good humoured crowd and was composed of men, women and children. How the latter survived the ordeal is a credit to their vitality but there were some who had to be pulled out by the police and taken to a place of safety. The crush at times was terrific and it calls for comment that the authorities should have permitted the trams to run as long as they did and that they did not put up some barricades. The running of the cars made matters worse and the poor girls and women in the crowd had a weary time while the mammoth cars were getting through. When the thoroughfare became packed the more venturesome spirit invaded the enclosure in front of Brunswick Chapel by climbing over the railings. Others climbed on to the roof and had a capital view. A sailor created much diversion for the crowd by climbing a lamp-post and knocking off the mantle in doing so."

The Bradford City team had arrived at Manchester Road station around the same time and were trying to make their way to Turf Moor. The road was a solid mass of people so they were escorted inside the Town Hall by the police and straight out of the back entrance to help them get to Turf Moor.

Opposite the Town Hall one group of Burnley supporters held up a banner which read,
"Long Live the Memory of Our Heroes," in silver and gold letters. They also sang a ragtime parody, part of which went -

> Burnley keeps on doing it, doing it, doing it,
> See little Mosscrop running up the line;
> Don't he put his centres in fine?

See Bert Freeman put it over the line;
It's a goal, It's a goal, It's a goal. - Well
Everybody's shouting it, shouting it, shouting it
Ain't that football thrilling your soul?
Hear the Burnley spectators brawl
Come along Bert, let's have another goal
Everybody's shouting it now.

The Mayor, Mayoress and members of the Corporation looked out from the upper floor town hall windows and at 4:40 pm the procession slowly came to a halt outside the Town Hall. The crowds were so thick the players could not get out of their vehicles. The Mayor came to the entrance steps of the Town Hall as far as he could and offered three cheers for the team. It was previously thought that at this point the team went inside the Town Hall and waved to the crowd from the balcony but the Burnley Express reports state that, "it was judged wisest for the footballers to go forward to Turf Moor - and this they did."

**Figure 67: The Scene Outside Burnley Town Hall
(Getty Images)**

The Express's report of the team NOT waving from the town hall balcony conflicts with another source, a recollection of the day written in 1963 by former Burnley chairman, Bob Lord,

"I stood as a youngster amid the mighty mass of people assembled near the Town Hall of Burnley to cheer home our Cup winners of 1914. That vast crowd was there, together with the city fathers, to welcome the Cup to Burnley for the first time. The team came out on the balcony, and there was Tommy Boyle, the captain, holding the Cup in triumph as high above his head as he could in order that all those people should see it. Even I, as a nipper of six, I could see it. How I thrilled!" *(Lord, 1963)*

After a short halt, the procession carried on down Manchester Road and on to Yorkshire Street where more crowds were waiting. By this stage the crowds from around the Town Hall had begun to slowly follow the procession. The cheering was deafening. At the end of Yorkshire Street the procession were in sight of Turf Moor and at the junction of Brunshaw and Belvedere Road, a banner proclaimed, "Welcome To The Victors." The procession came to a halt outside Turf Moor's Brunshaw Road stand where the players managed to dismount and go inside.

The turnstiles were already open for the evening game and many of the Burnley supporters that had followed the team at The Palace were already inside. They gave their team a rousing reception as Tommy Boyle came out onto the pitch with the Cup in his arms, and the band struck up "See the Conquering Hero Comes." By 6:30 pm and kick-off, a big turn-out gathered for the Clarets final game that would bring the curtain down on the 1913-14 season.

The Final Match of the Season

Sportsman thought that the Bradford game was one of the best games he had witnessed all season. Ronnie Sewell kept his place in goal and the only omission from the Cup winners was Eddie Mosscrop. His place was taken by Levi Thorpe with Billy Watson switching to the outside-left position.

Burnley v Bradford City, Turf Moor, Monday 27 April, Kick-Off 6:30 pm

The Teams lined up:
Burnley: Sewell, Bamford, Taylor, Halley, Boyle, Thorpe, Nesbitt, Lindley, Freeman, Hodgson, Watson.
Bradford City: Ewart, Potts, Boocock, McIlveny, Hargreaves, McDonald, Bond, Fox, Walden, Storer, Logan
Referee: Mr Palmer (Hucknall Torkard)

Tommy Boyle lost the toss and Burnley played against the wind toward the Cricket-Field End. Burnley began well and made several attacks on the Bradford goal with the Yorkshiremen kept on the defensive. On 15 minutes, City broke away and scored a goal against the run of play through Bond. Then Bert Freeman won the ball and proceeded one of his trademark dribbles on goal, "practically trying to walk the ball into the visitors net," said Sportsman, before Ewart ran out and grabbed the ball off him. Five minutes after City scored, they did it again, Bond scoring his second goal. A hush fell over the crowd as City looked like they intended to spoil the celebration party. And despite the Clarets making most of the headway in the game, it was Bradford who took a shock 2-0 lead into the half-time interval.

Burnley began brighter in the second half. Ewart was the much busier of the two goalkeepers for the first 20 minutes. Burnley attacked only to be beaten back by the City defence. A Billy

Nesbitt cross found Bert Freeman whose shot Ewart cleared only for McIlveny to then handle in the penalty area. Mr Palmer pointed to the spot and Tommy Boyle stepped up and converted the penalty to put the Clarets back in the game amid great cheers. Burnley then forced two corners and pressed for long periods but with little in the way of attacks from the visitors.

In the 85th minute Bert Freeman put in a great shot which Ewart saved under the crossbar and could only put the ball out for a corner. Boyle called for all his men to come forward. Nesbitt centred and running in from the edge of the box was full-back Dave Taylor who met the ball with his head, to give Ewart no chance and level the scores. The goal was greeted with tremendous applause. Boyle pushed his team forward again hoping for a winner. "Burnley had the better of the bout for the remaining minutes." The match finished at 2-2 and after Mr Palmer's final whistle had sounded, the crowd broke onto the pitch and gathered around the front of the stand, cheering frantically. "The scene was a really remarkable one and will live long in the memory of those present and the same jubilation was manifested outside the enclosure," said Sportsman.

At Full Time: Burnley 2 (Boyle pen, Taylor), Bradford 2 (Bond 2)
Attendance: 35,000 (Gate receipts £705)

---xxx---

The Cup was brought up to the front of the stand and was held up first by the Mayor and then Mayoress. Tommy Boyle appeared and as the Mayor was unable to congratulate the team at the Town Hall, he gave his thanks to the team from the stand. Bert Freeman's father Tom was present and also said a few words. Later that evening, the Burnley players visited Cronkshaw's Temperance Hotel for a late dinner and ended their evening at the Empire Theatre where in the interval, the team with the Cup, were invited up onto the stage to a cheering audience.

The following Tuesday evening, the Mayor invited the Burnley team and directors to dinner at the Bull Hotel. Guests included Mr G. H. Pullon JP, Mr J. N. Grimshaw, Mr J. H. Ashworth and Mr T. H. Freeman, father of Bert Freeman. The Mayor toasted, "The English Cup Winners"
Before Tommy Boyle rose to cheers and gave a short vote of thanks.

"Thank you Mr Mayor. On behalf of the players it was a great privilege and honour to have won the English Cup. We fought hard last year but were beaten in the semi-final. This year we had got it! [Cheers] I hope that next year we will be at the top of the First Division and can I sincerely thank you for the hospitality tonight." After dinner, the players and officials visited The Palace Theatre.

On Wednesday morning, the players drove to their training headquarters at Lytham to show off the Cup and then on to Southport in the afternoon before travelling to play cup-opponents Liverpool in a charity match at Anfield in the evening.

Figure 68: Burnley and Liverpool at Anfield, 29/4/1914

Wednesday's Burnley Express printed the following song from William Cheeseborough, titled, "Done It," to the tune of God Save The King.

DONE IT!

Burnley have won the Cup
Now let them fill it up
With good champagne
Good boys, Sir, every one;
On merit they have won
Let's hope what they have done
They'll do again.

We now with pride can say
Each man was fit to play
Before the King;
Bert Freeman did the trick
Dashing and fleet and quick
Say, boys, that he's a brick!
His praises sing.

Tom Boyle, the captain then,
Right ably led his men,
Before the King.
Royal was their display,
Each man shone in the fray,
On that historic day,
God save the King.

Burnley Collier in Trouble
One Burnley supporter had missed the train home and the homecoming celebrations having been arrested in London and spending the weekend in the police cells.

"A Burnley collier was charged at Old Street Police Court, London on Monday (27 April) with disorderly conduct and with assaulting the police. A constable stated that at 12.20 on Sunday morning the prisoner asked him the way to King's Cross Station. He directed him and without any provocation the prisoner punched him on the chest. He arrested him and then the prisoner then tried to trip him up. Prisoner said he was very sorry. He had come up from Burnley for the Cup Final and had got too much to drink.

Magistrate Mr Chester Jones: Is that the way you behave in Burnley? We do not allow such conduct in London. The prisoner murmured something about a "long day" and the magistrate imposed a fine of 10 shillings. The prisoner said he had no money left, but if allowed to return home would send the money. The Magistrate said: "Very well, you are on your honour. Pay on Saturday." *(Burnley Express, 29 April 1914)*

Figure 69: Burnley Team With The FA Cup.

Back Row L to R: Ernie Edwards (Trainer) Tommy Bamford, Ronnie Sewell, Dave Taylor
Middle Row: Billy Nesbitt, Richard Lindley, Bert Freeman, Teddy Hodgson, Eddie Mosscrop
Front Row: George Halley, Tommy Boyle, Billy Watson.

The busy week of engagements continued for the players. On Thursday there was a tour of local towns and villages travelling as far as the Ribble Valley, to show off the Cup. A fortnight later, the Burnley party departed on a month long European tour that took in several European countries and the team played several exhibition matches along the way.

Figure 70: Burnley on Tour in Earby.

**Figure 71: Burnley Players Outside the
Thorn Hotel in Burnley**

The summer of 1914 was one of the hottest on record in
Lancashire with temperatures of 100 degrees recorded in the
mills in Burnley. That summer, East Lancashire ruled the
football world, Burnley as FA Cup winners, and Blackburn
Rovers as First Division champions. Next seasons football
fixtures arrived before the Wakes Weeks holidays got underway on the first weekend in July. All seemed well as local holi-
daymakers packed their suitcases for a relaxing week at by
the seaside with no idea of the situation that was building
in Europe.

On the 4th of August 1914, war was declared and from that
point on the world would never be the same. The euphoric
summer came to an abrupt end. The 1914-15 football season

went ahead as planned and the FA Cup but by the summer of 1915, professional football in England was outlawed, the Football League was dismantled and the FA Cup mothballed. As the bloody war continued, the eleven members of the FA Cup winning team and all those who had been a part of Burnley's great season, found themselves involved in the war effort. By the end of the war some of them had become prisoners-of-war, some of them had been wounded in action and others were psychologically affected. Five of the players in the Burnley squad in 1913-14, including Teddy Hodgson, the leading goal-scorer in Burnley's 1914 Cup campaign, made the ultimate sacrifice for their country.

In 1920-21, two years after the Great War ended, Burnley won the Football League Championship for the first time with several of the players who had won the Cup. During that season the team went a record-breaking thirty League games undefeated. That record was held over sixty years until Arsenal bettered it in 2004. It was a great achievement, a great record, of that there is no doubt. But did winning the League in 1921 come anywhere close as winning the Cup and the historic welcome homecoming that followed during that amazing week in late April 1914? A hundred years on in 2014, we celebrate the great achievement Burnley made in winning the Cup in front of the King. The eleven heroes who made history that April day in 1914, may no longer be with us, but their legend lingers on.

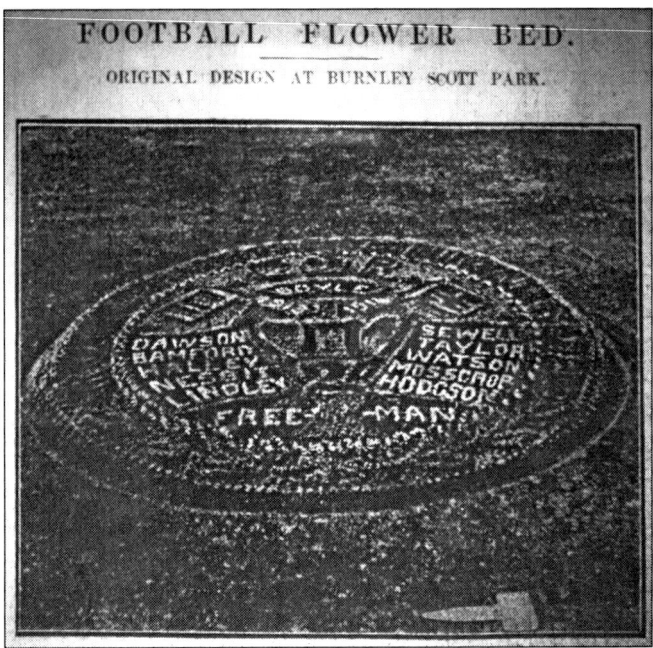

FOOTBALL FLOWER BED.

ORIGINAL DESIGN AT BURNLEY SCOTT PARK.

Figure 72: A flower bed in Burnley's Scott Park in the Summer of 1914, Celebrating the Burnley Teams Great Achievement.

Though nothing can bring back the hour
Of splendour in the grass, of glory in the flower;
We will grieve not, rather find
Strength in what remains behind;
In the primal sympathy
Which having been must ever be...
– William Wordsworth

The End

---xxx---

CHAPTER NINE

Player Profiles

Walter Ronald Sewell, Goalkeeper, (1890 - 1945)

**Figure 73: The Treaty of Commerce with
Ronnie Sewell Inset.**

Ronnie Sewell (his first name on his birth certificate is Walter) was born in Wingate, County Durham and joined local side Wingate Albion as a youngster. At the end of the 1910-11 season, Sewell signed for Second Division Gainsborough Trinity. Following the Second Round Cup tie at Turf Moor in

February 1913 when the Clarets won 4-1, Burnley bought Sewell and both the Gainsborough full-backs, Cliff Jones and Sam Gunter for a combined fee of around £2,400. (Also playing in the Gainsborough side that day was the Liverpool captian Henry Lowe who missed the 1914 Final through injury.) Ronnie Sewell made 55 first team appearances for Burnley between 1913-20. In 1920 he was sold to Blackburn Rovers where he went on to make 248 first team appearances between 1920-27, Sewell making his debut in February 1920 against Liverpool. Ronnie won one England cap in the Home Championship v Wales in 1923-24 and stayed at Rovers until 1927 before going back to Gainsborough Trinity where he spent two seasons before retiring from football at the end of the 1928-29 season.

In March 1934, Ronnie took on the licence of The Treaty of Commerce pub in High Street, Lincoln. The pub is located on the main street that leads to the shopping centre and Lincoln Cathedral. The Treaty was still open and serving beer in 2014. Ronnie was landlord there from his retirement from football until his death in February 1945, at the age of only 54.

---xxx---

Jeremiah Dawson, Goalkeeper, (1888 - 1970)

Born in Holme, near Cliviger, Jerry Dawson was the son of the village blacksmith and played his first match with Burnley Reserves in February 1907. Jerry took over as Burnley's first choice goalkeeper the following season. A one-club man all his career, Jerry played in goal for Burnley a record 569 times and made 522 League appearances. He played in goal for England and won two full international caps.

Jerry lived locally in Cliviger all his life and was a frequent visitor to Turf Moor in the 1950s, 60s and 70s. Along with Bert Freeman and Eddie Mosscrop he was a guest at the 1947 Cup

Final at Wembley between Burnley and Charlton Athletic. Jerry died in 1970 aged 82.

Following the Cup Final where he had stood down due to injury, another Cup medal was struck and awarded to Jerry which he is shown wearing on his watch-chain in Figure 74.

**Figure 74: Tom Bamford, Jerry Dawson and Dave Taylor
with Cup Medals (Getty Images)**

---xxx---

Thomas Bamford, Right Full-Back, (1887 - 1944)

Burnley right-back Tom Bamford was born in Horwich and was discovered playing at Darwen before signing for the Clarets in 1909-10. The Burnley Gazette described him as, "a fearless tackler but quiet type, well built, standing 5 foot 8 inches, and weighing 12 stone". Mr Reliable, Tommy only missed one game for Burnley in the entire 1913-14 season and that a Lancashire Cup tie at Ewood Park. Tom was in the Army Service Corps during WW1 where he drove motor transport. After making 157 first team appearances for Burnley, Tommy was transferred to Rochdale in September 1920. Tommy's final occupation is given as a motor wagon driver for a Blackburn coal merchants. He died aged 57 in Blackburn on the 9th of August 1944.

---xxx---

David Taylor, Left Full-Back, (1883 - 1949)

David Taylor was born at Bannockburn Scotland in 1883. Taylor's football career began at Motherwell before he was signed by Glasgow Rangers in 1906. He was loaned back to Motherwell in 1909 and a year later Taylor was transferred to Bradford City in September 1910. The 1911 Census shows Taylor aged 24 and living in a Bradford boarding house with two other Bradford City players. Taylor played against Burnley in Bradford's 1911 Cup winning season. After only 51 first team appearances for Bradford, John Haworth signed Taylor for Burnley in December 1911 and from then on he was rarely absent from the team.

During the First World War, like Tommy Bamford, Taylor joined the Army Service Corps as a driver. He played 11 first team games in the Championship winning season of 1920-21 and in total some 221 first team games for the Clarets. When his Burnley career ended he went into football management. His first club as manager was St. Johnstone where he stayed until 1931. He then took over at Dunfermline between 1936 and 1938. Taylor's last managerial post was at Carlisle United where he managed from 1938 until 1940. Following retirement from football Dave Taylor returned to his native Scotland and died in his home at Bridge of Allan, near Stirling in 1949. He was 65.

---xxx---

George Halley, Right Half-Back, (1887 - 1941)

Figure 75

George Halley was born in Cronberry, a small village south of Glasgow, on 29 October 1887. His first position was as an outside right for his local village team, the Glenbuck Cherrypickers, the same village team that would in 1930 give a debut to a 17 year old Bill Shankly. Halley was about to play for Ayr when Kilmarnock signed him. At the end of 1910-11 he signed to Bradford Park Avenue. Halley was secured by Burnley in March 1913 for the sum of £1,200. Following the 1914 FA Cup, George played the following League season until he became the first player in the Cup team to join up. Halley joined the Royal Engineers and served all over the world. He didn't return to Burnley until late October 1919, when he re-joined the team and picked up where he left off in the heart of the defence. Halley played a big part in Burnley's 1920-21 Championship winning season. He lived at number 12 Haven Street in Burnley, next door to centre-forward Joe Anderson, and in the same street as Teddy Hodgson and John Haworth, just a stones throw from Turf

Moor. Halley left Burnley in November 1922 for Southend United and played later in non-League football with Bacup Borough. Halley was a skilled plasterer and after his playing career had ended in 1930 he took up part-time study at Ruskin College in Oxford. George Halley died in Victoria Hospital in Burnley on the 18th of December 1941. He was 54.

---xxx---

Thomas William Boyle, Centre Half, (1886 - 1940)

Figure 76

Tommy Boyle was born in the pit village of Platts Common, south of Barnsley in January 1886. Like his father and brother, Tommy's working career began in the local pit as a miner. He was a good runner before he was a footballer and after playing semi-professional football locally with Elsecar Athletic, Boyle joined Barnsley as a professional in 1906. Boyle led Barnsley to the 1910 Cup Final where they played Newcastle United at The Crystal Palace, drawing 1-1 before losing the replay at Goodison Park 2-0. Tommy signed for Burnley the following year and became Burnley captain shortly after. When war was declared,

Tommy joined the Royal Artillery along with Bob Kelly and several other Burnley players. He saw active service at Messines Ridge and Ypres in July 1917, when he was wounded in the leg by shell fragment. It looked at the time he would not play football again. He recovered, and in 1921, led Burnley to the League Championship. After a spell coaching the 'A' and Reserve teams at Burnley, in 1923 he joined Wrexham and played the first part of the 1923-24 season before being suspended by the club. The following year he had a season coaching in Germany at the Tennis Borussia Club based in Berlin. Tommy returned to Blackpool and took up crown-green bowling as a pastime but in 1932 he suffered mental illness. He died in Whittingham Mental Hospital in January 1940, aged 53.

In April 2010, Burnley and Barnsley football clubs jointly paid for an engraved headstone for Tommy and the family. The Boyle family grave is in St. Helens Church at Hoyland.

His life story is told in, *Tommy Boyle - Broken Hero.*

---xxx---

William Watson, Left Half-Back, (1890 - 1955)

Figure 77

Billy Watson was born in Birkdale, Southport and on leaving school became a skilled painter and decorator. He joined his local team, Southport Central FC where he was spotted by a Burnley scout. Billy was signed by Spen Whittaker and joined Burnley during the 1908-09 season, making his first team debut in October 1910.

During WW1, Billy served in the Army Service Corps and spent time overseas. He returned home from France on the same Southport train with Eddie Mosscrop in 1919. Billy played in the 1920-21 League Championship winning team and was part of the 'holy trinity' of Halley, Boyle and Watson. Billy had a seventeen-year career at Burnley, during which he won three England caps. In 1925, Billy signed for Accrington Stanley and the season after that, Blackburn Rovers. When his football career ended, Billy picked up his job as a master painter and decorator again. Billy's 1914 Cup Final shirt was sold at Sotheby's in London in 1999. He died aged 64 in September 1955 in Southport.

---xxx---

William Nesbitt, Outside Right, (1891 - 1972)

Figure 78

Billy was born in November 1891 in Todmorden and began playing football at 16 with local side, Cornholme before later joining Portsmouth Rovers. It was while at Portsmouth he was discovered by John Haworth. In 1911 Haworth managed to sign the nineteen-year-old, first as an amateur and gained permission for him to be released from his apprenticeship as a wood turner. Billy made his first team debut at Bradford in February 1912. Billy was acutely deaf all his life. His partnership with George Halley and Dick Lindley on Burnley's right flank was remarkable in the way his team mates communicated with him using a variety of methods, from shirt-pulling, hand signalling and lip-reading. Nesbitt drove referees wild as he could not hear the whistle when straying offside. Billy won a League Championship winners medal in 1921 but was injured in the following 1921–22 season. He recovered his fitness, but following a dispute with Burnley over a second benefit match he left and joined Bristol City. Billy later moved to London and had a spell playing with Clapton Orient. When his football career ended, Billy opened a tobacconist and sweet shop in Paddington. He eventually returned to his native Todmorden and died in hospital in Halifax on 11 January 1972 aged 80.

---xxx---

Richard Lindley, Inside-Right, (1884 - 1958)

Figure 79

Richard Lindley was one of eight children and was born in Bolton on the 13th December 1884 and began his working life as a joiner like his father. Lindley arrived at Burnley in the summer of 1908 and made his first team debut a year later aged 23. The 1911 Census shows Richard as age 27, occupation, 'Professional Footballer – Burnley FC.' He was still living at home with his family in Bolton. Lindley had made 100 appearances for the Clarets by December 1913 and was a regular at inside-forward for twelve seasons at Turf Moor. In 1920 he joined Bradford City for one season before moving to Coventry City in 1921. He retired from football in 1922. Dick returned to Burnley where he ran the Empress Hotel in the town centre. He later became the custodian of the Queens Hotel in Lytham, located on Central Beach across from the spot where the Clarets trained in 1914. Dick lost his FA Cup winners medal and it was later found by a member of the public in Westgate, Burnley who handed it back. Richard died in October 1958 aged 76.

---xxx---

Bertram Clewley Freeman, Centre-Forward, (1885 - 1955)

Figure 80

Bertram Clewley Freeman was born on 13 October 1885 in Handsworth, Staffordshire, to parents Thomas Holt and Sarah Jane Freeman (née Clewley). Bert's father was a jeweller and worked in Birmingham. Bert played first for Aston Villa before moving to Arsenal a year later in 1905. He joined Everton in 1908 and in the 1908-09 season became the Football Leagues record goal-scorer with 38 League goals, a record Bert held until 1926. Bert is shown on the 1911 Census, as 25 years old, 'Professional footballer with Everton' and living in Walton, Liverpool. Shortly after the 1911 Census was taken, Bert became a Burnley player. The Everton minute book entry of April 19, 1911 states, "The Secretary reported the transfer of these players; Bert Freeman (£550) and Harry Mountford (£300) to Burnley F.C. at a fee of £850 payable as to one half forthwith and the balance secured by a bill to be dated November 30th 1911."

Bert won five England caps while at Everton and scored three goals for his country. When he moved to Burnley he lived in Royle Road and shared rooms with Tommy Boyle when he arrived at the club in September 1911. He saved Tommy Boyle's life on the night after he celebrated his 29th birthday, when Boyle was nearly asphyxiated after leaving the gas switched on. During WW1, Bert was engaged in the Royal Flying Corps as an engineer and another account mentions that he worked on "important government work in the Midlands" for the war effort. In 1919 Bert married the Burnley director and town mayor, Edwin Whitehead's daughter, Margaret. After his career at Burnley ended in April 1921, Bert signed for Wigan Borough, scoring thirteen goals in twenty-five appearances. The Freemans' moved to Birmingham and Bert continued playing football part-time with Kettering Town and later at Kidderminster Harriers. In 1924 he set up a cutlery business in Birmingham and his last recorded employment is given as a lift operator. Bert died on the 11th of August 1955 at his home in Birmingham at the age of sixty-nine. His Cup Final shirt and winners medal is on display in the Burnley boardroom in the Bob Lord Stand.

---xxx---

Edward Hodgson, Inside Left, (1886 - 1919)

Figure 81

Teddy was born in Chorley and played for the same Lancashire Combination side as a teenager. He was signed by Burnley in 1911 and made his debut at Barnsley in September 1911 in the same game as Tommy Boyle. He became a regular in the Burnley forward line. In the 1913-14 FA Cup run, Teddy was Burnley's leading scorer with five goals in the eight Cup matches which included his hat-trick against Derby County. When war broke out, Teddy joined the 52nd Manchester's' Regiment and saw action in France and in other theatres of the war. He was promoted to Sergeant Instructor and continued to play for Burnley in the wartime league when he was home on leave. In 120 games, he scored 53 goals for Burnley. While serving in Germany after the war ended in July 1919, Teddy was taken ill and he was brought home to Whalley Military

Hospital. Sadly Teddy died on the 4th August 1919 following the illness brought about by his war experience. At his funeral, Tommy Boyle, Bert Freeman, Billy Watson, Tommy Bamford, Dick Lindley and Jerry Dawson carried his coffin into the little church in Burnley cemetery. The funeral procession left his home on Haven Street and passed Turf Moor, taking the opposite route the Cup winners took five years before in 1914. The roads were lined with Burnley people all paying their last respects. Teddy was only 33 years old when he died.

---xxx---

Edwin Mosscrop, Outside-Left, (1889 - 1980)

Figure 82

Edwin 'Eddie' Mosscrop was the youngest son of three boys. He was born in Eccleshall Bierlow, in Sheffield on 16 June 1889 before the family moved to Southport. Eddie's father was a travelling salesman and then became a coal merchant and his two elder brothers joined him in the family business. Eddie is listed on the 1911 Census as aged 21, and is among a list of students at teacher training college in Chelsea. Eddie's first teaching post was at a School in Salford before he obtained a permanent position in a Southport school. Throughout his career Eddie's teaching duties came first and football second and Burnley worked around that. Eddie played at first for Blowick FC, based at Blowick Sports ground, a suburb of Southport. While at training college in London he played for Shepherds Bush and Middlesex. He was discovered by Burnley playing at Southport Central. Eddie made his first appearance for Burnley on September 7 1912. After starting off at outside-right he was switched to outside-left that December. (He would often be switched over on the wings with Billy Nesbitt) Eddie was also an amateur up to 1912 but turned professional. Following the Cup Final in 1914, Mosscrop went straight back to the classroom the week after while the Clarets toured the county and later Europe. He re-joined his team-mates in August 1914 after war had broken out. When all the Burnley players joined up in 1915, Eddie joined the Royal Army Medical Corps where he saw action in France and Salonika. He also played for the RAMC football teams while abroad. He returned from France in 1919 having spent six weeks on his journey home from Salonika sleeping under blankets on the deck of a troopship.

A committed teacher for over forty years and with a dry sense of humour, the red-haired Mosscrop managed a professional football career with his regular day job as a schoolteacher.

What stories he must have told his pupils. Known as 'Mossy' to his teammates and Mr Mosscrop to his pupils, he was good friends with Billy Watson who lived nearby in Southport where Eddie lived with his wife Gertrude Mary and their two boys. Highly intelligent and of slight build, Mosscrop wore spectacles. On one occasion he didn't convince the Sunderland gatekeeper at Roker Park that he was a footballer and he wouldn't let Eddie in the ground! After retiring from professional football, Eddie played cricket. He retired aged sixty from his post as headmaster at Bury Road School in Southport in 1949.

Eddie died in Southport on the 14th of March 1980 at the ripe old age of 90. At his funeral held at All Saints Parish Church in Southport, one of the hymns sung was, *Abide With Me*. Eddie's Cup Final shirt, Cup winners' medal and some of his other football mementoes, were auctioned at Bonhams on 2nd February 2011. Burnley Football Club bought Eddie's shirt and Cup medal and these now are on display in the Boardroom at the football club. (See Bonhams Website and the Appendix for more details.)

---xxx---

James Bellamy Outside Right, (1881 - 1969)

Figure 83

James Francis Bellamy played outside right for Burnley from 1912 to 1914. His playing career saw him play professional football at a number of clubs; Arsenal, Portsmouth, Norwich City, Dundee and Motherwell before arriving at Turf Moor in mid-1912 where he played for two seasons. He suffered a number of injuries at Burnley and was in and out of the team, Billy Nesbitt taking his place. Jimmy was transferred to Fulham in July 1914 and by the end of the War, he was 37. Once his playing days ended, Jimmy took up a football coaching career on the continent. Working first in Germany and moving later to Italy, Jimmy arrived in Spain as head coach at Barcelona in early 1929. Jimmy led Barca to win the very first La Liga title in 1929. He later won the Catalan championship twice in 1930 and 1931. Jimmy died in 1969 aged 88.

---xxx---

Robert Kelly, Inside-Right, (1895 - 1969)

Figure 84

Robert Kelly was born in Ashton-in-Makerfield and on the 1911 Census, he was 16, living in Harphurey and working as an ironworker. Kelly signed for Burnley from Lancashire Combination side, St. Helens Town on the 1st November 1913, two weeks before his 19th birthday. He went on to make 277 appearances for Burnley, scoring 88 goals and winning 14 England caps, scoring 8 goals in the process. He scored his first goal for the Clarets on his debut against Aston Villa, the day before his nineteenth birthday.

The sporting headlines the day after his debut were full of praise for Burnley but especially for the youngster, Kelly.

The Daily Dispatch, "A born footballer." The London Express, "Burnley have to thank Kelly for the extent of their four goals." The Daily Mail, "Kelly has a rare gift…" The Burnley Express, "Aston Astonished" ran the football page headline in the mid-week issue. Kelly came into the Burnley team more during 1915 and played in the wartime League until 1920 when he was home on leave. Like Tommy Boyle and several other Clarets, Bob joined the Royal Artillery and saw action in France. After the war, Kelly came into the Burnley side with the death of Teddy Hodgson in 1919. After winning a championship winners medal in 1921, Kelly got better and better. In 1925, Kelly was transferred to Sunderland for a transfer record-breaking fee of £6,550. His transfer came as a massive shock to Burnley supporters as he was the best player Burnley had at the time. After Sunderland he later played for Huddersfield Town, Preston North End and finally Carlisle United. When his playing career ended in 1936, Kelly was 41, and he went into football management. He was the player-manager at Carlisle until 1938 then had a two-season spell managing at Stockport County. After the Second World War, Kelly travelled to Portugal where he managed Sporting Club for a season before moving to the Swiss side, FC St. Gallen. His longest spell in management was at FC Heerenveen in Holland for four years until 1955. After spells managing at Kooger FC (now AZ Alkmaar), Bob returned to England and lived in Blackpool where he became a school caretaker before retiring in1960. He died in Fylde in 1969 aged 74.

---xxx---

Harry Windle, Burnley Chairman, (1877 - 1938)

Figure 85

Harry Windle was born at Wilsden near Keighley in 1877. His family arrived in Burnley in 1887 and as a youth Harry was an enthusiastic footballer playing in local teams including the Young Britons and Burnley Lane Reform Club. Windle worked full-time as a tea merchant's clerk for Abraham Altham's (the Burnley-based tea merchant and travel company) and was a keen Burnley supporter. In 1901 aged 24, with Burnley relegated and struggling financially, Windle led a supporters' fundraising campaign to sponsor the purchase of a player with a shilling subscription and managed to raise fifty pounds for the club's funds. In 1903 he was formally asked by the directors to chair a committee to look at fundraising and four years later, in July 1907, he joined the board as full director. After becoming Vice Chairman in 1908, on the 11th June 1909 he was elected Burnley Chairman.

Following the death of Burnley manager Spen Whittaker in April 1910, Windle's appointment of John Haworth as the new manager that summer, was possibly the best decision he ever made. Windle oversaw the rebirth of Burnley as a football club and he backed his project with hard cash. He spent the club's money wisely and with Haworth brought in the best players.

During his years in charge, Windle developed Turf Moor, increasing its capacity from 20,000 to 50,000 on either side of the Great War. His time, devotion and investment paid off, with massive attendances and First Division football after promotion in 1913. In addition to promotion, FA Cup and League success during Windle's tenure, twenty-nine international caps were awarded to Burnley players serving at the club.

Harry Windle resigned as chairman before a meeting of shareholders in January 1930, three-months prior to the team's relegation later that year. He was replaced by W.E. Bracewell. Windle continued on the Burnley board and later became chairman of the Lancashire Football Association. Harry Windle completed twenty-seven years of service with Burnley FC and managed the Club while also working for Abraham Altham's in Burnley. He lived at 259 Brunshaw Road, a five minute walk away from Turf Moor. Harry Windle died in July 1938 while on holiday in Bournemouth with his wife Amelia and family. He was 61 years old and is buried in Burnley Cemetery.

---xxx---

John Haworth, Burnley Secretary-Manager (1876 - 1924)

Figure 86

John Haworth came from a football family. A photograph of his uncle George, 'Jud' Howarth, and his England international cap are on display in the National Football Museum collection in Manchester. John was born in Accrington in 1876 and played football as a full-back with local Accrington side, Meadow Bank Rovers. He became their team manager in 1894. Three years later the club disbanded and Haworth brought his players to Accrington Stanley where he became a committee member. Haworth later took over as Accrington Stanley manager in 1897-98 and saw the team win the North East Lancashire league. After Spen Whittaker's death in 1910 he applied for the post and was appointed the new Burnley Manager. (His actual job title in the 1913 Burnley v Newcastle United programme is given as, 'Secretary-Manager.')

Under Haworth's stewardship, Burnley FC won footballs two biggest prizes, the FA Cup in 1914 and Football League Championship in 1921. The 1911 Census shows that a year after he was appointed manager, Haworth lived at 11 Mizpah Street with his family. He later moved later to 25 Haven Street where he lived in the same street as a number of Burnley players. The 1911 Census gives his occupation as "Company Secretary Burnley Football Club." John married Gertrude in 1907 and in January 1911 the couple had a son, John Walter Haworth, who is shown as three months old on the 1911 Census.

John Haworth had the ability to recognise talent and nurture it, with youngsters like Bob Kelly, Billy Pickering and Billy Nesbitt. He knew how to balance a team and his policy was based on a strong defensive back line, fast attacking wing play and aerial power. In many of the match reports of the day, Haworth's name is rarely mentioned. His name is usually only given in regard to staffing issues and player signings, and very little credit is given to his input into team tactics or the way the game was played on the pitch. In the 1914 Cup Final banquet for example, he was not among the speakers and it was difficult to find any news sources of interviews with him or what his comments were. Haworth is rarely shown on team photographs, and he isn't on the FA Cup-winning photograph for example, that being trainer, Ernie Edwards. I believe John Haworth deserves more credit than he was given at the time. He was a major influence in building two teams, pre-and post-War. During his years in charge Burnley won promotion, the FA Cup, made three FA Cup semi-final appearances and won the League Championship. Quite a record.

Howarth's death in 1924 from pneumonia was a major tragedy for the football club. He was only 48 years old. Five seasons after his death, Burnley were relegated and stayed in the Second Division wilderness until after World War Two. On the day of his funeral, thousands of Burnley people lined the funeral route to pay their respects, all the way from Turf Moor to Haworth's home town of Accrington where he is buried in the town cemetery. Football clubs from across England and Scotland and the Football authorities all sent representatives to the funeral to commemorate John's impact on the game, spanning over thirty years in football management.

---xxx---

Ernest Stanley Edwards, Burnley Trainer

As the directors couldn't agree terms with former Burnley trainer Jerry Jackson at the end of the 1913-14 season, a new trainer was brought in. Ernie Edwards began working with the Burnley players from August 1913. Edwards hailed from Plymouth. An all-round sportsman, Edwards previous duties were as a trainer for four years at Plymouth Rugby club. He had played football for Penzance, playing in a team that had won the Cornwall County Cup. A short-distance sprinter, Edwards had ran the 100 yards in 10.8 seconds and was a Southern area athletics gold medal winner, apparently winning a hundred trophies during his sporting career. The Burnley

News described him thus, "Standing six feet high, weighing 11st 9½ lbs, and with an almost soldierly bearing, Mr Edwards is a fine specimen of alert athletic manhood." Ernie Edwards is the suited man in the photograph with the Burnley players and the FA Cup (Figure 69). Ernie must have had an impact on the player's preparation for the final and his training methods must have been a factor in Burnley's success in 1914.

---xxx---

Herbert Sydney Bamlett, Cup Final Referee, (1882 – 1941)

Herbert Sydney Bamlett was born in Sunderland before his family moved to Gateshead. He was a railway worker according to the 1901 and 1911 Census and was shown in 1911 still living at home with his mother Clara in Gateshead, when he was 29. Bamlett never played football professionally and became a referee with the Durham Association in 1901 at only 19. In 1914, at 32, he was the youngest referee to ever officiate a FA Cup Final. In the infamous 1909, 'Snowing' game, Bamlett was allegedly too cold to blow the whistle and let United's Charlie Roberts do it. Allegedly.

After refereeing the Cup Final in August 1914, Bamlett suddenly gave up refereeing and moved into football management. With no previous experience of managing, at 33 he took over as manager at Oldham Athletic for the 1914-15 season. In his first season as a manager, Oldham finished runners-up to champions Everton, missing out on the title in April 1915 by only one point; the closest Oldham have ever come to winning the Football League title. Bamlett had seven seasons in the manager's seat at Oldham where he stayed until the summer of 1921. He then dropped down into the Third Division North and took on the managerial vacancy at League newcomers, Wigan Borough. Bamlett's first game in charge was against Nelson FC and making his debut for Borough was Bamlett's first signing, former Burnley centre-forward Bert Freeman. Freeman scored 13 goals in 25 appearances in Wigan's first League season.

Bamlett moved to Middlesbrough in 1923 and had three seasons in charge in the north-east seeing them first relegated, then promoted and then relegated again. Bamlett's last management post was at Manchester United, arriving at Old Trafford in April 1927. His four year tenure at Old Trafford wasn't exactly groundbreaking. His win ratio was only 31.32%. In 182 games United Won 57, Drew 43 and Lost, 82. Statistics show Bamlett was United's worst ever manager. He was sacked by the Old Trafford chairman on April Fools Day in 1931 after United had lost all their first twelve League games of the 1930-31 season. Herbert Bamlett died in Barton, Lancashire in October 1941 aged 59.

---xxx---

And Whatever Happened To...

The 1914 FA Cup Final Ball

At the end of the Cup Final, Burnley captain Tommy Boyle claimed the match ball. Along with the match ball for the 1920-21 League Championship match v. Everton, Boyle had both match balls mounted and embossed in gold letters. These became part of his collection that he displayed behind the bar at The Pedestrian Inn in Burnley in 1923-24. In 1947, the Cup Final ball apparently re-surfaced again after it was found in an attic in a house in Burnley in good condition. Sadly, neither the 1914 or 1921 ball has been seen since.

This Ball Won the Cup—1914

This is the ball with which Burnley won the Cup Final of 1914 against Liverpool. It was returned to the club this week after being retrieved from a Burnley attic by Mr A. Aspinall, of Montague-road. Billy Morris and Jack Chew are wondering if it is a lucky sign that they will emulate the success of those former Clarets!   "Express" Photo.

Figure 87: Jackie Chew and Billy Morris with the 1914 Cup Final Ball

---xxx---

Liverpool Football Club

A year after the Cup Final, in April 1915, Liverpool took on Manchester United in a League match at Old Trafford. The match referee and several observers claimed that Liverpool had shown a 'lack of commitment' during the game, which they lost, 2-0 to United, both goals scored by George Anderson. After the match, handbills started to appear, alleging that a large amount of money had been bet at odds of 7/1 on a 2–0 win to United. The Football Association investigated and found three of United's players, Enoch West, Sandy Turnbull and Arthur Whalley along with four Liverpool players, Jackie Sheldon, Tom Miller, Bob Pursell and Thomas Fairfoul, all guilty. The result of the inquiry was released to the press on Christmas Eve 1915. All seven players plus another player, Cook of Chester, were banned from playing professional football for life. The ban went as far as the eight players ever setting foot inside a football stadium.

After the First World War, all four Liverpool players and two of United's, (not West) had their bans lifted by the FA in recognition of their war service. Sandy Turnbull was killed during the war and was given a posthumous reinstatement. Enoch 'Knocker' West had to wait until 1945 to receive his pardon.

Following the 1914 Final, it took another 50 years before Liverpool won the FA Cup. Liverpool led by manager Bill Shankly beat Leeds United in the Cup Final held at Wembley stadium, 2-1 on the 1st May 1965. They have since won the Cup seven times.

---xxx---

The Crystal Palace

Shortly after the Burnley v Liverpool Cup Final, in August 1914, the Crystal Palace was commandeered by the War Office and the Park and all its facilities became, *HMS Victory VI*, used for naval training and stores. After the War ended, in 1919 the Imperial War Museum was temporarily located there. On the 30th November 1936, a fire burned down the Palace building which sadly was not fully insured, which prevented its rebuilding. Various activities took place in the Park over the years, including motor-racing, concerts, and in 1964 the Crystal Palace National Sports Centre was built in the Park, on the spot where the football pitch stood in 1914.

The latest plans to develop the site are proposals put forward by a Chinese consortium in late 2013 and supported by the London Mayors Office. The ambitious plans are to rebuild the Crystal Palace building and restore the rest of the Park to its former glory of 100 years ago.

Figure 88: Artists Impression of the Proposed New Crystal Palace (ARUP Ltd.)

---xxx---

APPENDICES

Figure 89

Bibliography

Ackroyd, Peter (2000) <u>London - The Biography</u>, Chatto & Windus, London

Atterbury, Paul (2010) <u>An A-Z of Railways: A Nostalgic Tour of Britain's Railways</u>, David & Charles, Newton Abbott, Devon.

Ashworth, Frank (1981) <u>Burnley – A Town Amidst The Pennines</u>, published by Mid-Pennine Arts Association

Barrett's, (1914) <u>Directory of Burnley</u> (copy available at Burnley Reference Library)

Beaver, Patrick (1986) <u>The Crystal Palace – A Portrait of Victorian Enterprise</u>, Phillimore, Sussex.

Bevan, Ian, Hibberd Stuart and Gilbert, Michael (1999) <u>To the Palace for the Cup: An Affectionate History of Football at The Crystal Palace,</u> Replay Publishing Limited, Beckenham, Kent.

Bostridge, Mark (2014) <u>The Fateful Year: England 1913</u>, Viking Books, London.

Boujaoude, Charbel, et.al (2013) <u>Manchester United: Legends of a Bygone Era</u>, Empire Publications, London

Bradshaw, Robert (1981) <u>Burnley Football Club – Centenary Handbook 1981-2</u>, Burnley Football Club.

Briggs, Asa (1983) <u>A Social History of England,</u> Book Club Associates, London

Butler, Byron, (1998) <u>The Official Illustrated History of the FA Cup</u>, Headline Publishing.

Davidson, Lester & Mark (2008) <u>A Pictorial Guide to the Programmes and Ephemera of Burnley Football Club,</u> Hudson and Pearson publishers, Burnley.

Chapples, Leslie (1986) <u>The Taverns In The Town: A walk round the pubs of Burnley of the 1920-30s</u>, published by Burnley Historical Society.

Dunning, Eric et al. (1988) <u>The Roots of Football Hooliganism: An Historical and Sociological Study,</u> Routledge, London

Emerson, Charles (2013) <u>1913: The World before the Great War,</u> PublicAffairs Publishing, London

Firth, Peter (1992) The Mule Spinning Industry in N.E Lancs. to 1914: An Assessment of Decline, Burnley Reference Library, Local Collection, 054404029 Lib Ref 338.4767 (Lists typical local wages in Burnley up to 1914)

Fort, Keith (1988) Burnley Since 1900, Archive Publications, Manchester

Hackett, Robin (2011) Billy Meredith - Welsh Wizard, (date accessed 12/12/2013) http://espnfc.com/columns/story/ /id/969222/ the-mavericks:-billy-meredith?cc=5739

Harding, John (1998), Football Wizard: The Billy Meredith Story, Robson Books, London.

Hawksley, Lucinda (2013) March, Women, March: Voices of the Women's Movement From The first Feminist to Votes for Women, Andre Deutsch Publishers, London.

Hayes, Dean (2001) East Lancashire Derbies: Blackburn Rovers v. Burnley, Sigma Publishing, Cheshire

Hill, Tim (2006) A Photographic History of English Football, Parragon Publishers, Bath

Hopkin, Roger, (2009) Hopkin's History of the Football League: Volume One 1888-1946, Desert Island Books, Southend on Sea

Hutchinson, John (1982) The Football Industry, Richard Drew Publishing, Glasgow.

Inglis, Simon (1987) The Football Grounds of Great Britain, Willow Books, London

Inglis, Simon (1988) League Football and the Men who Made It, Willow Books, London

Krieger, Eric (1983) Good Old Soccer: The Golden Age of Football Picture Postcards, Longman, London

Kynaston, David (2011) City of London: The History, Chatto & Windis, London

Lee, Edward & Simpson, Ray (1991) Burnley A Complete Record, Breedon Books, Derby.

Lee, Christopher (1999) This Sceptred Isle – Twentieth Century, BBC Books, London

Lord, Robert William (1963) My Fight For Football, Stanley Paul, London.

Lowe, John (1985) Burnley, Phillimore &Co, Chichester, Sussex

Major, John (2012) My Old Man: A Personal History of the Music Hall, Harper Press, London.

McMeekin, Sean (2013) July 1914: Countdown to War, Basic Books, London

Midwinter, Eric (2007) Parish to Planet: How Football Came to Rule The World, Know The Score Books, Warwickshire.

4444444

Myers, Simon (2008) Football The Early Years Fineprint, Stockport.

Pine, Leslie Gilbert (1983) A Dictionary of Mottoes, Routledge, London

Quinn, Tom (2008) Memories of Steam: Reliving The Golden Age of Britain's Railways, David & Charles, Newton Abbott, Devon.

Ronay, Barney (2009) The Manager: The Absurd Ascent of the Most Important Man in Football, Sphere, London

Riches, Adam (2009) Football's Comic Book Heroes, Mainstream Publishing, Edinburgh.

Saunders, Ann (1984) The Art and Architecture of London, Phaidon Press, London.

Simpson, Ray (2007) The Clarets Chronicles: The definitive History of Burnley Football Club 1882 – 2007, printed by Nayler Group, Church.

Smith, Mike (2011) Tommy Boyle - Broken Hero, Grosvenor House Publishers, Guildford,

Storey, Nicholas (2011) History of Men's Sporting Etiquette: A Guide to the Sporting Life, Pen and Sword Books, Barnsley, UK.

Taylor, Matthew (2008) The Association Game: A History of British Football, Pearson, London

Taylor, Matthew (2005) The Leaguers: The Making of Professional Football in England, 1900-1939, Liverpool University Press, Liverpool.

Tennant, John (2001) Football- The Golden Age: Extraordinary Images from 1900 to 1985, Bounty Books, London.

Tibballs, Geoff (2008) Football's Greatest Characters: Amazing Stories of Hard Men, Hellraisers and Crowd Pleasers, JR Books, London

Wilson, A. N. (2004) London: A Short History, Phoenix , London

Wilson, Jonathan (2013) Inverting the Pyramid: The History of Football Tactics, Second Ed. Orion, London

Wiseman, David (1973) Up The Clarets: The Story of Burnley Football Club, Robert Hale, London.

Wiseman, David (2006) A Case of Vintage Claret: Fifty of the best Burnley Footballers of all-time, Hudson and Pearson Publishers, Burnley

Whalley, Phil (2001) Images of Sport: Accrington Stanley Football Club, Tempus Publishing.

Wolmar, Christian (2007) Fire & Steam: How the Railways Transformed Britain, Atlantic Books, London.

Wolmar, Christian (2004) The Subterranean Railway: How London Underground was built and How it Changed the City Forever, Atlantic Books, London.

Newspapers Consulted

The Athletics and Cyclists News (Microfilm – at the British Library St. Pancras)

British Newspapers 1600-1900 (Gale, online under Library license) www.britishnewspaperarchive.co.uk

The Burnley Chronicle

The Burnley Express and Clitheroe Advertiser – from 1906 to 1924 archived on microfilm and can be accessed at Reference Section, Burnley Library, Grimshaw Street, Burnley.

The Burnley News 1900 to 1933 (microfilm set located in Burnley reference library)

The Burnley Gazette

The Times Newspaper Archive (Online)

The Daily Mirror (UK Press Online)

The Daily Express (UK Press Online)

The Daily Mail (British Newspapers Online accessed at The British Library)

The Guardian and Observer Online (formerly the Manchester Guardian)

The London Gazette – www.london-gazette.co.uk/

Football Journals and Magazines

Programme Monthly http://www.pmfc.co.uk/

Soccer History http://www.soccer-history.co.uk/about-soccer-history.asp

Sport In History http://www.sporthistinfo.co.uk

When Saturday Comes http://www.wsc.co.uk/

Websites

Bonhams – The Eddie Mosscrop Collection – a number of Eddie's items were auctioned February 2011 at Chester including his Cup Final medal, match shirt, international caps etc. Some of these items were purchased by Burnley Football Club. (Lot 442) http://www.bonhams.com/auctions/18747/57774/#r1=253&m1=1

The Briercliffe Society – www.briercliffesociety.co.uk/ - an excellent local archive of Burnley images and photo archive.

British Film Institute - Several old clips of Burnley are available from the British Film Institute. http://www.bfi.org.uk/nationalarchive/

Burnley Football Club http://www.burnleyfootballclub.com/

British Pathe www.britishpathe.com

Have an excellent clip of the 1914 Cup final squad relaxing in 'mufti.'
http://www.britishpathe.com/record.php?id=19620

The Burnley Historical Society – local group dedicated to historical research in the Burnley area www.burnleyhistoricalsociety.com

ClaretsMad – an excellent source of information, news, archive resources, and arguably the best debating forum in football, edited by dedicated Burnley fan, Tony Scholes. www.clarets-mad.co.uk

The Everton Collection an excellent resource for football historians - the minute books especially which you can search on. http://www.evertoncollection.org.uk/home

The Football Association www.TheFA.com

Getty Images has several photographs covering the 1913 Cup semi-final v Sunderland and the 1914 Final v Liverpool.

Graham Budd Auctions – click on catalogue and sale results to search on Burnley items.
www.grahambuddauctions.co.uk

Historical Kits – football kits for teams down the decades http://www.historicalkits.co.uk/

Historical Cup Final Kits – 1910-15 Showing the Burnley shirts with the Royal Arms v Liverpool http://www.historicalkits.co.uk/English_Football_League/FA_Cup_Finals/1910-1915.html

ITN Source also has footage of Burnley at www.itnsource.com

Lancashire Archives http://www.lancashire.gov.uk/corporate/web/?siteid=4528&pageid=30539&e=e

Lancashire Museums http://new.lancashire.gov.uk/museums

London Transport Museum http://www.ltmuseum.co.uk/collections

Movietone News - www.movietone.com

Mirrorpix – Daily Mirror photo archive – www.mirrorpix.com/index

The National Archives – http://www.nationalarchives.gov.uk/records/looking-for-subject/photographs.htm

The National Football Museum - http://www.nationalfootballmuseum.com/

The North West Film Archive http://www.nwfa.mmu.ac.uk/

Wigan Borough, www.wiganborough.bernardramsdale.com

Wiganworld - George Chilvers examples of colourised mono photographs. http://www.wiganworld.co.uk/album/photo.php?opt=7&id=17671&gallery=Wigan+Highfield+Rugby+Team&offset=0

Yorkshire Film Archive http://www.yorkshirefilmarchive.com/

Some Facts About the 1913-14 FA Cup

The 1913-14 final was the 43rd FA Cup Final to take place since 1871-2.

The 1914 Final was the 20th and last time the Cup Final was held at The Crystal Palace.

A total of 476 teams competed in the 1913-14 competition.

There were 13 rounds of competition including the final. The competition began on the 13th September 1913 with two preliminary rounds followed by five qualifying rounds. Twenty four clubs making it through these stages were added to the 20 League Division One and 20 League Division Two clubs, making up the 64 clubs to enter the draw for the First Round proper.

The Cup Final was held at the Crystal Palace, Sydenham on Saturday the 25th April 1914 and the kick-off time was 3:30pm.

It was the first occasion that a reigning monarch had attended the Cup Final, His Majesty, King George V.

It was the first time two Lancashire clubs had reached the Final and the first time both Liverpool and Burnley had reached the Final.

The King wore a red rose at the Final to signify the red rose county clash.

Burnley had defeated five First Division clubs on the way to winning the Cup, then a record.

The stadium had been substantially improved for the 1914 Final following the previous years Final (Aston Villa v. Sunderland) which had seen an attendance of **121,919**. During that final, crowd congestion, poor visibility and one stand suffered a collapsed roof with a number of spectators injured.

There were no reported accidents at the 1914 Final.

Burnley lined up with nine English and two Scotsmen while Liverpool lined up with seven Scottish players, three Englishmen and an Irishman.

The FA's official attendance for the 1914 Final was given as **72,778**, 49,000 fewer than the previous years final despite the monarch's attendance.

Other sources state the attendance figure was **74,500**.

Supporters travelled to London to see the Cup Final on 170 special trains.

Burnley sold out their ticket allocation of 8,000 tickets (priced at five shillings and at 2s 6d) plus a further 8,000 ground tickets at one shilling.

You could also pay-on-the-turnstile to watch the Final for one shilling.

There may well have been more Burnley supporters in the ground than the football club's ticket sales.

What the Cup Winners Received

The Football Associations financial reward for teams progressing through the various rounds of The Cup was a sum of money to be shared among the participating players. In 1914 the sums of money were as follows;

The Cup Winning team - £275. For the twelve Burnley players (including Jerry Dawson) taking part in the eight games, each player would therefore have received a maximum fee of £22 10s.

Runners-Up Liverpool received £220 for all their players to share.

Semi-Finalists Aston Villa and Sheffield United both received £165.

Fourth Round teams each received £110.

Third Round teams each received £55.

Second Round teams each received £22.

UK Currency in 1914

The currency used in Britain up to February 1971 when the country switched to decimal currency was based on a Roman system, the 'd' standing for denarius or denari. £1 = One Pound = 240 pennies, or 240d.

Coins
¼d = a farthing, four in a penny (withdrawn from circulation 31/12/1960)
½d = a halfpenny of h'apenny, two in a penny.
1d = a penny
3d = threepence, threepenny bit or 'thruppence'
6d = sixpence or sometimes called a 'tanner'.
1/- or 1s = one shilling = twelve pennies often called - 'a bob.'
2/- or 2s = two shillings, or one florin, often called 'two bob.'
2s 6d = two shillings and sixpence, = 30 pennies = 'half a crown.'
5/- or 5s = five shillings, a crown, (four crowns in £1)

Paper currency
10/- = ten shillings, or 'ten bob.'
£1 = one pound, or 'a quid.'

Other denominations
1 guinea = 21/- twenty one shillings often used for purchasing goods and services.

Converting pre-decimal currency to decimal

Post 1971 (Decimal coinage)	Pre-decimal coinage - as 1914
£1 = 100pence or 100p	£1 = 240 pennies or 240d
50p	10/- ten shillings or 120d
20p	4/- four shillings or 60d
10p	2/- two shillings or 24 pennies
5p = five pence	1/- one shilling or 12 pennies
2p = two pence	Approximately equal to 6 pennies
1p = one pence	Approximately equal to 3 pennies
½ = half pence (no longer used)	One penny

The Cost of Watching Football in 1914

Typical wages for a Burnley weaver in 1914 would be £1 5s., or 25 shillings a week for a 48 hour working week including a Saturday morning shift.(See Peter Firth, 1992)

An adult season ticket in the Brunshaw Road stand at Burnley FC, 1913-14 = 25 shillings.

A match day programme in 1913-14 cost 1d, a penny.

Adult ground admission to Turf Moor was 6d, sixpence. Juveniles and Ladies 3d.

(For FA Cup Ties past the third round, admission prices doubled to a shilling for adults)

A pint of local Massey's beer (brewed in Westgate, Burnley) cost 2½d (tuppence-ha'penny).

Ground admission to the FA Cup Final, Crystal Palace was 1/- standing (one shilling), top price stand seats were 5/- there was uncovered seating at 2s 6d.

In London

Dinner at the Savoy Hotel in London in April 1914 cost from 7s 6d.

Overnight hotel accommodation in the Strand, with Bed and Breakfast cost 6s.

A front row seat at the Opera House Covent Garden to see Nelly Melba in April 1914 cost one guinea (21 shillings).

Transport costs

Underground tube fares in 1914 were 2d for a single journey (it was called the tuppenny tube).

Return train fare from Burnley to London for the Cup Final with Althams' for a one-day ticket cost 12/- twelve shillings.

A three-day return ticket from Burnley to London cost 17/- seventeen shillings.

A 1914 model bicycle with pneumatic tyres and a three-speed Sturmey-Archer gear change from H. Fitzpatrick in Burnley cost £15 10s.

To get away from the football in 1914, Abraham Althams' were offering a five-day escorted tour to Paris and Europe from £4 17s 6d.

A one-way ticket to America on board the Titanic in 1912 cost £7 9s.

A brand new 16-20 Wolsey car with hood and screen cost £460 at the Mitre Garage in Burnley in 1914.

Calculating Burnley's Attendances From Gate Receipts

In looking at the actual attendances at Burnley's First Division games in 1913-14, it is difficult to obtain an accurate figure. In 1913-14, football clubs reported in the press the gate receipts received rather than the true attendance figure. It is difficult to accurately estimate the actual gate based on gate receipt figure as prices varied. It was (3d) for children and ladies, 6d for adult men and a higher fee for the enclosure and for covered seating in the stand. Gates printed in the press were often rounded up, or down.

Taking the typical costs per adult males of 6d for a League match (in the latter rounds of the FA Cup, the ground entrance fee was doubled to a shilling) it is possible to give a close estimate to what the League gate might have been, based on the largest group, adult males, based on their each paying sixpence for ground admission.

Before the start of the 1913-14 season, Everton and Burnley had agreed to pool their income from gate receipts and share the money equally. (The Everton minutes don't show why the clubs did this.) At the end of the 1913-14 season, the Everton minute book entry for the 4th May 1914 states that the match receipts for the Everton v Burnley match at Goodison Park equalled £974 7s 1d, and for the Burnley v Everton match at Turf Moor, £542 6s 6d, giving a total of £1,516 13s 6d. With the 'pooling' arrangements therefore, a cheque for £216 0s 3d was sent to Burnley.

Working on a 6d admission fee per adult. (£1 = 20 shillings = 40 sixpences = 240 pennies.)
With fees received of £974 7s 1d = 233,760 pennies)
Dividing this by six (sixpence) = would give an all adult male, all standing attendance at Goodison park of **38,974.**
The gate figure given in the newspapers for the match was **35,000.**

While £542 6s 6d would be approximately equal to an attendance of **21,693** for the Burnley v Everton game at Turf Moor by the same guidelines.

The gate figure given in the newspapers for the match was **20,000**.

The figures here don't account for those paying the higher fees to go in the stand (two shillings) and enclosure or the lower fee for ladies and children (3d). Without knowing the sales of stand tickets or the numbers of ladies and children attending the calculation can only be a rule of thumb at best.

Burnley's Progress in the FA Cup: 1885 to 1914

Season	Round	Cup-tie	Comment/ income	Attendance/ gate receipts
1872-85		Did not participate		
1885-86	1	Burnley's first entry into the FA Cup. Darwen Old Wanderers 11, Burnley 0	Burnley sent their reserve side, the first team being ineligible.	
1886-87	1	Astley Bridge 3, Burnley 3 Burnley 2, Astley Bridge 2 (replay)	Burnley disqualified (players did not have requisite residential qualifications)	
1887-88	1	Burnley 4, Darwen Old Wanderers 0 - walk-over.		
	2	Accrington 3, Burnley 2		
1888-89	1	Burnley 4, Old Westminster's 3	Football League's first season.	
	2	West Bromwich Albion 5, Burnley 1		
1889-90		Sheffield United 2, Burnley 1		
1890-91	1	Burnley 4, Crewe Alexandra 2	Extra time played when scores were 2-2	
	2	Notts County 2, Burnley 1		

350

Season	Round	Cup-tie	Comment/ income	Attendance/ gate receipts
1891-92	1	Everton 1, Burnley 3	This was a	
	2	Burnley 1, Stoke City 3	replayed match, Burnley having won 4-2	
1892-93	1	Burnley 2, Small Heath 0		
	2	The Wednesday 1, Burnley 0		
1893-94	1	Notts County 2, Burnley 1		
1894-95	1	Newcastle United 2, Burnley 1		
1895-96	1	Burnley 6, Woolwich Arsenal 1		
	2	Burnley 1, Stoke City 1		
	replay	Stoke City 7, Burnley 1		
1896-97	1	Burnley 0, Sunderland 1		
1897-98	1	Burnley 3, Woolwich Arsenal 1		
	2	Burnley 3, Burslem 0		
	3	Burnley 1, Everton 3		£800 gate a then record v Everton
1898-99	1	Burnley 2, Sheffield United 2		
	replay	Sheffield United 2, Burnley 1		
1899-00	1	Burnley 0, Bury 1		
1900-01	1	Newton Heath 0, Burnley 0		
	replay	Burnley 7, Newton Heath 1		
	2	Small Heath 1, Burnley 0		

Season	Round	Cup-tie	Comment/ income	Attendance/ gate receipts
1901-02	1	Bishop Auckland 2, Burnley 3		
	2	Walsall 1, Burnley 0		
1902-03	1	Reading 1, Burnley 0		
1903-04	1	Burnley 8, Keswick 0		
	2	Darwen 3, Burnley 0		
1904-05	1	Burnley 1, Lincoln City 1		
	replay	Lincoln City 3, Burnley 2		
1905-06	1	Tottenham Hotspur 2, Burnley 0		
1906-07	1	Aston Villa 3, Burnley 1		
1907-08	1	Burnley 1, Southampton 2		
1908-09	1	Bristol Rovers 1, Burnley 4	The Alec Leake –	7,269, / £190
	2	Crystal Palace 0, Burnley 0	Walter Abbot Clarets team.	18,000, / £773
	replay	Burnley 9, Crystal Palace 0		12,161, / £393
	3	Tottenham Hotspur 0, Burnley 0		21,872, / £1,390
	replay	Burnley 3, Tottenham Hotspur 1		23,000, / £1,152
	4	Burnley 1, Manchester United 0 (abandoned) Burnley 2, Manchester United 3	The 'stop the game it's showing game.' (United win the Cup.)	15,471, / £1,089 16,850, / £1,036

Season	Round	Cup-tie	Comment/ income	Attendance/ gate receipts
1909-10	1	Burnley 2, Manchester United 0		16,625, / £871
	2	Swindon Town 2, Burnley 0		10,000 / £500
1910-11	1	Burnley 2, Exeter City 0		14,225, / £340
	2	Burnley 2, Barnsley 0	Dave Taylors	23,357, / £726
	3	Burnley 5, Coventry City 0	Bradford City go on to win the FA Cup	11,714, / £503
	4	Bradford City 1, Burnley 0		40,000, / £1,640
1911-12	1	Fulham 2, Burnley 1		
1912-13	1	Leeds City 2, Burnley 4 (abandoned, snow)	Sewell signs.	13,000, / £505
		Leeds City 2, Burnley 3		13,110, / £463
	2	Burnley 4, Gainsborough Trinity 1		18,092, / £586
	3	Burnley 3, Middlesbrough 1	Boyles winner at Ewood	27,824, / £1,679
	4	Blackburn Rovers 0, Burnley 1	Park	43,000, / £3,003
	SF	Burnley 0, Sunderland 0 (Bramall Lane)		33,655, / £2,263
	replay	Burnley 2, Sunderland 3 (St. Andrews)		30,000, / £1,880

Season	Round	Cup-tie	Comment/income	Attendance/gate receipts
1913-14	1	Burnley 3, South Shields 1		16,000 / £598
	2	Burnley 3, Derby County 2		29,992 / £1,025
	3	Burnley 3, Bolton Wanderers 0		32,000, / £2,153
	4	Sunderland 0, Burnley 0		34,581, / £2,196
	replay	Burnley 2, Sunderland 1		49,734, / £2,858
	SF	Burnley 0, Sheffield United 0 (at Old Trafford)		55,812, / £3,777
	replay	Burnley 1, Sheffield United 0 (at Goodison Park)		27,266 / £1,831
	F	Burnley 1, Liverpool 0 (at the Crystal Palace)	Burnley win the FA Cup 25 April 1914	72,778 / £6,687

Football League First Division All-Time Leading Goal scorers

	Name	League Goals	Club	Season
1	William 'Dixie' Dean	60	Everton	1927-28
2	Tom Wareing	49	Aston Villa	1930-31
3	William 'Dixie' Dean	44	Everton	1931-32
4	Dave Halliday	43	Sunderland	1928-29
5	Ted Harper	43	Blackburn Rovers	1925-26
6	Ted Drake	42	Arsenal	1934-35
7	Vic Watson	41	West Ham United	1929-30
8	Jimmy Greaves	41	Tottenham Hotspur	1960-61
9	W G Richardson	39	West Bromwich Albion	1935-36
10	Bertram Clewley Freeman	38	Everton	1908-09
11	Joe Smith	38	Bolton Wanderers	1920-21
12	John Charles	38	Leeds United	1956-57

Bert Freeman's record of 38 League goals in a season stood for 17 seasons until Blackburn Rovers Ted Harper broke it in 1926 after scoring 43 League goals.

1913-14 FA Cup Round by Round

#	First Round	Second Round	Third Round	Fourth Round	Semi Final	Final
1	BURNLEY (h) 3	BURNLEY (h) 3				
2	South Shields 1					
3	Derby County(h) 1	Derby County 2				
4	Northampton 0		BURNLEY (h) 3			
5	Bolton Wanderers (h) 3	Bolton Wand (h) 4	Bolton 0			
6	Port Vale 0					
7	Swindon (h) 1	Swindon 2		BURNLEY 0 2		
8	Manchester United 0			Sunderland (h) 0 1		
9	Sunderland (h) 9					
10	Chatham 0	Sunderland (h) 2				
11	Plymouth A (h) 4	Plymouth A 1	Sunderland (h) 2			
12	Lincoln City 1		Preston N E 0			
13	Preston North End (h) 5					
14	Bristol Rovers 2	Preston N E 1			BURNLEY 0 1	
15	Glossop (h) 2	Glossop (h) 0			Sheff U 0 0	
16	Everton 1				(At Old Trafford)	
17	Sheffield United 5				Replay at	
18	Newcastle United (h) 0	Sheffield U (h) 3			Goodison Park	
19	Bradford P A (h) 5	Bradford P A 1	Sheffield U 4			
20	Reading 1		Millwall (h) 0			
21	Millwall (h) 0 1	Millwall (h) 1				
22	Chelsea 0 0					
23	Bradford City (h) 2	Bradford City 0		Sheff Utd 0 0 1		
24	Woolwich Arsenal 0			Man C (h) 0 0 0		
25	Manchester City 2					
26	Fulham 0	Man City (h) 2	Man City 2			
27	Tottenham Hotspur 5 2	Tottenham H 1	Blackburn R (h) 1			
28	Leicester Fosse (h) 5 0					
29	Blackburn Rovers (h) 3	Blackburn R (h) 2				BURNLEY 1
30	Middlesbrough 0	Bury 0				LIVERPOOL 0
31	Bury 0 2					
32	Hull City (h) 0 1					
33	Notts Forest 2 0		Brighton & H 0			
34	Clapton Orient (h) 2 1	Clapton O 1	Sheff Wed (h) 3			
35	Oldham (h) 1 0	Brighton & H (h) 3				
36	Brighton and Hove 1 1					
37	Southampton 1			Sheff Wed (h) 0		
38	Wolves (h) 3	Wolves (h) 1 0		Aston Villa 1		
39	Notts County 2	Sheff Wed 1 1				
40	Sheffield Wed. (h) 3					
41	Gainsborough 2		West Brom 1			
42	Leeds City (h) 4	Leeds City (h) 0	Aston Villa (h) 2			
43	Grimsby 0	West Brom 2			Aston Villa 0	
44	West Brom (h) 2				LIVERPOOL 2	
45	Portsmouth (h) 0				(at White Hart lane)	
46	Exeter City 4	Exeter City (h) 1				
47	Stoke City 0	Aston Villa 2				
48	Aston Villa (h) 4					
49	London Caledonians 0		Birmingham (h) 1			
50	Huddersfield Town (h) 3	Huddersfield 0	QPR 2			
51	Southend United 1	Birmingham (h) 1		QPR 1		
52	Birmingham City (h) 2			LIVERPOOL (h) 2		
53	Merthyr Town 0					
54	Swansea Town (h) 2	Swansea T. (h) 1				
55	Bristol City 2 0	QPR 2				
56	QPR (h) 2 2		West Ham U (h) 1 1			
57	Norwich City 1	Crystal Pal 1	LIVERPOOL 1 5			
58	Crystal Palace (h) 2	West Ham (h) 2				
59	Chesterfield 1					
60	West Ham United (h) 3					
61	Blackpool 0					
62	Gillingham (h) 1	Gillingham 0				
63	Barnsley 0 0	LIVERPOOL (h) 2				
64	LIVERPOOL (h) 0 1					

Cup Winners' Record Profit

BURNLEY CLUBS' HAPPY POSITION

Yesterday there was issued to the shareholders of the Burnley Football Club the annual balance sheet, and this is a revelation in football finance. After a remarkable season the club has an unprecedented profit of £12,883 2s 9½d against £1,917 13s 5d last season.

In their 17th report the director's state,

"Both from a financial and a playing point of view it has been a record, having to report a profit of no less than £12,883 2s 9½d on the revenue account. We also had a record attendance on the occasion of our English Cup tie - replayed Fourth Round tie with Sunderland when 49,771 paid for admission, the receipts totalling £2,859 9s 5d, this showing the continued enlargement of the accommodation has been fully justified. From a playing point of view we congratulate the players on winning the English Cup for the first time in the club's history, one of the most pleasing features being the universal acknowledgement of the clean and sporting play of the team.

"The directors have the pleasure in recommending payment of the maximum dividend (free of income tax) allowed by the Football Association, viz, five percent."

Income:

According to the balance sheet, the total income was £24,048 11s 9d. The gross gate receipts at home were £18,547, 10s 7d and the receipts from away matches were £5,562 14s 2d., but from these amounts there was paid to visiting teams £3,557 15s 10d., to the Football Association as percentage of Cup ties £368, and compensation for loss of gates to other clubs, £540 making the net gate receipts £19, 644 8s 11d. Season ticket sales brought in £2,866 8s, transfer of players, £1,137 10s., advertisements and refreshment privileges £71 10s., profit on programmes £195 10s 10d, rent for use of ground £125 1s and donations £8 3s.

Expenditure:
Players wages and merit money £5,165 9s., travelling expenses £1,351 11s 10d., players outfits £99 1s., training and medical expenses £530 1s., transfer of players £1,230., match expenses £321 10s 4d., referees and linesmen £139 18s 7d., office expenses £286 15s 4½d., printing and postage £380 18s 5d., ground expenses £804 0s 11½d., rates, insurance £112 15s 10d., ground and rent and income tax £88 19s., sundries £58 7s 2d., national Insurance payments £32 8s 10d., police £194 19s 3d., interest and bank commission £82 5s 4d., gas and coal £68 7s 4d., Football League and Association fees £56, discounts to shareholders £28 17s, loan and debenture interest £133 2s 8d.

The profit and loss account shows there was a balance from last season's account of £1,065, 7s 5½d., £2 13s 6d was received for share transfer fees and the balance profit from income and expenditure account was £12,883 2s 9½d making a credit total of £13,951 3s 9d. As stands pavilion was depreciating to the extent of £1,077, there is a balance of £12,874 3s 9d to be carried to the next account.

The company's assets amount to £19,259 5s 10d, made up of pavilions, stands etc as per last account of £4, 861 9s additions during year £9, 516 9s 10d., sundry debtors £250, cash in bank £4,631 7s. The principal liabilities are Share capital £1,059, depreciation £1,077, debenture holders £2,400 sundry creditors £1, 810 15s 6d.

(The Burnley Express and Advertiser, June 24 1914)

Notes

Lightning Source UK Ltd.
Milton Keynes UK
UKOW04f2211091214

242911UK00001B/118/P